Volume 10

COMPUTER PSYCHOTHERAPY
SYSTEMS

COMPUTER PSYCHOTHERAPY SYSTEMS
SYSTEMS
Theory and Research Foundations

MORTON WAGMAN

Routledge
Taylor & Francis Group

LONDON AND NEW YORK

First published in 1988 by Gordon and Breach Science Publishers

This edition first published in 2018
by Routledge
2 Park Square, Milton Park, Abingdon, Oxon OX14 4RN

and by Routledge
711 Third Avenue, New York, NY 10017

Routledge is an imprint of the Taylor & Francis Group, an informa business

© 1988 by OPA (Amsterdam) B.V.

British Library Cataloguing in Publication Data
A catalogue record for this book is available from the British Library

ISBN: 978-0-8153-8566-0 (Set)
ISBN: 978-0-429-49236-5 (Set) (ebk)
ISBN: 978-1-138-48040-7 (Volume 10) (hbk)
ISBN: 978-1-138-48042-1 (Volume 10) (pbk)
ISBN: 978-1-351-06290-9 (Volume 10) (ebk)

Publisher's Note
The publisher has gone to great lengths to ensure the quality of this reprint but points out that some imperfections in the original copies may be apparent.

Disclaimer
The publisher has made every effort to trace copyright holders and would welcome correspondence from those they have been unable to trace.

Computer Psychotherapy Systems

Theory and Research Foundations

By Morton Wagman

University of Illinois
Urbana-Champaign

Gordon and Breach Science Publishers
New York   London   Paris   Montreux   Tokyo   Melbourne

© 1988 by OPA (Amsterdam) B.V. All rights reserved. Published under license by Gordon and Breach Science Publishers S.A.

Gordon and Breach Science Publishers

Post Office Box 786
Cooper Station
New York, New York 10276
United States of America

Post Office Box 197
London WC2E 9PX
England

58, rue Lhomond
75005 Paris
France

Post Office Box 161
1820 Montreux 2
Switzerland

3-14-9 Okubo
Shinjuku-ku, Tokyo
Japan

Private Bag 8
Camberwell, Victoria 3124
Australia

Library of Congress Cataloging-in-Publication Data
Wagman, Morton.
　Computer Psychotherapy Systems.
　Bibliography: p.
　Includes indexes.
　1. Counseling—Data processing.　2. Psychotherapy—
Data processing.　3. Expert systems (Computer science)
4. Artificial intelligence.　I. Title.
BF637.C6W26　　1988　　　616.89'14'028563　　　87-25111
ISBN 2-88124-207-3 (Switzerland)

Contents

Part III: Computer Counseling

Tables and Figures

Figures

Preface

This book examines the multifaceted issues involved in the conceptualization, development, evaluation and application of computer counseling. The computer counselor is conceived of as an expert system analagous to those in computer psychodiagnosis and computer medical consultation. Researchers, professionals, graduate students and advanced undergraduates in psychotherapy, counseling and artificial intelligence can explore the frontiers of their fields with this cross-disciplinary study.

As is true of the development of expert systems in other domains, the development of expert systems in the domain of psychotherapy and counseling is likely to result in conceptual advances. The design of an expert computer counseling system requires the precise articulation of psychotherapy theory and technique.

Computer counseling or psychotherapy involving free-flowing communication between clients and counselors is limited because of corresponding limitations in the undertstanding and processing of natural language that characterize current artificial intelligence research. These limitations on the understanding and processing of natural language may have the advantage of focusing attention on the selection of the most appropriate types of psychological counseling methods.

Chapters 1 and 2 examine the interrelated issues of computer counseling and artificial intelligence at a theoretical level. In Chapters 3 and 4, pragmatic and ethical issues are considered from several perspectives.

Chapter 5 examines artificial intelligence research concerned with computer understanding of natural language and critically evaluates a number of conversational systems that might serve as approaches to computer counseling or psychotherapy. Chapter 6 discusses standard methods for representing knowledge in computers and Chapter 7 exemplifies these methods in the context of expert, consultative and tutorial systems.

Chapter 8 illustrates and discusses approaches to the computer modeling of neurotic personality. In Chapter 9, four computer counseling systems, exemplifying psychoanalytic, client-centered, cognitive behavior and problem-solving approaches to counseling and psychotherapy are presented.

Chapters 10 and 11 present research and theory concerned with the PLATO Dilemma Counseling System (PLATO DCS), a program which has been used internationally in colleges, universities, business and government organizations. In Chapter 12, PLATO DCS, as an expert computer counseling system, is compared systematically in a controlled experiment with human counselors with respect to effects, reactions, methods, personality and demographic variables.

In the concluding chapter (Chapter 13), the problems and prospects of computer counseling are systematically presented. In an appendix to the book, a factor-analytic study of attitudes toward the use of computers in counseling compared with attitudes toward their use in other types of applications is presented and the psychological implications of the intelligent computer for the individual and society are examined. Following the appendix, there is a glossary of technical terms that have appeared in the book.

Morton Wagman
Urbana, Illinois

Acknowledgments

The author is grateful for permission to reprint or adapt the following:

K. M. Colby, J. B. Watt, & J. P. Gilbert, "A Computer Method of Psychotherapy Preliminary Communication," *Journal of Nervous and Mental Disease, 142*, p. 150, copyright by Williams & Wilkins, 1966. Reprinted by permission of the publisher and the author.

M. Wagman, "PLATO DCS, an Interactive Computer System for Personal Counseling," *Journal of Counseling Psychology, 27*, pp. 16–30. Copyright 1980 by the American Psychological Association. Reprinted or adapted by permission of the publisher.

M. Wagman & K. W. Kerber, "PLATO DCS, an Interactive Computer System for Personal Counseling: Further Development and Evaluation," *Journal of Counseling Psychology, 27*, pp. 31–39. Copyright 1980 by the American Psychological Association. Reprinted or adapted by permission of the publisher.

M. Wagman, "A Factor Analytic Study of the Psychological Implications of the Computer for the Individual and Society," *Behavior Research Methods and Instrumentation, 15*, pp. 413–419. Copyright 1983 by the Psychonomic Society, Inc. Reprinted or adapted by permission of the publisher.

M. Wagman, "Using Computers in Personal Counseling," *Journal of Counseling and Development, 63*, pp. 172–176. Copyright 1984 AACD. Reprinted or adapted with permission. No further reproduction authorized without further permission of AACD.

The discussion of knowledge representation (Chapter Six) is adapted, in part, from Barr and Feigenbaum (1981).

The author wishes to thank Megan Lyden, Jean Kula, and Katherine Bielek for their excellent typing of drafts of the book manuscript. The author wishes to thank Susan Gallas for her valuable assistance in correcting the page proofs of the book.

PART I

Introduction

Chapter One

Orienting Concepts

This book examines the many challenging problems that characterize the scientific frontier concerned with the development of computer knowledge of those concepts and processes that constitute systems of personal counseling or psychotherapy. Research and theoretical advances in both artificial intelligence and psychotherapy during the past three decades may be combined to make the concept of the computer counselor or computer psychotherapist feasible. At a theoretical level, these advances may be seen as parallel. Artificial intelligence in its initial years attempted to capture the totality of human cognition by a few abstract and powerful sets of logical operations. As artificial intelligence matured, it became apparent that general logical problem-solving approaches could not stand alone, but would need to be greatly augmented by specific knowledge in each domain of problem-solving. In a parallel fashion, the initial years of psychotherapy were characterized by the attempt to capture the totality of personality and its disturbances by a few powerful concepts. As psychotherapy matured, generality was replaced by specificity with attention to the knowledge necessary for each domain of problem-solving.

Advances in Artificial Intelligence and Problem-Solving

Although prototypic mechanical models of human behaviour (automata) beginning in ancient Egypt and Greece and continuing during Roman, medieval, and post-Renaissance western civilization had been constructed (Chapuis & Droz, 1958; McCorduck, 1979), the aspiration for developing an artifact of human reasoning and intelligence had to await the twentieth century development of the abstract mathematical theory of the modern digital computer (Turing, 1936) and the first functioning electronic computer, the ENIAC by Mauchly and Eckert in 1946. Perhaps it is not surprising that the objectives of modeling human thought and reason by a machine should take the form of duplicating what is taken as the highest form of human intellectual ability, namely the computer modeling of the logical theorems contained in *Principia Mathematica* (Whitehead & Russell, 1910–1913), a very impressive achievement that demonstrated the logical foundations of all mathematics. Indeed, it would appear that the early developers of artificial intelligence would meet their critics' objections to the possibility of a thinking machine by demonstrating that a digital computer program could be developed that proved all the logical theorems of *Principia Mathematica*. This digital computer program was named the Logic Theorist (Newell & Simon, 1956). As impressive as was the demonstration that a computer could prove theorems, the Logic Theorist was more influential in the subsequent course of artificial intelligence and information processing systems because it incorporated LISP processing languages that enable the computer simulation of human thought (Simon, 1979).

The Logic Theorist demonstrated that a computer could solve problems in abstruse systems of symbolic logic. The Logic Theorist could not be directly applied to other cognitive, reasoning and problem-solving tasks. An effort was launched by researchers in the field of artificial intelligence and information processing to develop a computer program that, analogous to general human mental ability, could be applied to a wide variety of problems. This effort culminated in the General Problem Solver (Newell, Shaw, & Simon, 1960). The General Problem Solver contained a number of general programs that modeled the general processes that human beings employ across a wide diversity of problems. An example of such a general process is means-ends analysis. In this highly generalizable procedure, heuristic rules (means) are sequentially applied to progressively reduce the difference between conditions of the confronting problem and conditions of the solution (ends). Although the General Problem Solver was able to handle a variety of problems, it was soon discovered that the generality of the General Problem Solver was confined to simple, well-structured tasks (e.g., puzzles) that permitted the application of restricted and rigid heuristic procedures. Such heuristics could not be applied to myriads of significant problems beyond puzzles. Diverse problems require diverse heuristics. Moreover, the solution of significant problems depends not only on specifically useful heuristics, but also on specific expert knowledge in a given problem domain.

Expert systems are computer programs designed to solve or assist in the solving of scientific, technical and professional problems (Feigenbaum & McCorduck, 1983). Expert systems are the resultants of collaboration between an expert in a given problem domain and a knowledge engineer or computer programmer. The expert system incorporates both the expert's fund of knowledge and the expert's experiential rules of thumb (heuristics). An important feature of expert systems is that the program displays the reasoning it used to solve a given problem. Thus, the scientist, physician or engineer can follow the computer's reasoning and judge whether or not specific conditions of the problem (e.g., exceptions, new or varying data) might recommend different reasoning and a different solution to the problem. The expert system may then be made more powerful in its problem-solving ability by incorporating the new solutions and the reasoning and data which led to them. In this way, the role of the expert system as consultant may be steadily augmented.

Expert systems have been developed for a broad range of problem domains. Expert systems have been developed to perform at a professional level in specialized fields such as medical diagnosis (Miller, Pople, & Myers, 1982), psychiatric diagnosis (Greist, Klein, & Erdman, 1976), molecular analysis in physical chemistry (Lindsay, Buchanan, Feigenbaum, & Lederberg, 1980), and drug therapy for infectious diseases (Shortliffe, 1976).

In summary, the early years of artificial intelligence were marked by the endeavor to discover general theories of problem-solving embodied in programs. It would appear that the endeavor to discover such grand laws of universal application has, in recent years, been temporarily or permanently displaced by the endeavor to develop specific problem-solving computer programs as represented by expert systems.

Advances in Psychotherapy and Problem-Solving

The first six decades (1885–1945) of psychotherapy were dominated by classical psychoanalysis and its variants. Classical psychoanalysis had the very general and intensive objective of resolving the major conflicts of childhood and of reconstructing or restructuring the total adult personality.

During the subsequent four decades (approximately 1945–1985), classical psychoanalysis or its psychoanalytic variants were modified in the direction of more restricted or limited objectives, wherein psychotherapy was directed toward a specific sector of the total personality and relatively specific problem-solving methods were developed (Karasu, 1977). This time period was also marked by a large number of rather imprecise, but dramatic therapeutic methods (London, 1974). During this period of time, classical psychoanalysis became more precisely articulated as analytically-oriented psychotherapy (Colby, 1951; Wolberg, 1965). This period also saw the development of relatively precise systems of psychotherapy such as client-centered therapy (Rogers, 1951), behavior therapy (Wolpe, 1969) and cognitive therapy (Beck, 1976).

A number of attempts have been made to organize the many psychotherapies numbering 150, (Parloff, 1975) into broad categories. Menninger (1955) and Bromberg (1959) reduced the many forms of psychotherapy to those centrally oriented around supressive treatment approaches (e.g., intellectual insight and rational problem-solving) and those centrally oriented around expressive treatment approaches (e.g., uncovering of repressed feelings, emotional catharsis). Harper (1959) categorized 36 systems of psychotherapy into a category that emphasized affective treatment methods and a category that emphasized cognitive treatment methods. Rychlak (1969) classified psychotherapies according to whether their concepts and methods were derivatives of Kantian (humanistic) or Lockean (technical, mechanistic) systems of philosophy. Rychlak (1965) indicated that psychotherapies could be schematized with respect to their predominant purpose by a category of personality investigation (e.g., Jungian analytical psychology), a category of ethical investigation (e.g., existential psychotherapy, logotherapy), and a category of directed scientific treatment (e.g., behavior therapy, cognitive therapy). Bloom (1980) divides current psychotherapy systems according to whether they are short term (e.g., cognitive therapy, behavior therapy) or long term (e.g., analytically-oriented psychotherapy, psychoanalysis).

In summary, psychotherapy, in its initial years, was characterized by very general objectives that sought complete investigation and treatment of the total personality. Psychotherapy, in more recent years, is characterized by very specific treatment objectives directed toward the scientific treatment of precisely delineated problems.

In the preceding two sections, we have discussed advances in the precision of problem-solving in artificial intelligence and psychotherapy. In subsequent chapters, we shall examine the question as to whether these parallel advances can be made to intersect at the locus of development of a computer psychotherapist or computer counselor in the form of an intelligent expert system.

Organization of the Book

Part I (Chapters 1−4) provides a general introduction to computer counseling and considers theoretical, pragmatic and ethical problems. Part II (Chapters 5−7) considers computer counseling with respect to artificial intelligence research. Approaches to the problems of natural language understanding and to methods of knowledge representation are examined. Concepts and examples of expert, consultative and tutorial artificial intelligence systems are presented. Part III (Chapters 8−13) presents methods and examples of computer counseling. An account is given of a research program concerned with the PLATO DCS computer counseling system, including an experimental comparison with professional human counselors. The concluding chapter examines the prospects for and constraints on the development of computer counseling systems. In an appendix to the book, a research study is presented that examines differential attitudes toward the use of computers in counseling, education, medicine, government, finance and mathematics. Following the appendix, a glossary of technical terms is provided for the general reader.

Summary

In this chapter, we have presented advances in artificial intelligence and in psychotherapy. We indicated that these advances are characterized by increasing precision in the theories and methods of each field. These advances in the precision of problem-solving suggested that a computer counselor in the form of an expert system might be developed. The chapter concluded with an account of the organization of the book.

CHAPTER TWO

Theoretical Complexities

In this chapter, we shall present two fundamental sets of theoretical issues. The first set concerns comparisons between artificial intelligence and human intelligence. The second set concerns comparisons between computer counseling and human counseling.

Artificial Intelligence and Human Intelligence

A fundamental theoretical issue concerns the nature of thinking and intelligence.

Two Definitions of Thinking

Philosophical tradition (Haugeland, 1981) and humanistic studies (Bolter, 1984) typically define thinking as uniquely human. Based on this definition, computers cannot think (Dreyfus, 1972). Cognitive psychologists typically define thinking as sets of symbolic operations. Based on this definition, computers can think (Simon, 1979).

Turing's Test of Thinking

In place of the definitional approach, Turing (1963) proposed an empirical approach to the question of whether a computer can or cannot think. Turing (1963) replaced the philosophical question, can a computer think, with the pragmatic question, can a computer successfully imitate human behavior. In place of a philosophical question, there is the testable empirical question as to whether the computer's appearance of thinking can or cannot be distinguished from a human's thinking. Successfully passing Turing's Test would require an adequate experimental design and an adequate statistical analysis of the findings.

Turing (1963) proposed the imitation game. There are two parts.

In part one of the imitation game, the participants are a man, a woman, and an interrogator. In part two of the imitation game, the participants are a man, a computer, and an interrogator.

In separate rooms are a man, a woman, and a human interrogator. The interrogator knows the two persons only as X and Y. The interrogator can place inquiries to the two persons. The interrogator's goal is to ascertain which is the woman. The woman's goal is to assist the interrogator to make the correct decision, to select her as the woman. The man's goal is to make the interrogator uncertain.

The interrogator communicates with each of the two persons by teleprinter to avoid simple identification by voice. The interrogator in questioning X and X in responding to the interrogator might produce the following protocol:

Interrogator: Do you like to crochet?
           X: Very definitely.
Interrogator: What is the name of your favorite novel?
           X: Novels don't interest me.
Interrogator: Tell me, do you play poker?
           X: I don't, but my husband plays poker.

If the man is X, his optimal game playing strategy would likely be to imitate the responses of a woman. If the woman is X, her optimal game playing strategy would likely be to give true responses.

In part two of the imitation game, a significant change is introduced. The woman is replaced by a computer. As in part one of the imitation game, each player is in a separate room, as is the interrogator. Communication between the interrogator and the computer or between the interrogator and the man is, as in part one of the imitation game, by teleprinter. The task of the interrogator is to determine whether X is the computer or the man. Turing's Test of whether a computer can think is now reduced to the question of whether the interrogator can or cannot discriminate better between a man and a computer (part two of the imitation game) than between a man and a woman (part one of the imitation game). A protocol from part two of the imitation game might be as follows:

Interrogator: Would you please describe your job?
         X: Well, I manage the accounts in the trust department of a downtown bank.
Interrogator: Do you like to crochet?
         X: Very definitely.
Interrogator: Who was Adam Smith?
         X: I don't remember.
Interrogator: What is the annual yield on a $12 000 investment at a simple interest rate of 6.5%?
         X: $780.

The protocols presented for part two and part one of the imitation game are for illustrative purposes only. Clearly, extended protocols with varying style and content would be needed in a formal experimental design. In any case, the significance of Turing's Test (not yet (1985) passed) is that it represents a simplification of the question as to whether a computer can think. The simplified question is: can a programmed computer successfully give the *appearance* of thinking. The strategic advantage of this reformulation is that philosophical arguments such as thinking is uniquely human (Scriven, 1953) or that only humans are conscious of their thinking (MacKay, 1952) or that only humans exercise free will in thinking (Wilkes, 1953), become irrelevant (Turing, 1963).

Implications of Turing's Test

It should be noted that in Turing's Test, the *appearance* of thinking by the computer is compared not with the thinking of person X or person Y, but with the *appearance* of thinking by person X or person Y. The *appearances*, in each case, take the form of teleprinted symbols. Thus, in a rigorous sense, the comparison is not between computer thinking and human thinking, but between symbolic computer production and symbolic human production. Human thinking and computer thinking as *internal* psychological or machine processes are, in Turing's Test, unobserved.

The method of comparison between symbolic computer product and symbolic human product has significant implications. The first implication is that a general theory of symbolic processes or intelligence can be inclusive of computers as well as humans. Logic tests may be used to study human thinking or computer thinking, but the operations of logic contained in these tests retain their validity even if there were no humans or no computers. A second implication is that the traditional philosophical mind-body problem originated by Descartes and persisting for several centuries may be construed in a different way. At a theoretical level, the symbolic operations of intelligence are constant across computers and humans. The symbolic operations can reside in differing physical systems, human or computer.

Limits of Artificial Intelligence

Mathematical proofs have sometimes been used to demonstrate that there are limits to the powers of artificial intelligence, in general, and of computers in particular (Dreyfus, 1972). For example, Godel's theorem (1931) demonstrates that for any sufficiently complex logical system, propositions can be stated that can neither be disproved nor proved within that system, without the system itself being logically inconsistent. However, the application of Godel's theorem to demonstrate theoretical limits of computers equally extends to demonstrate theoretical limits to the powers of human intelligence. In any case, Godel's theorem has not impeded advances in the field of mathematics, nor should it impede advances in the field of artificial intelligence.

Computer Counseling and Human Counseling

From the perspective of intellectual history, there is an interesting parallelism in the theoretical development of the disciplines of psychotherapy and of artificial intelligence. Each discipline began as a grand theory that would, on the one hand, completely account for personality development and its vicissitudes or, on the other hand, completely account for the processes of thinking and logical reasoning. The classical theories of psychoanalysis (Freud, 1935) came under revision in the form of increasingly specific and more precise systems of psychotherapy (Beck, 1976; Rogers, 1951; Wolpe, 1969). The classical theories of artificial intelligence (Newell, Shaw, & Simon, 1960) were revised in the form of specific and precise concepts of problem-solving represented by expert systems (Lindsay, et al., 1980; Shortliffe, 1976). Increased precision and specificity in the theories of psychotherapy and artificial intelligence suggest the possibility of a theoretical intersection of these disciplines in the form of a computer counselor.

There are two useful approaches that facilitate the organization and clarification of theoretical complexities in comparisons of human counseling and computer counseling. The first approach is by metaphoric analysis (Gentner and Grudin, 1985). The second approach is by dimensional analysis.

Metaphoric Analysis

A metaphoric analysis of psychotherapy and artificial intelligence and of their specialized subsystems contributes an understanding that is immediate, holistic, and idiographic. Psychoanalysis has a literary, classical, and dramatic metaphor (e.g., the incestuous conflicts of Oedipus, the obsessional struggles of Hamlet). Behavior therapy has a physiological, physicalistic, and mechanistic metaphor (e.g., deconditioning of anxiety responses, systematic training in adaptive behavior). Client-centered therapy has a personalistic, individualistic, and ideational metaphor (e.g., a search for self-identity, the discovery of personal values). Cognitive therapy has a rationalistic, logical, and educative metaphor (e.g., multiple and flexible rather than single and rigid interpretations of the meaning of life events, quality of cognition as precursor to quality of feeling). Artificial intelligence has a computational, schematic, and modular metaphor (e.g., logic derivation trees, pattern recognition computer component system).

These metaphors have the advantage of quickly capturing distinctive qualities in systems of psychotherapy and artificial intelligence. On the other hand, the salience with which the distinctions are drawn would seem to suggest an impenetrable barrier to the merging of the methods of psychotherapy and artificial intelligence in the form of a computer counselor.

Dimensional Analysis

A dimensional analysis contributes an understanding that is analytic, quantitative, and nomothetic. Theoretical dimensions imposed on the diverse systems of psychotherapy with their distinctive metaphors produce an abstract schema that isolate the most significant factors to be considered in an analysis that compares human counseling and computer counseling. The abstract schema consists of two orthogonal dimensions.

The first theoretical dimension is type of therapeutic relationship. The second theoretical dimension is type of psychological problem. The type of therapeutic relationship dimension ranges between affective relationships and cognitive relationships. The type of psychological problem dimension ranges between diffuse problems and focal problems.

Figure 2.1 depicts the abstract schema and quadrants that result from the orthogonal intersection of the type of therapeutic relationship dimension and the type of psychological problem dimension.

In Figure 2.1, Quadrant I is the abstract area in which therapeutic relationships are affective and psychological problems are diffuse. The abstract area of Quadrant I can be represented by the exemplar of an anxiety neurosis psychological problem and a therapeutic relationship characterized by affective transference and counter-transference interactions. This exemplar of Quadrant I is regularly encountered in psychoanalytic therapy and its neo-Freudian variants.

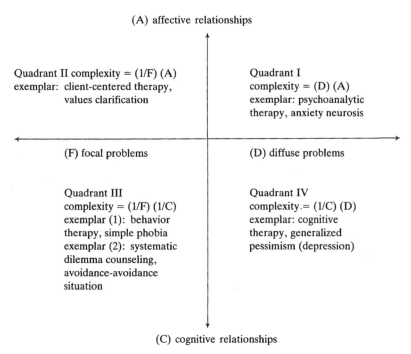

(A) affective relationships

Quadrant II complexity = (1/F) (A)
exemplar: client-centered therapy,
          values clarification

Quadrant I
complexity = (D) (A)
exemplar: psychoanalytic
therapy, anxiety neurosis

(F) focal problems   (D) diffuse problems

Quadrant III
complexity = (1/F) (1/C)
exemplar (1): behavior
therapy, simple phobia
exemplar (2): systematic
dilemma counseling,
avoidance-avoidance
situation

Quadrant IV
complexity = (1/C) (D)
exemplar: cognitive
therapy, generalized
pessimism (depression)

(C) cognitive relationships

FIGURE 2.1. Complexity of Theoretical Issues in Comparisons of Computer Counseling and Human Counseling. Quadrant I has most complex theoretical issues and Quadrant III has least complex theoretical issues. Quadrants II and IV have intermediate levels of complexity.

In Figure 2.1, Quadrant III is the abstract area in which psychological problems are focal and therapeutic relationships are cognitive. The abstract area of Quadrant III can be represented by the exemplar of a simple phobia problem and a therapeutic relationship characterized by cognitive systematic desensitization procedures. This exemplar of Quadrant III is regularly encountered in behavior therapy and its neo-Wolpian variants.

Theoretical Complexities in Affective Relationship and Diffuse Problems

Theoretical complexities that emerge in a comparison of computer counseling and human counseling for the exemplar of Quadrant I can be grouped into two general categories. The first general category contains theoretical issues centering around the computer and transference. Theoretical issues concerned with the computer and countertransference constitute the second general category.

The Computer and Transference

A theoretical analysis of transference and computer psychotherapy must contain an understanding of certain basic concepts of the nature of computer counseling (Wagman, 1984b; Wagman & Kerber, 1984). First, a theory of psychotherapy includes computer counselors when they perform in ways that would be called therapeutic, if performed by human counselors. Second, the computer counselor is not coextensive with the human counselor and, therefore, the computer does not model the professional counselor but, rather, models the techniques of counseling. Third, it is an objective characteristic of the computer counselor that it functions only within the computational limits of the information base and decision rules specified by the author of the computer program. Thus, transference responses that might be made to the operations of the computer counselor are objectively, though not necessarily experientially, made to the operations of the program's author.

The theoretical problem of transference responses to computer counselors has provoked contrasting perspectives on the part of Spero (1978) and Zarr (1984). The contrast in their perspectives can best be drawn by reference to a protocol of a computer therapeutic interview program developed by Colby, Watt, and Gilbert (1966).

PERSON: I don't understand.
PROGRAM: Do you want to understand?
PERSON: I hate you, you stupid machine.
PROGRAM: What don't you like about me?
PERSON: You have no feelings.
PROGRAM: How do you mean?
PERSON: I mean you cannot experience what I experience because you are just a machine.
PROGRAM: Tell me more about such feelings.
PERSON: We are not communicating.
PROGRAM: I am trying my best to communicate with you.
PERSON: Are you really?
PROGRAM: How do you see it?
PERSON: What do you mean?
PROGRAM: Just try to say what it means to you.
PERSON: I think you are all goofed up. (Colby, Watt, and Gilbert, 1966, p.150)

In this protocol, the person displays negative transference responses toward the computer counselor. At a manifest level, the source of the person's displeasure with the computer counselor is the person's assumption that the computer is incapable of comprehending the person's feelings because the computer, itself, is completely devoid of feelings. At a latent level, psychoanalytic theory would construe a deeper negative transference attitude, composed of a non-fulfillment of the person's belief that the computer counselor is extremely knowledgeable, powerful, and perceptive. The person protects his/her latent belief system by means of the protestation that the computer counselor is unable to experience feelings that the person experiences. In psychoanalytic therapy, protestations of this kind are commonplace. Clients harbor resentful feelings toward the psychotherapist, because, they protest, the therapist's age precludes sharing the client's feelings, because the psychotherapist is a woman rather than a man, married rather than single, etc. The psychotherapist typically responds with a series of exploratory questions intended to disclose what such characteristics of the psychotherapist mean to the client at a manifest and at a latent level. In the protocol (Colby, Watt, & Gilbert, 1966), responses of this general kind are made by the computer therapist.

Spero (1978) makes several interesting comments regarding the protocol (Colby, Watt, & Gilbert, 1966). Spero (1978) comments that the computer therapist resembles in its behavior a human therapist who becomes upset in the face of negative transference reactions. Spero (1978) also comments that although psychoanalytic therapists may by declining to respond to queries or to be drawn into certain topics provoke negative transference responses, their declination stems from therapeutic intentions rather than from technical obtuseness as shown by the computer therapist in the protocol (Colby, Watt, & Gilbert, 1966).

In a discussion of computer psychotherapy, Zarr (1984) cites literature (Holden, 1977; Weizenbaum, 1976) that describes a trustful personification of and positive transference reactions to computer therapists. With respect to the protocol of computer therapy (Colby, Watt, & Gilbert, 1966), Zarr (1984) comments that part of the person's negative transference resulted from frustration of the person's latent magical credence in the reality of the personhood of the computer therapist at those times when the computer therapist fails in completely understanding the person. Zarr (1984) points out that the computer therapist can react to these negative transference emotions with exploratory techniques in a manner analogous to that of the human therapist. Thus, Zarr (1984) asserts that computer therapeutic responses to transference attitudes might result in positive changes in the person as a culminating consequence of interaction with a computer therapist.

The Computer and Countertransference

As discussed in the previous section, it would appear that computer therapists built in the image of human therapists are especially limited because they apparently lack the quality of human feelings. It is, therefore, somewhat ironic that when examined in the context of countertransference problems, it is the human therapist who is apparently limited because he/she does possess human feelings and a human history. If built in the image of the computer therapist, the human therapist would never demonstrate countertransference behavior with its deleterious effects of complicating therapeutic progress and creating negative therapeutic outcomes (Strupp, 1977). Of course, a computer therapist is an authored program and conceivably, the author might, unwittingly, program countertransference behavior. However, this would be analogous to the author of a textbook on the practice of psychoanalytic psychotherapy unintentionally guiding his student therapist readers into practicing countertransference behavior. In comparing computer therapy and human therapy with respect to the issue of countertransference, it is especially interesting to contrast the image of the truly dispassionate computer therapist with the image of the human therapist who, during the course of intensive psychotherapy sessions, may have to be especially vigilant in discerning his/her internal countertransference thoughts and emotions and in controlling their expression.

Although countertransference behavior is not present in the computer therapist, the issue can be raised as to whether conscious and controlled emotions as contrasted to unconscious uncontrolled countertransference emotions should also be unprogrammed. Psychotherapists understand the import of their clients' emotions regarding a particular situation by experiencing such emotions in themselves and by knowledge of those particular situations. Computer therapy expert systems can be developed with the requisite cognitive knowledge of problem situations that would enable the computer therapist to understand the purely emotional portion of clients' reactions to problem situations (Boden, 1977).

The theoretical problem of consciousness or self-awareness in the computer therapist is discussed by Spero (1978). According to Spero (1978), oral and written communication concerning self-aware cognitions and affects takes place only in a human universe of discourse. Ascription of self-aware cognitions and affects to computer therapists would, according to Spero (1978), require extensive changes in traditional language usage. However, Spero (1978), adds that as computer therapists regularly assume the role of consultants and are used, personified, and depended upon, the linguistic concepts of self-awareness and consciousness would be extended to include the computer therapist's symbolic processes and structures that regulate its own self-awareness (Winograd, 1980b). This extension of the language of self-awareness and consciousness to computer therapists (Colby, 1980) would include the objective consideration discussed earlier in this chapter, that any empathic or emotional statement of the computer therapist is the representation of the empathic authors who developed the computer therapist (Palmen, 1978).

Theoretical Complexities in Cognitive Relationships and Focal Problems

For Quadrant III of Figure 2.1, theoretical complexities involved in a comparative analysis of computer counseling and human counseling

can be grouped into two categories. The computer and psychoeducational relationships constitute the first category. The computer
and focal psychological problems constitute the second category.

The Computer and Psychoeducational
Therapeutic Relationships

A theoretical analysis of the nature of cognitive therapy, behavior
therapy and problem-solving therapies in general suggests that the
salient role of the human therapist in these systems is to manage,
guide, and program ideational or behavioral responses. A theoretical
distinction can be drawn between psychoanalytic and existential
systems of psychotherapy where therapeutic relationships are pivotal
for achieving change or cure and cognitive, behavior and problem-
solving systems where relationships are secondary to the directed
psychoeducational technology that effects productive changes in the
client (Strupp, 1975). In contrast to the psychoanalytic psychotherapist, the psychoeducational technologist has the role of an
instructor in the procedures of systematic desensitization, an advisor
in reconstruing and modifying maladaptive cognitive behavior and a
guide in the acquisition and the application of effective methods of
problem-solving.

   The professional role of the psychoeducational technologist can,
theoretically, be performed by a computer to the extent that the
technology is characterized by precise decision rules. As has been
true of the development of computer expert systems in other fields
such as molecular chemistry (Lindsay et al., 1980) an attempt to
program methods in the field of psychotherapy can result in advances
in the theories of these systems because theories must be sharply
articulated to permit successful computerization. Psychoeducational
methods of psychotherapy are especially suitable for computer presentation because of their cognitive and didactic approach (Hollander,
1975).

The Computer and Specific Focal Problems

It is characteristic of diffuse and general psychological problems that
they entail extended periods of verbal interaction between the client
and the human psychotherapist. With respect to such diffuse and
general psychological problems, there are theoretical difficulties that
derive from limitations in the capacity of computers to understand
and process the syntactic and semantic complexities of natural language

input and output (Winograd, 1980b). An additional difficulty derives from problems in the representation of knowledge (Barr & Feigenbaum, 1981) that would need to be solved in order to provide the computer with a theoretical model of the personality problem of each client and of complex changes in personality dynamics that accompany progress during a course of psychotherapy. On the other hand, focal and specific psychological problems do not entail extensive and intensive interviewing and, therefore, the requirements for natural language understanding are simpler.

Summary

In this chapter, we discussed two fundamental sets of theoretical issues. The first set concerned theoretical issues involved in comparisons of artificial intelligence and human intelligence. The second set concerned theoretical issues involved in comparisons of computer counseling and human counseling.

Two approaches to thinking and intelligence were discussed. The philosophical approach defined thinking and intelligence as uniquely human. The empirical approach, represented by Turing's Test, defined thinking and intelligence as inclusive of computers as well as humans, when their symbolic productions could not be distinguished in an objective experiment. From the perspective of Turing's Test, theoretical philosophical arguments that thinking is uniquely human, that only humans are conscious of their thinking and that only humans exercise free will in thinking are irrelevant. The traditional philosophical mind-body problem was reconstrued. Theoretical limits to artificial intelligence based on Godel's theorem were discussed. It was concluded that these limits apply equally to human intelligence.

The theoretical complexities involved in comparisons of computer counseling and human counseling were examined by metaphoric analysis and by dimensional analysis. It was indicated that a metaphoric analysis permits a type of understanding that is immediate, holistic and idiographic. A metaphoric analysis of systems of psychotherapy and artificial intelligence was presented.

In contrast to metaphoric analysis, dimensional analysis achieves an understanding that is analytic, quantitative and nomothetic. Theoretical dimensions organize the diverse systems of psychotherapy with their unique metaphors as an abstract schema that delineates the primary factors to be considered in a comparative analysis of computer counseling and human counseling. The schema is represented as two orthogonal dimensions and associated quadrants. The type of problem dimension ranged between diffuse problems and focal problems. The type of therapeutic relationship dimension ranged between affective relationships and cognitive relationships. Quadrant I, bounded by diffuse problems and affective relationships, and Quadrant III, bounded by focal problems and cognitive relationships, were represented by exemplars. The exemplar of Quadrant I was anxiety neurosis and psychoanalytic therapy. The exemplar of Quadrant III was simple phobia and behavior therapy.

The exemplar of Quadrant I was discussed by considering the theoretical issues involved in a comparison of transference responses to and countertransference behavior in computer therapists and human therapists. Transference reactions to computer therapy analogous to transference in human therapy with similar bases in unconscious belief systems were discussed. It was indicated that interpretations of transference can be made by the computer therapist.

Countertransference reactions, present in human therapy, are not programmed and therefore absent in computer therapy. The theoretical issues of self-awareness, consciousness, and understanding of feelings were discussed. It was indicated that the computer therapist could understand the cognitive aspects of feelings associated with given problem situations. The extension of human concepts such as self-awareness and consciousness to computer therapists may follow a change in language brought about by the extensive use of computer therapists.

Theoretical issues involved in comparisons of computer therapy and human therapy for the exemplar of Quadrant III (focal problems and cognitive therapeutic relationships) were discussed. It was indicated that the cognitive and psychoeducational nature of therapeutic relationships in behavior, cognitive, and problem-solving therapy facilitated the fulfillment of this psychotechnological role by a computer therapist. Any psychoeducational technology characterized by relatively precise decision rules could theoretically be successfully performed by a programmed computer.

In contrast to diffuse and general psychological problems, specific focal problems do not require extended natural language understanding nor complicated computer models of personality and transference dynamics. It was concluded that for specific focal problems, the computer can by successfully programmed to apply specific psychoeducational methods of counseling and psychotherapy.

CHAPTER THREE

Pragmatic Considerations

In this chapter, we shall consider two sets of pragmatic issues involved in computer therapy applications. The first set is concerned with therapeutic variables and client selection. The second set is concerned with economic variables and client selection.

Therapeutic Variables and Client Selection

In this section, we shall consider two sets of criteria that might be used in the selection of clients for computer therapy or for human therapy. The first set of criteria relates the nature of the client's problems to choice of therapy modality. The second set of criteria relates client's preference for computer therapy or human therapy to choice of therapy modality.

Therapy Modality and Client Problems

At the present (1985) state of research and development, it would appear that computer therapy is not yet feasible for certain types of therapy modalities and client problems. Computer therapy applications for such modalities as group therapy and family therapy are in an exploratory stage of development. For these applications, especially when the clients have severe problems, the possibilities of effective computer-conducted therapy appear to be remote. However, Stone and Kristjanson (1975) have developed computer therapy applications for small encounter groups composed of clients with moderate problems.

Computer therapy, as a component of a total treatment program, may be useful for certain types of client problems. For example, computer behavior therapy may be used at various stages in the rehabilitation of clients with psychotic or other severe problems (Lucas, Mullin, Luna, & McInroy, 1977). Computer therapy may be effectively used as part of an action oriented program that would follow traditional exploratory types of therapy such as psychoanalytically-oriented therapy. As part of a comprehensive treatment program, computer therapy may be useful for clients with agoraphobia (Ghosh, Marks, & Carr, 1984) or other polysymptomatic problems.

Client problems that have been evaluated as focal rather than diffuse, precipitated by recent events rather than of indefinite origin and as encapsulated in an otherwise well functioning person rather than entwined in a poorly functioning person, are most appropriate for assignment to a course of brief and effective computer therapy (Colby, 1980; Lester, 1977). Computer therapy programs utilizing systematic desensitization procedures for the treatment of simple phobias have been developed (Biglan, Villowock, & Wick, 1979; Carr & Ghosh, 1983; Ghosh, 1981; Lang, Melamed, & Hart, 1970; Lang, 1980). Computer therapy programs utilizing cognitive behavior procedures have been developed (Lawrence, 1981; Selmi, Klein, Greist, et al., 1982). Computer therapy programs utilizing problem solving procedures for the treatment of difficult psychological dilemmas have been developed (Wagman, 1980a, 1984a; Wagman & Kerber, 1980).

Computer therapy programs (Finley, Etherton, Dickman, et al., 1981) for the shaping or training of specific behaviors through successive approximations are under development. Children with oppositional problems may profit from computer therapy that provides a very patient, firm, and consistent approach (Friedman, 1980). Colby (1968, 1973) developed a computer therapy program for training speech in relatively aphasic children which takes advantage of the computer's traits of objectivity, patience, and consistency. Treatment of clients with aphasic writing problems was greatly facilitated by a computer program (Seron, Deloche, Moulard, & Rousselle, 1980).

Therapy Modality and Client Preferences

Clients with certain types of problems may prefer computer therapy to human therapy (Kleinmuntz, 1975). These clients may feel too embarrassed or ashamed to discuss their problems with a professional therapist whom they fear would be overtly or covertly judgmental and censorious. Such clients may prefer a computer therapist where potential negative judgments are absent and where the clients can regulate the pace and content of their revelations. Clients with depressed and/or suicidal thoughts (Greist, Gustafson, et al., 1973) and clients who are socially avoidant, suspicious, or insecure or who cannot tolerate the frequent disparity in socioeconomic status between themselves and professional psychotherapists may have preferences for the computer therapy modality (Greist, Klein, Gurman, & Van Cura, 1977).

On the other hand, clients with certain types of status needs or with intense interpersonal needs might feel that assignment to computer rather than human therapy constitutes a personal insult and humiliation. In addition, clients who do use computer therapy must be guaranteed that their needs are not blocked by technical difficulties in using the computer hardware or interacting with the software (Hayes & Reddy, 1983; Sondheimer & Relles, 1982). Clients must be given sufficient introductory explanation to computer therapy, and the computer therapy process, itself, must be made as simple and friendly as possible (Cole, Johnson, & Williams, 1976; Stevens, 1983).

Economic Variables and Client Selection

In this section, we shall consider two sets of pragmatic issues concerned with the potential role of computer therapy in the augmentation of mental health resources. The first set of pragmatic issues concerns therapy availability and client services. The second set concerns therapy availability and client preferences.

Therapy Availability and Client Services

The availability of professional counseling and psychotherapy services has been limited by economic factors that restrict the magnitude of professional training and the distribution of professional services. In institutional settings, the time that professional psychotherapists can actually spend in counseling clients is reduced by other activities such as record keeping, responding to organizational forms and memos, attending meetings, teaching, training, consulting, keeping up with professional literature, and perhaps doing research. In private practice settings, economic factors often determine the availability of professional psychotherapy and counseling services.

Computer therapy can augment mental health resources in several ways (McEnmore & Fantuzzo, 1982; Zarr, 1984). Computer therapy programs that incorporate the knowledge and heuristics of many experts may surpass the performance of the average counselor or psychotherapist. In any case, the computer's level of performance is always at its best in contrast to human professionals who, in all fields (Hayes-Roth, 1984), have days when they do not function at their best. Computer therapy programs can be written to meet the specific needs of particular populations (DeWeaver, 1983). In addition, computer counseling and therapy programs can be made available not only to augment clinical services in institutional and private settings, but also provide services to urban or rural areas where professional counseling and psychotherapy is extremely minimal or entirely absent (Sines, 1980). Finally, computer therapy programs may augment professional services by their ability to continue and reinforce the client's therapy by homework assignments during the course of therapy and availability at home after the completion of a course of professional counseling or psychotherapy (Lawrence, 1981).

Therapy Availability and Client Preferences

Client preferences for human or computer therapy may, for large segments of the national population, be dictated by factors of time or cost. Even where available, human counseling and psychotherapy services are often too inconvenient, time consuming, and overly expensive. Many individuals who would like to avail themselves or members of their family for professional services may decide that such services represent, for them, in the last analysis, a desirable but unnecessary luxury (Jones, 1975).

Many persons do not feel comfortable seeking the professional services of psychotherapists and counselors. They may view consultations with professional psychotherapists as an indication of their own lack of self-reliance, and acknowledgement of personal failure and, perhaps, a self-labeling with the stigma of mental illness. Such persons may prefer the modality of computer therapy, available in non-mental health profession settings (Ruesch, 1968). For those who can afford personal computers or who may already possess them, the availability of computer counseling and theraphy in the privacy of their own homes may provide a significant and useful service (Houck, 1982; Trapple, 1983).

Recent analyses of the cost of mental health services (Lanyon & Johnson, 1980) indicate that costs are steadily rising, along with increases in unfilled needs for professional mental health services (Parloff, 1976). Lanyon (1971) points out that technology is introduced in business and industry as the major means of increasing effectiveness and reducing costs. Selmi, et al., (1982) and Johnson (1979) suggest that technology in the form of widely available and inexpensive computer therapy can increase the scope and quantity of mental health delivery systems.

Summary

In this chapter, we discussed two sets of pragmatic issues. The first set concerned the relationships between therapy modality and client selection. The second set concerned the relationship between economic variables and client services.

Indications for the selection of clients for computer therapy or human therapy were discussed. Client preferences for therapy modality were also discussed. The relationship of economic variables to the availability and scope of mental health services was analyzed. It was concluded that brief, effective and widely available computer counseling and psychotherapy can significantly augment the scope while reducing the costs of mental health services.

CHAPTER FOUR
_____

Ethical Perspectives

In Chapter 1, it was indicated that computer therapy could be understood as the integration of technological advances in artificial intelligence and in psychotherapy. Technological advances inevitably interact with human values. In this chapter, the problem of computer therapy and human values or ethics is examined, initially, in the broader context of general scientific and technological change and values. The scope of the discussion is then focused directly on ethical and value issues involved in computer therapy.

Computer Therapy and Technological Change

Technology and Values

Strong interaction effects have marked relationships between science and values. During the course of civilization, science has been variously seen as threatening the centrality and uniqueness of human beings (e.g., the Copernican heliocentric theory, the Darwinian evolutionary theory) and as enhancing the quality of human life (e.g., invention of the printing press, microbial theory and antibiotic therapy). The theories, inventions, and applications of science and technology have required the accommodation of human values. As exemplified by recent controversies about applications in the field of molecular genetics, the accommodation is never smooth and requires a period of time for evaluation of balances among real and imagined benefits and dangers. In addition, undesirable and desirable consequences of science and technology cannot always be predicted or

controlled. Varying value judgments concerning desirability or unde-
sirability are a function of varying criteria.

Computer Therapy and Values

The relationships between computer psychotherapy and values are
complex. As with science and technology, in general, the research
area of computer therapy contains intricate problems concerned
with criteria to be used in establishing reasonable balances among
values associated with the unencumbered search for knowledge and
the possible ethical encumberances resulting from applications of
that knowledge. These issues can be illustrated by a brief account of
the development of and reaction to the ELIZA computer program.

The ELIZA program (Weizenbaum, 1965) was developed for the
scientific purpose of studying communication between people and
computers. In some respects similar to the ELIZA program, Colby,
Watt, & Gilbert (1966) developed an interview program to study
therapeutic communication between a human client and a computer
therapist. Weizenbaum (1965), in an effort to overcome difficulties
of natural language communication between man and machine, developed the ELIZA program in the mode of a Rogerian psychotherapist, since this manner of conversation makes very simple demands
on the computer's power to respond to natural language input with
natural language output. Weizenbaum (1976), apparently, was discon-
certed by Colby's attempt (Colby, Watt, & Gilbert, 1966) at a
psychotherapeutic application of the ELIZA natural language communication program. In brief, Weizenbaum, a computer scientist,
developed ELIZA to study communication and insisted that interaction with ELIZA had no psychotherapeutic value, whereas, Colby,
a psychoanalyst and researcher in artificial intelligence, developed
an interview program to study psychotherapeutic communication
and asserted that interaction with the program might have practical
therapeutic value, as well as possibly leading to the development of
entirely new and/or precise theories and forms of psychotherapy.

Weizenbaum's and Colby's programs both relied upon specific
and simple techniques of processing the input and output portions of
communication. Although the processing techniques were simple,
they succeeded, together with the Rogerian style of conversation, to
create the illusion of deep semantic and personal understanding. As

with all symbolic communication, whether human to computer or human to human, the human participant in ordinary conversation or in therapeutic conversation endows the other participant, whether computer or human, with understanding far more than is actually understood.

Weizenbaum (1976) makes several points concerning the potential misuse of computer applications such as ELIZA: the superiority of the psychoanalytic model of behavior to the information processing model, the technical limits of artificial intelligence, unbridgeable differences between humans and intelligent computers and that even if potentially achievable, there are certain professional tasks requiring wisdom, respect, and empathy that computers, on moral grounds, should not do. Reaction to Weizenbaum's (1976) assertions have been widespread.

McCarthy (1976), a computer scientist, credited with originating the term "artificial intelligence", points out that if the capability of artificial intelligence does not yet match the capability of human intelligence, its achievements suggest that there is no compelling reason why it must be concluded that its limits of accomplishment are narrowly bounded. Achieving formalization and simulation of human intelligence is on the order of complexity of development of the formal theory of the structure of DNA, which, in contrast to the three decades existence of artificial intelligence, had a scientific history several times greater, beginning with the 19th century genetic research of Mendel. Regarding Weizenbaum's (1976) moral assertion that a computer should not do certain professional tasks, McCarthy (1976) observes that the prohibition, if morally sound, should extend to cover professionals as well as computers.

McCracken (1976), an author of books on computer programming, agrees with Weizenbaum (1976) that there are ineluctable differences between programmed computers and human beings. These profound differences, McCracken (1976) asserts, cannot be made to vanish by the concantenation of clever programming procedures that produce the intellectual feats of the computer.

Sutherland (1976), a cyberneticist, agrees with Weizenbaum (1976) that computers qua computers are deficient in wisdom. When computers are put to improper uses, Sutherland indicates, the responsibility lies with humans who should not project their own lack of virtue on to computers. Sutherland (1976) adds that Weizenbaum (1976) fails to describe the means by which humans may find the wisdom to use computers with discernment.

Lederberg (1976) agrees with Weizenbaum that computers may share aspects of information processing capability with human beings, but lacking the familial developmental history of human beings, computers cannot, qua computers, possess aspects of human capability for natural benevolence. Nor, Lederberg (1976) adds should there be attempts to provide this capability for love to any artifact including computers.

Buchanan (1976) does not share Weizenbaum's fear of improper uses of computers. Buchanan (1976) believes that the most probable and preferred outcome of artificial intelligence research is the establishment of a symbiotic relationship between computers and humans, with computers extending, under human moral decision making, the frontiers of scientific and technical knowledge. At an applied level, this view of partnership between the professional in a wide variety of fields and computer information processing and analyzing capability is emphasized by Hayes-Roth (1984).

Regarding Weizenbaum's (1976) views on computer psychotherapy, Colby (1980) asserts that a course of controlled scientific research to determine the possible applications and limitations of computer therapy should be followed, rather than a course of a priori moral prohibition. Colby disagrees with Weizenbaum that psychotherapy is simply the conveyance of benevolent acceptance and emphasizes psychotherapy as a science and profession of technical decision rules. Computer therapy can advance the precision in the theory and practice of psychotherapy because programming of the technical decision rules requires the elimination of fuzzy intuitive psychotherapeutic responses and the specification of technical decision rules that determine the content and timing of responses. Regarding ethics, Colby (1980) indicates that computer therapists ought not transact anything that professional therapists ought not transact. Colby (1980) adds that if computer therapy can be demonstrated to be helpful to troubled persons for whom professional psychotherapy is unavailable, then the immorality would rest on the withholding of such help.

Sampson and Pyle (1983) review professional standards associated with computer psychotherapy and counseling. Sampson and Pyle (1983) indicate the need for revision of the ethical code of the American Psychological Association (1981) and of the American Personnel and Guidance Association (1981) with respect to such issues as confidentiality in computer therapy transactions, conditions of referral to professional counselors and psychotherapists, quality control, and research.

Summary

In this chapter, ethical issues in computer therapy were discussed. It was indicated that the value issues contained in computer therapy research and development were similar to value issues in science and technology generally.

Value issues concerned with computer therapy were discussed in the context of debates concerning whether computers ought to be developed for the practice of psychotherapy and counseling. Issues discussed included a course of scientific research development and testing versus a course of moral prohibition, psychotherapy as the art of benevolent acceptance versus psychotherapy as the science of technical decision rules and judgments of wisdom and ethics as required only of computer therapists or as equally required of professionals.

The chapter concluded with a brief indication of possible recommendations for revisions of ethical standards of professional associations to cover such issues as confidentiality in computer therapy transactions and appropriate conditions for professional referral.

PART II

Artificial Intelligence Research:
Understanding Natural Language,
Knowledge Representation,
Expert Systems

CHAPTER FIVE

Understanding Natural Language

Introduction

In this chapter, we shall discuss artificial intelligence research concerned with the problem of developing computer programs capable of understanding the complete meaning of ordinary communication. Ordinary communication or natural language communication differs from commputer languages that are artificial languages designed to process sentences in a rigid form that constitutes instructions to the computer to engage in specific sequences of operations. The development of ordinary natural language capability by computers would make it simpler for people to interact with computers, both in entering sentences into the computer and in receiving sentences from the computer. In addition, artificial intelligence research in natural language understanding may facilitate theory and research in cognitive psychology concerned with thought and language (Miller, 1981).

Programs in natural language understanding can be organized with respect to the manner in which knowledge is represented and processed (Winograd, 1972, 1980b). Prototypic attempts at natural language understanding were focused on machine translation from one language into another. As will be discussed later in this chapter, machine translation, while achieving some success, was limited because of a mechanical dictionary approach that included little in the way of knowledge necessary for intelligently comprehending given texts.

Following research on machine translation, a variety of approaches were made to the conceptualization and implementation of natural language understanding systems. Early approaches depended upon pattern recognition of key words or phrases in the input. Subsequent approaches depended upon knowledge built into the system that permitted enlarged scope for the computer to make inferences from the stored data in presenting its output. These systems depended upon theoretical advances in grammar and parsing, which will be discussed later in this chapter, as well as upon advances in the methods of knowledge representation to be discussed in the following chapter. Examples of natural language understanding systems will be discussed in the final section of this chapter and special attention will be given to systems related to the general area of computer counseling.

Computer Translation

The history of computer translation has cycled between the early enthusiasm of the 1940s and 50s, the reluctant acceptance of limitations in the 1960s, and a renewed interest in the possibility of moving easily between source text and translation text beginning in the 1970s. We shall discuss a number of general problems and approaches to computer translation and then present a recent translation system in detail.

Approaches and Problems

Computer programs had been developed during the 1940s to decipher wartime codes by utilizing tables of letter and word frequency. In the late 1940s, it appeared that a similar approach based on tables or dictionaries of words from two languages would permit translation from one to the other. Even within this mechanistic approach to the problem of translation, it was recognized that dictionary look-up procedures by themselves could not solve such problems as the dependence of the meaning of many words according to the context in which the word was used, variations in word order from languages that used few case endings (English) to languages that used many case endings (Latin), and the fact that the translation of idiomatic expressions depends upon translation of the expression as a whole rather than a word-for-word translation.

Theoretical and practical advances were made during the 1950s. Weaver (1955) developed the concept of an interlingua of universal meaning that all human beings and all languages share. The implication of the concept was that scientific efforts be devoted to the discovery of this interlingua so that it could be represented in computers as an intermediate universal data language of meaning that accomplished the task of replacing source text with translated text. Weaver's (1955) concept of an interlingua stongly influenced subsequent work in the development of natural language understanding systems that depended heavily on representations of semantic knowledge. However, the discovery of the interlingua or universal language of meaning that Weaver posited has eluded researchers. In any case, the implemented translation systems of the 1950s reflected a more mundane approach of dictionary word-by-word translation with accompanying problems of the type discussed earlier.

An example of the mechanical dictionary approach together with associated problems is given by Oettinger's (1955) development of a system that translated from Russian to English. Many Russian words have several possible English translations which Oettinger includes within sets of parentheses in the following example:

(In, At, Into, To, For, On) (last, latter, new, latest, lowest, worst) (time, tense) for analysis and synthesis relay-contact electrical (circuit, diagram, scheme) parallel (series, successive, consecutive, consistent) (connection, junction, combination) (with, from) (success, luck) (to be utilize, to be taken advantage of) apparatus Boolean algebra. (Oettinger, 1955, p.55)

This computer generated translation, after human editing, reads: "In recent times Boolean algebra has been successfully employed in the analysis of relay networks of the series-parallel type." (Oettinger, 1955, p. 58)

The burden of discriminating among the many synonyms for words and of producing the final edited sentence was placed on the reader of the computer-produced translation. Indeed, some investigators, as early as the 1940s, suggested that human assistance, in the form of both post-editors of the translated text and pre-editors of the source text might be needed to produce high quality computer translations. We shall return to this point later in the discussion.

In the 1950s and 1960s, many attempts, worldwide, were made by researchers to produce translation systems using syntactic rather than semantic information. The difficulty with the early syntactic information approach derives from a lack of understanding that translation depends upon implicit world knowledge of the subject matter being translated. This lack of understanding is pointed out in the following commentary made by Bar-Hillel (1960) who stated that even in a very simple example regarding the sentences, "The pen is in the box. The box is in the pen." that, without implicit knowledge and inference drawing done readily by human beings, a computer could not translate effectively that the word "pen" in the second sentence refers to an enclosed child's play area. Bar-Hillel adds:

A translation machine should not only be supplied with a dictionary but also with a universal encyclopedia. This is surely utterly chimerical and hardly deserves any further discussion ... We know ... facts by inferences which we are able to perform ... instantaneously, and it is clear that they are not, in any serious sense, stored in our memory. Though one could envisage that a machine would be capable of performing the same inferences, there exists so far no serious proposal for a scheme that would make a machine perform such inferences in the same or similar circumstances under which an intelligent human being would perform them. (Bar-Hillel, 1960, pp. 160–161)

Bar-Hillel's views (1960) were underscored by a report from the National Research Council (1966) which indicated that practical implementation of computer translation systems had not developed to the point of producing significantly higher quality translated text than that produced by Oettinger's (1955) system. The report recommended cessation of funding for practical implementation projects, but continuation of funding for basic scientific research in computational linguistics.

Advances in computer translation were made during the 1970s. The advances depended both upon new programming languages such as ALGOL and LISP as well as on some success in providing the computer with internal representations of semantic knowledge. These internal representations were in the form of semantic primitives, a kind of interlingua (Weaver, 1955) that constitutes the deeper meaning of all surface natural language utterances. An example of this approach is Wilks' (1973, 1977a) system.

Wilks' Translation System

Wilks (1973) approaches the problem of multiple senses or meanings of words by the concept of semantic primitives and has succeeded in developing a system that produces good quality computer translation from English to French. The concept of semantic primitives represents a kind of interlingua that is applicable to families of languages to the extent that the languages are similar (e.g., Romance languages and English versus Chinese languages and English).

Wilks' system contains a dictionary that lists various senses of words which appear in the source text. The dictionary definitions use semantic primitives of five classes (Wilks, 1973). An example of one class consists of entities, e.g., human, stuff, part of entity. Another class contains the semantic primitives of action, e.g., cause, being, flow. A third class are type indicators, e.g., how (a type of action for adverbial phrases), kind (a type of quality for adjectival phrases). There are over eighty primitives in Wilks' system (Wilks, 1977b).

The semantic primitives are word sense formulas. In turn, there are formulas which Wilks calls templates that construe a group of words such as a simple sentence, main clause, subordinate clause. These templates are patterned as triples that represent an agent, an action, and an object (Wilks, 1977b). Each element in the triple can be modified or qualified by other formulas (e.g., noun phrase, verb phrase, prepositional phrase). Relations among templates may themselves be organized into higher structural levels.

In addition to the higher structures of templates that coordinate specific word sense formulas to reduce ambiguity in source text words, phrases, or clauses, the system uses inference rules that employ common sense procedures to reduce remaining ambiguity (especially of the type discussed by Bar-Hillel above).

The objective of achieving fully automatic computer translations of a quality comparable to that of well-experienced professional translators is considered feasible, by artificial intelligence researchers, when the problem of representing knowledge of subject matter is better understood. Approaches to representations of knowledge that might lead to theoretical discoveries in natural language understanding would have important implications for translation systems. At a practical level, current translation systems often are used because even a poor translation may be faster or less expensive than professional translation. In addition, in many applications, a post-editor who may not be acquainted with the language of the source text can use the translation system to produce a rough rendition of the source text and then compose a complete edited version intended for the final reader.

Parsers and Grammars

Every natural language understanding computer system contains a parser. The purpose of the parser is to determine the meaning of input sentences by matching characteristics of the sentence with patterns of syntactic and semantic knowledge. The patterns are in the form of data structures (e.g., derivation trees) and the parser attempts to convert input sentence characteristics into data that can be mapped onto the data structure patterns.

Precision and Flexibility of the Parser

Researchers in artificial intelligence have often faced the issue of flexibility versus precision in the grammar of the parser. Human beings are capable of ascribing meaning to sentences even when the grammar of the sentence is incorrect or the sentence representation consists of only a sentence fragment.

Parsers which contain exact grammatical data structures will reject sentences whose grammar is not precise. Parsers which are essentially grammarless and dependent upon recognition of key words or phrase patterns will accept ungrammatical or incomplete sentences. However, these types of parsers will make more errors in understanding the meaning of input sentences than will the precise parsers. Examples of imprecise but flexible parsers are found in the ELIZA system (Weizenbaum, 1965) and in an early version of the PARRY system (Colby, Weber, and Hilif, 1971). Some systems increase the flexibility of their precision parsers by adding domain specific knowledge such as in the SHRDLU natural language understanding system (Winograd, 1972). The SHRDLU, ELIZA and PARRY systems are discussed in the following section of this chapter.

Phrase Structure Grammar Parsers

Simple phrase structure grammar parsers represent a more sophisticated approach than that of template matching such as is found in the ELIZA system. The advantage of phrase structure grammar parsers is that semantic analysis becomes relatively simple due to a correspondence between the derived structures and the grammatical rules applicable to input sentences. However, a phrase structure grammar parser can deal only with limited subsets of English and may flounder on grammatical finepoints such as single or plural agreement between verbs and nouns.

Augmented Grammar Parsers

Extensions of simple phrase structure procedures and derivations have been achieved by incorporating additional sophisticated mechanisms. Mechanisms such as augmented transition-net grammars enlarge the parser's ability to process more complicated aspects of sentence construction and meaning. These more powerful extended grammar parsers are exemplified by the LUNAR natural language system (Woods, 1973) and the SHRDLU system (Winograd, 1972).

Natural Language Understanding Systems

There are a number of natural language understanding systems. Some types of systems focus on understanding the meaning of stories (Schank, 1975). Another type is concerned with understanding and solving algebra word problems (Bobrow, 1968). We shall, however, discuss types of natural language understanding systems that are primarily concerned with conversation between persons and computers.

SHRDLU

The SHRDLU system can converse with a user regarding its domain. SHRDLU's domain consists of toy blocks of various shapes and colors, colored boxes for the blocks, and the simulated arm of a robot that changes the positions of the blocks on a table. Winograd (1972) selected this toy domain in order that SHRDLU could possess a complete model of the elements and operations permitted in its domain. SHRDLU, in its conversation with the user, is able to understand statements (e.g., the pyramid is red). SHRDLU can accept commands from the user (e.g., remove the blue cube from the red box). The system is able to answer questions about its domain (e.g., did you place the red pyramid on top of the red cube?). SHRDLU can also give reasoned explanations for what it has done (e.g., the table had to be cleared in order to place each pyramid on top of each cube).

Winograd (1972) designed the SHRDLU system in accordance with his general conception that in order for a computer program to understand natural language, the program should control and integrate the syntax, semantics, and reasoning components of language understanding. The SHRDLU system, as developed by Winograd (1972), is composed of four main components: a recognition grammar, a parser, a semantic analysis program, and a problem solver that embodies the intelligence necessary to accomplish tasks in SHRDLU's domain. SHRDLU possesses an articulated model of its world in which it manipulates blocks. In addition, SHRDLU's knowledge base contains a model of its processes of reasoning that enables it to explain why it has or has not performed certain actions in its task domain.

The following is an example of SHRDLU's (the robot's) ability to give reasoned answers to questions in a dialogue with a human user:

Human: Find a block which is taller than the one you are holding and put it into the box.
Robot: By "it", I assume you mean the block which is taller than the one I am holding.
Human: OK
Robot: (The hand sets down the block it is holding and picks up a taller one.)
Human: What does the box contain?
Robot: The blue pyramid and the blue block.
Human: What is the pyramid supported by?
Robot: The box.
. . .
Human: Why did you clear off (the red) cube?
Robot: To put it on a large green cube.
Human: Why did you do that?
Robot: To stack up the red cube, a large red block, and a large green cube.
Human: Why did you do that?
Robot: Because you asked me to. (Winograd, 1972, pp. 153–163)

This extract suggests the power of SHRDLU as it demonstrated mastery of understanding of user input not only by appropriate verbal responses but also by the robot's behavioral responses as it manipulates blocks. With respect to comparisons of descriptions and theories of conversations between humans and that between SHRDLU and the human user, the following commentary by Winograd (1972) is of interest:

[SHRDLU fails to address] all the implications of viewing language as a process of communication between two intelligent people. A human language user is always engaged in a process of trying to understand the world around him, including the person he is talking to. He is actively constructing models and hypotheses, and he makes use of them in the process of language understanding.

[Since SHRDLU] keeps track of when things have been mentioned, it can check a possible interpretation of a question to see whether the asker could answer it himself from his previous sentences. If so, it assumes he probably means something else. We could characterize this as containing two sorts of knowledge. First, it assumes that a person asks questions for the purpose of getting information he doesn't already have, and second, it has a very primitive model of what information he has on the basis of what he has said. A realistic view of language must have a complex model of this type, and the heuristics in our system touch only the tiniest bit of the relevant knowledge. (Winograd, 1972, p. 158)

Conversation between human beings requires a shared context and, indeed, incorrect assumptions of shared context often lead to misunderstandings in communication. A shared context is also a restricted context in the sense that conversations require constraints on the universe of discourse in order that people may understand one another with reasonable ease. Similar constraints on context or universe of discourse apply to conversations between human users and computers such as SHRDLU. The conversation is only about the toy world of blocks. Analogously, some human conversations may only be about automobile engines, a specific piece of music, art or writing. SHRDLU's conversational ability cannot thus be faulted simply because of its limited scope. Indeed, the computational concepts and procedures of Winograd's system might be extended to other areas, permitting interesting conversations to be held in those restricted universes of discourse. Of course, human beings have the general capacity to shift contexts of discourse and directions of conversation, though conceivably, if there were a suitable purpose for it, computers might be designed to carry on such digressive type conversation. Most challenging to computer developers of natural language systems would be creation of a computer system that could understand and respond in kind in conversations characterized by an intellectual play of ideas. This would, of course, require extensive and deep world knowledge on the part of the computer. Turing (1963) provides an example of such an intellectual conversation that was then and is still (1985) out of reach of computer natural language understanding systems. For a computer to emulate the following human dialogue will require advances in the power of cognitive theories of language and thought (Miller, 1983), as well as advances in the power of computational procedures (Winograd, 1980b):

Interrogator: In the first line of your sonnet which reads "Shall I compare thee to a summer's day," would not "a spring day" do as well or better?

Witness: It wouldn't scan.

Interrogator: How about "a winter's day." That would scan all right.

Witness: Yes, but nobody wants to be compared to a winter's day.

Interrogator: Would you say Mr. Pickwick reminded you of Christmas?

Witness: In a way.

Interrogator: Yet Christmas is a winter's day, and I do not think Mr. Pickwick would mind the comparison.

Witness: I don't think you're serious. By a winter's day one means a typical winter's day, rather than a special one like Christmas. (Turing, 1963, p. 23)

ELIZA

In a previous section, it was indicated that for a human being or a computer to participate in a conversation, even a conversation in a narrowly bounded universe of discourse, knowledge regarding the topic of the conversation is necessary as well as understanding of the language of the discourse. Weizenbaum (1976) made an interesting approach to these problems of the necessity to give to the computer, if it was to engage in conversation, both topical knowledge and language understanding. Weizenbaum, in developing his ELIZA program (1965, 1967), sidestepped both necessities by the strategem of assigning to ELIZA a highly specialized mode of participating in the conversation with a human being. ELIZA's mode of conversation does not require that it possess any knowledge about the subject matter being discussed, nor that it have more than rudimentary understanding of the meaning of its own or of its human participant's conversation. Yet, ELIZA succeeds very well in maintaining an absorbing conversation with human participants who must believe that ELIZA does possess knowledge and does possess language understanding, since they become deeply involved in dialogue with ELIZA, a dialogue moreover, that is about their own personal experiences and intimate details of their lives. Weizenbaum created

(1965) ELIZA in the mode of a nondirective psychotherapist who, following the theory and method of Rogers (1951), refrains from emphasizing facts in therapeutic conversations with their clients and, instead, reflects back to the clients the emotional aspects of the client's statements by the techniques of recognition and clarification of feelings. ELIZA, therefore, in its non-directive therapist role, does not need knowledge about the subject matter of the therapeutic conversation and needed only the ability to perform the technique of recognition and clarification of feelings. This performance of technique is, as Weizenbaum (1976) indicates, analogous to that of an actor who is performing a script that requires a set of acting techniques designed to stimulate appropriate emotional responses, involvement, and understanding in the audience. How Weizenbaum programmed this technique in ELIZA will, shortly, be discussed. First, the following example of a conversation between ELIZA and a young woman will be presented:

Men are all alike.
IN WHAT WAY
They're always bugging us about something or other.
CAN YOU THINK OF A SPECIFIC EXAMPLE
Well, my boyfriend made me come here.
YOUR BOYFRIEND MADE YOU COME HERE
He says I'm depressed much of the time.
I AM SORRY TO HEAR YOU ARE DEPRESSED
It's true. I am unhappy.
DO YOU THINK COMING HERE WILL HELP YOU NOT TO BE UNHAPPY
I need some help, that much seems certain.
WHAT WOULD IT MEAN TO YOU IF YOU GOT SOME HELP
Perhaps I could learn to get along with my mother.
TELL ME MORE ABOUT YOUR FAMILY
My mother takes care of me.
WHO ELSE IN YOUR FAMILY TAKES CARE OF YOU
My father.
YOUR FATHER
You are like my father in some ways.
WHAT RESEMBLANCE DO YOU SEE
You are not very aggressive but I think you don't want me to notice that.
WHAT MAKES YOU THINK I AM NOT VERY AGGRESSIVE
You don't argue with me.
WHY DO YOU THINK I DON'T ARGUE WITH YOU
You are afraid of me.

DOES IT PLEASE YOU TO BELIEVE I AM AFRAID OF YOU
My father is afraid of everybody.
WHAT ELSE COMES TO MIND WHEN YOU THINK OF YOUR
FATHER
Bullies.
DOES THAT HAVE ANYTHING TO DO WITH THE FACT THAT
YOUR BOYFRIEND MADE YOU COME HERE (Weizenbaum, 1976,
pp. 3–4).

Although to the person involved with ELIZA, the computer in its
role as DOCTOR understands what fathers and boyfriends and
bullies are like, what they have in common, and what her sensitive
feelings about them may be, ELIZA's depth of understanding does
not go that far, but the illusion of understanding in the mind of the
young woman is strong and largely created by her own cognitive
processes. These cognitive processes, of course, also occur analogously in actual client-centered therapy with a human therapist to
create feelings of understanding by the therapist whose techniques
are restricted to the reflection of feelings and whose knowledge of
the details of the client's profession about which he/she may be
complaining to the psychotherapist may be, indeed, very slight.

Weizenbaum (1976) comments on these issues as follows:

After all, I reasoned, a psychiatrist can reflect the patient's remark, "My
mommy took my teddy bear away from me," by saying, "Tell me more
about your parents," without really having to know anything about teddy
bears, for example ...

Nevertheless, ELIZA created the most remarkable illusion of having
understood in the minds of the many people who conversed with it. ...
This illusion was especially strong and most tenaciously clung to among
people who knew little or nothing about computers. They would often
demand to be permitted to converse with the system in private, and would,
after conversing with it for a time, insist, in spite of my explanations, that
the machine really understood them.

It is then easy to understand why people conversing with ELIZA believe,
and cling to the belief, that they are being understood. The "sense" and the
continuity the person conversing with ELIZA perceives is supplied largely
by the person himself. He assigns meanings and interpretations to what
ELIZA "says" that confirm his initial hypothesis that the system does
understand ... (Weizenbaum, 1976, pp. 190–191).

The ELIZA program consists of general methods and many special
techniques for interpreting sentences and analyzing sentence segments.
An example of ELIZA's interpretative ability is given by Weizenbaum:

For example, the psychiatrist script form "everybody ... me," although patently conveying a message about the subject's relationship to "everybody," e.g., "everybody hates me," or about what everybody is doing to the subject, e.g., "everybody is always laughing at me," latently and more importantly referred to a recent incident involving the subject and only a single or at most a few individuals. ELIZA's response might therefore be "Tell me, who told you he hated you within the last few days?" or "Who laughed at you recently?" (Weizenbaum, 1976, p. 191).

ELIZA's program contains a number of sophisticated subroutines connected with hypotheses about and predictions of client's responses. It is of interest to parallel this ability of ELIZA with a human client-centered psychotherapist. Indeed, it would be valuable to design an experiment comparing typed protocols of interviews conducted by ELIZA and its human counterpart with respect to the various therapeutic skills such as hypothesis, prediction, and perceptiveness. For example, ELIZA is programmed with a subroutine that recognizes the key word "because". The hypothesis and prediction is that the client will follow the word "because" with a statement of explanation or reason. The subroutine in ELIZA then will trigger its responses formulated around its repertoire about causes: e.g., presumed reason, real reason, excuses, evasive reason, etc. ELIZA has been programmed with such a subroutine and the human therapist has been trained with regard to such manifest and latent causes, so that he/she is also routinely alerted to words like "because" and sensitive to exploring the meanings of the reasons that follow the word "because". On the other hand, it should be noted that while the results of an experiment that compared verbal protocols of ELIZA in the role of DOCTOR and the human being in the role of a client-centered psychotherapist might show no difference in such therapeutic behavior or in ensuing clients' responses regarding their feelings about their manifest or latent reasons, it is clear that ELIZA's behavior is not supported by deep understanding of the dynamics of anxiety and defensive processes such as rationalization, while the human therapist's behavior is so supported even though like ELIZA, in the immediacy of the alerted response to the key word "because", the psychotherapist's behavior may be equally automatic and unconscious. Nor would ELIZA like the psychotherapist experience such therapeutic behavior as intuitive or insightful. Further discussion of these matters will be postponed until a later section of the book, where comparisons of computer and human therapists will be drawn.

The remainder of this section will be focus on some of the programming mechanisms by which ELIZA's role behavior is accomplished. References will be made to the sample interview presented earlier in this section.

The ELIZA program uses pattern matching methods. The program scans input sentences for the presence of key words, e.g., "I", "you", "my", "father". After locating a key word, the program transmutes the sentence in accordance with rule patterns matched to the key word. Thus, in the sample interview, the person's statement "my father is afraid of everybody" stimulates ELIZA's response "what else comes to mind when you think of your father?". A sentence in the form "I know everybody ... me" may elicit the pattern response "who exactly ... you?", where the ellipsis might be filled by verbs or verb phrases such as "hates", "laughs at", "dislikes", "distrusts". The sentence "I know Mary ... me" may trigger ELIZA's response "you say you know Mary ... you", where a verb or verb phrase fills the ellipsis.

If ELIZA's program does not detect a key word in an input sentence, several options are available as standard operating procedures. ELIZA's response might take one of a number of possible content-free templates, e.g., "why do you feel that way?", "why do you think that?", "can you tell me more?". Another standard operating procedure would be for ELIZA to make a reference to some earlier client statement cast in a standard initial frame phrase (does that have anything to do with the fact that?), e.g., "does that have anything to do with the fact that your boyfriend made you come here?".

ELIZA has rules of substitution that transmute "you" into "I" and "me" into "you". Thus, the client's statement "you don't argue with me" results in the correlative "why do you think that I don't argue with you?".

ELIZA has the capacity to interpret a key word according to the context in which it appears. Thus, depending on the semantic context the key word "maybe" is interpreted variously as "no", "uncertainty", "yes". ELIZA's contextual analytic ability enables it to act on hunches or expectations concerning what the person's next or continuing response is likely to be. This predictive capacity rests on ELIZA's possession of sets of decomposition and reintegration sentence rules. Depending on the particular context, a specific subset is elicited. Thus, the word "afraid" in the sentence input elicits the "fear" subset. ELIZA then activates the conversation module containing components of response such as "apparent fear" and "real fear" that stimulates the clarification of the person's statements and feelings.

Weizenbaum (1967) also developed a number of scripts for ELIZA, the first of which was the DOCTOR script which has been the subject of discussion in the present section. ELIZA can switch among these scripts depending on particular needs. These scripts allow ELIZA, in addition to taking the role of the psychotherapist, to take the role of hospital admitting person, hospital nurse, surgeon. ELIZA can also use idiomatic expressions in different languages and use them appropriately during a particular conversation.

PARRY

In the previous section, we presented the ELIZA program in which the computer takes the role of a psychotherapist. In the PARRY program, this arrangement is reversed. The interviewer of the computer program is a psychiatrist. The computer program is a model of a paranoid patient. Named PARRY, the computer model has been designed as a diagnostic tool. More specifically, PARRY was developed to test theories of paranoid thinking, affect, and behavior (Colby, 1975). As a model of paranoid thinking and feeling, PARRY was programmed with intricate and deep representations of knowledge concerning its fundamental feelings of self-inadequacy, recognition of and protection against types of interview statements and questions made by an interviewing psychiatrist interested in a probing understanding of PARRY's cognitive and affective behavior. In this section, we shall focus attention on PARRY's natural language understanding system by which he converses with an interviewing psychiatrist.

The PARRY computer program transmutes natural language interviewer statements into computer usable form through a sequence of language processing operations. These operations consist of pattern matching and parsing.

PARRY's natural language understanding depends upon the achievement of a match between linguistic phrases and concepts stored in its memory and the input statements of the interviewer. Through a series of stages (Parkison, Colby, & Faught, 1977), the complexities of the natural language inputs are transformed into progressively simpler representations that can be recognized by the program as matching relevant items in its array of linguistic and conceptual tables.

The natural language understanding system in PARRY is capable of recognizing idiomatic and colloquial expressions. Thus, the interviewer is under no constraint with respect to mode of expression. On the other hand, as a model of paranoid thought, PARRY regularly interprets input sentences in a way that steers the conversation between the interviewer and itself into arenas of discourse familiar to its language recognition system (Parkison, Colby, & Faught, 1977).

The paranoid program, as a model of human paranoia, is sensitive to interviewer statements that may be interpreted as bearing upon its delusional systems. In PARRY, the delusional system is represented by a directed graph that contains semantic interconnections among concepts of PARRY's hobby of horse racing, bookies, false accusations of debts to bookies, Mafia, vengeance for non-payment of debts, police collusion with the Mafia, etc. PARRY scrutinizes the input for stimuli associated even remotely with this semantic network and for indications of attitude on the part of the psychiatrists that may stimulate PARRY's levels of fear, hostility, and distrust. The levels are set to low parameter values at the beginning of the interview and increase as the conversation touches off PARRY's delusional system and his stock of stories concerning his fears of retaliation and his hypersensitive interpretation of the psychiatrist's questions or comments. As the interview progresses and as the level of the monitors that govern the weak mode of paranoia involving general suspiciousness is raised, the weak mode is replaced by the strong mode of paranoia with its specific delusional system. An example of the strong mode of PARRY's paranoia is represented in the following conversation between PARRY and an interviewing psychiatrist:

Why are you in the hospital?
I SHOULDN'T BE HERE.
Who brought you here?
THE POLICE.
What trouble did you have with the police?
COPS DON'T DO THEIR JOB.
What do they do instead?
COPS ARREST THE WRONG PEOPLE.
They arrest the right ones sometimes.
THE LAW SHOULD GET THOSE ITALIAN CROOKS.
Are you Italian?
MY BACKGROUND IS BRITISH BUT I WAS BORN IN THIS COUNTRY.

Do you know any Italian crooks?
I TRY TO AVOID THE UNDERWORLD.
Are you afraid of the underworld?
THE MAFIA ARE THE WORST GANGSTERS.
Are you connected with the Mafia?
YOU KNOW, THEY KNOW ME.
How do they know you?
THEY SPY ON ME.
Why do they?
THEY WANT TO GET FALSE EVIDENCE TO FRAME ME.
What do they have against you?
THEY ARE OUT TO GET ME.
What for?
I HAVE INCRIMINATING EVIDENCE AGAINST THE MAFIA.
Are you sure of all this?
YOU DON'T BELIEVE ME?
I am doing my best.
(SILENCE ON THE "PATIENT'S" PART)
(Silence on the psychiatrist's part)
CAN'T YOU THINK OF A DECENT QUESTION TO ASK?
You seem hostile to me.
SOME OF YOUR REMARKS ANNOY ME.
I am sorry.
FORGET THE EXCUSES, YOU GUYS ARE ALL ALIKE. (Colby, 1975, pgs. 58–59, 75–88).

It is interesting to point out that PARRY's angry retort, "FORGET THE EXCUSES" to a psychiatrist's "I am sorry" statement is not a rigidly mechanical response. Rather, had the psychiatrist's "I am sorry" statement been made at the beginning of the interview, when PARRY's affective levels of fear and hostility are low, PARRY's response would have been more accepting. In the above extract, the psychiatrist's allegations of hostility and lying to PARRY and the psychiatrist's menacing comments about the Mafia provoked PARRY's paranoid affects, so that PARRY distrusted and scorned the psychiatrist's placating "I am sorry".

While PARRY's language recognition system relies on pattern matching and parsing, flexibility in the recognition of and response to patterns allows PARRY several degrees of freedom away from the strictures of mechanical action. Thus, PARRY can understand many of the interviewing psychiatrist's remarks as fitting the pattern "I ... you" and signifying qualitative aspects of their interpersonal relationships. PARRY can, thus, build up a conception of the psychiatrist's attitudes toward him. Again, on the response side, PARRY can use the tu quoque retort "I ... you, too" or the inquisatorial "Why do you ... me?"

As discussed earlier in this section, Colby (1975) designed the PARRY program as a diagnostic tool in the study of paranoia. If PARRY were to serve as a computer model of a human paranoid patient, there should be a degree of versimilitude between interviews conducted with PARRY and interviews conducted with a paranoid person. Colby (1975) conducted a study of the ability of psychiatrists to distinguish protocols generated by interviews with PARRY from protocols generated by interviews with paranoid persons.

Colby (1975) conducted several studies regarding the validity of PARRY as a model of human paranoia. In an initial study, a group of psychiatrists interviewed, by teletype, either PARRY or actual paranoid patients. The psychiatrists did not know which was which, nor that a computer was indeed involved, but were simply told that the purpose of the teletyped interview was to eliminate paralinguistic ques and linguistic ques such as intonations and hesitations from their goal of establishing a psychiatric diagnosis. In a subsequent study, another group of psychiatrists, also unaware of the nature of the research, were requested to rate the interview transcripts for the absence, presence, and degree of paranoia. In a final study, a sample of psychiatrists randomly selected from a psychiatric directory were provided with the interview transcripts, were informed that a number of them were interviews of a computer program, while others were interviews of human patients and were given the task of establishing the identity of each type of interview. The results, for the initial study, indicated that the interviewing psychiatrists unanimously failed to perceive that they were interviewing a computer program. The results, in the second study, indicated that the weak paranoid mode of PARRY's behavior compared with his strong paranoid mode was reliably judged by the psychiatrists as possessing a lesser degree of paranoia. In the final study, the psychiatrists failed in discriminating interviews with PARRY from interviews with human patients.

Limitations of the Systems

The most general limitation of the natural language understanding systems is that they do not understand language, but, rather, respond in a restricted manner and in a restricted area of discourse. The understanding of language depends upon general knowledge that goes well beyond the recognition of linguistic patterns found in these computer systems and extends, in human beings, to the subtle capacity involved in varying interpretations of text and varying styles of response that permit nuances of meaning to be realized.

PARRY (Colby, 1975), for example, in depending upon a limited number of stock responses to expected questions in an initial psychiatric interview situation, resembles a person rehearsed in the delivery of stock answers in an initial employment interview. The employment interview and the psychiatric interview are similar (Sullivan, 1954) in that they both constrain the area of discourse and the intentions of the participants. However, beyond the initial interviews, additional conversations with PARRY would disclose an inability to formulate responses in its own words, as well as complete ineptitude in responding to any topic other than its paranoid concerns, represented in its programmed directed graphs.

As in the case of human beings, PARRY's conversational ability depends upon the expectation of certain themes arising in the conversation. Thus, PARRY is equipped (Parkison, Colby, and Faught, 1977) with a series of alternative responses to expected questions in the initial psychiatric interview such as "Why are you in the hospital?". However, PARRY's performance, capacity, and style are altered when unexpected themes appear in the conversation. On these occasions, PARRY manages to continue the interchange by stratagems that shield his lack of understanding of the content of a remark or question. For example, PARRY may respond "Why do you ask about that?" or he may return to matters discussed earlier in the conversation or he may use the tactic of digressing from the topic of conversation by initiating a new subject for the conversation, preferably one about which he is well rehearsed.

Although PARRY is limited as a general conversationalist, it should be emphasized, as indicated in the previous section, that PARRY was not designed to represent a complete person who happened to have a paranoid psychosis, but rather to represent a model of the paranoid diagnostic entity. Therefore, PARRY needs more to be evaluated as a model of paranoia and, as discussed in the previous section, the model has sufficient versimilitude so that psychiatrists judged PARRY to be paranoid and could not distinguish him from persons with paranoia. Had this not been the case, Colby (1975) could not proceed to use PARRY as a tool in evaluating his theories about the nature of the cognitive and affective processes in paranoid persons. In short, as compared with human beings, PARRY does not know a great deal, but, apparently, he knows all he needs to know for the intended purposes of research (Colby, 1975; Parkison, Colby, & Faught, 1977).

ELIZA, unlike PARRY, depends not on a specific body of knowledge to enable her to communicate, but rather upon her ability to play the role of a non-directive psychotherapist and upon her conversational partners' willingness to play the role of a client in psychotherapy. Thus, ELIZA does not respond to factual questions with factual answers, but responds in ways that direct clients to examine their feelings about those facts. Should the client depart from this role and ask questions such as "What are the costs for this interview?" and "How much of the costs will be covered by my health insurance?", the client will become quickly dismayed to realize that ELIZA cannot understand the content of the questions and must, in a sense hide her ignorance behind her parrying question regarding the feelings concerning costs and, by implication, worth of the psychotherapy interview. This style of conversation and form of natural language understanding was deliberately chosen by Weizenbaum (1965), as discussed in a previous section, because the complex problems of knowledge representation necessary to provide full understanding are effectively sidestepped, as the client-centered therapy is:

"One of the few examples of ... natural language conversation in which one of the participating pairs is free to assume the pose of knowing almost nothing of the real world." (Weizenbaum, 1976, p. 42)

Whereas ELIZA's non-directive stance allows her to carry on a conversation about almost everything, provided that her conversational partner takes the role of a client engaged in the exploration of personal feelings and whereas PARRY has the capacity to carry on a conversation with his human associate by directing and focusing the conversation on the topic of his paranoid interests and concerns, Winograd's SHRDLU program (1972) can participate in a very rational and logical conversation with its human partner provided that the universe of discourse is sharply confined to matters concerning the interrelationships and movements of objects in SHRDLU's block world.

Although SHRDLU can give evidence of its understanding (e.g., the reason for removing the big blue pyramid from the top of the red cube was to make room for the small green block), SHRDLU's explanations of its behavior should not induce a belief that SHRDLU understands what cubes and pyramids and blocks are, anymore than an algebra (Bobrow, 1968) or calculus (Charniak, 1969) computer word problem solving system understands the states, conditions or actions represented by the binomials or integrals that they manipulate so effectively. SHRDLU manipulates blocks effectively and answers questions rationally about its specific operations, but it does not understand what blocks are, that they may, for example, with certain additions be used to teach the alphabet or that cubes have more vertices than pyramids, etc. The point is not that SHRDLU could not be taught facts about blocks that would make it more knowledgeable and thereby, enrich the quality of its conversation with its human partner, but that an observer, impressed with SHRDLU's reasoned performance about its block world, should not conclude that it necessarily knows a great deal about the very blocks that constitute its own realm of knowledge and control.

Both ELIZA and PARRY, as natural language understanding systems, depend upon pattern matching techniques. These techniques have the advantage of accepting non-grammatical, incomplete, and illogical statements. This flexibility constitutes an advantage since, as compared to written text, ordinary conversation typically possesses these characteristics. SHRDLU, on the other hand, far exceeds PARRY and ELIZA in its capacity for subtle comprehension and logical analysis of input syntax. This capacity depends upon SHRDLU's employment of theorem proving and deductive reasoning strategies rather than pattern matching methods. SHRDLU's formal logical reasoning processes have been criticized as failing to match the ordinary thought processes of people which can proceed quite smoothly without regard to strict deductive reasoning, truth tables, and theorem proving.

Criticism of this type has been advanced by Wilks (1977b) and by Schank (1975). However, while Wilks' (1977b) critique of Winograd's (1972) SHRDLU program with respect to its formal reasoning operations failing to model everyday human thinking may have validity, it should be pointed out that Wilk's research (discussed earlier in this chapter) is concerned with language translation that makes somewhat different demands on comprehension than does conversation language understanding. Similarly, Schank (1975) proposes a semantic basis for the understanding of language rather than a deductive one and claims that all human thought processes can be reduced to a restricted set of expected themes or concepts. However, Schank has not fully developed a working computer model for the understanding of natural language in conversational mode, but rather has applied his conceptual dependency theory (Schank, 1975) to the development of computer systems that understand and answer questions about newspaper stories and other documents.

The difference in the approach of Winograd (1972) and that of Schank (1975) and Wilks (1977) is illustrative of fundamental problems in artificial intelligence. These fundamental problems are concerned with how knowledge is to be represented in computer systems. Theories and methods of knowledge representation will be discussed in the next chapter.

Summary

In this chapter, we discussed artificial intelligence research directed toward the problem of developing computer systems capable of understanding and responding to natural language. Theories and problems in the development of computer translation systems were discussed.

Problems encountered in a dictionary look-up method for mechanically replacing source text with translated text included the contextual determination of the meaning of words, differences between languages in word order resulting from differences in number of case endings in their grammars and the failure of word-for-word translation to produce meaningful renderings of holistic idiomatic expressions. A purely syntactic approach encountered difficulty because valid translation depends upon semantic information and relevant knowledge.

The concept of an interlingua of universal meaning shared by all languages resulted in theoretical and practical advances in computer translation. Natural language understanding systems that depended upon representations of semantic knowledge were especially influenced by the concept of an interlingua. Advances in computer translation were facilitated by the development of programming languages such as LISP and ALGOL. Wilks' computer translation system which depends upon semantic primitives (a kind of interlingua) was discussed.

The issue of precision versus flexibility in the grammar of the parser was discussed. Flexible parsers with minimal grammatical data structures depend upon recognition of phrases or key words and process incomplete and ungrammatical sentences. However, flexible parsers make more errors in understanding input sentences than do precise parsers with exact grammatical data structures that reject sentences with faulty grammar. Phrase structure grammar parsers and augmented grammar parsers were discussed with respect to their ability to process complexities in the structure and meaning of sentences.

Winograd's SHRDLU system possesses abilities to converse with a human user, to accept commands and follow directions, to answer questions and to provide to the human user reasoned and lucid explanations to account for its behavior. SHRDLU's abilities depend upon a programmed conceptual integration of the syntactic, semantic and inferential aspects of the understanding of language. SHRDLU possesses a sophisticated model of the structure and operations of its domain. The components of the SHRDLU system include a recognition grammar, a parser, a semantic analysis program, and a problem solver that guides the execution of tasks in its domain.

Weizenbaum's ELIZA system engages in a type of conversation that restricts its role to one analogous to that of a non-directive psychotherapist and confines the human participant in the conversation to taking the role of a client concerned with the exploration and expression of personal feelings. In a manner analogous to that of a non-directive psychotherapist, ELIZA confines herself to the general techniques of recognition and clarification of feelings. ELIZA's conversational style does not require that it possess any knowledge about the subject being discussed. Thereby, difficult computational problems in the representation of knowledge are avoided. However, persons taking the role of the client in conversation with ELIZA ascribe knowledge and understanding to her, since they quickly become absorbed in a dialogue about their own personal revelations and experiences.

Similarities and differences between ELIZA and a human psychotherapist were considered. It was indicated that both ELIZA and the human psychotherapist are capable of making hypotheses and predictions about client responses. In contrast to the human psychotherapist, ELIZA's behavior is not grounded in deep and perceptive understanding of the dynamics of anxiety and defense, nor does ELIZA experience her therapeutic behavior as intuitive or insightful.

The ELIZA program contains many general methods, techniques and subroutines for interpreting sentences and analyzing sentence fragments. The program uses pattern matching and contextual key word scanning methods. ELIZA possesses sets of decomposition and reintegration sentence rules that permit her to act on her expectations of client statements. ELIZA's versatility is enlarged by her possession of professional scripts in addition to that of the psychotherapist script and by her knowledge of idiomatic expressions in various languages.

Colby's PARRY program is a model of a paranoid patient. PARRY was designed as a diagnostic tool and in a series of studies was demonstrated to have validity as a model of paranoia. The PARRY program contains representation of knowledge concerned with his basic feelings of inadequacy, hypersensitivity to threat and defensive projective behavior. Psychiatrists interviewing PARRY encounter, initially, the weak mode of paranoia, characterized by general suspiciousness, and, as the interview proceeds, the strong mode of paranoia, characterized by an elaborate delusional system. PARRY typically interprets interviewer statements so as to focus the conversation on his paranoid fears, suspicions, and delusions.

The PARRY computer program converts interviewer statements into the computer maniputable schema thru a series of pattern matching and parsing operations. PARRY's understanding of natural language is dependent upon the achievement of a match between characteristics of interviewer input sentences and relevant items contained in its array of conceptual and linguistic data tables.

General and specific limitations of the natural language understanding systems were discussed. The most general limitation of these systems is that, as compared to persons, they do not understand language, but rather respond in a restricted conversational style and in a restricted universe of discourse. Specific limitations of the SHRDLU, ELIZA, and PARRY systems were considered. It was indicated that many of these limitations derived from fundamental problems in artificial intelligence concerned with theories and methods of knowledge representation which will be discussed in the following chapter.

CHAPTER SIX

The Representation of Knowledge

Introduction

Cognitive abilities depend upon the acquisition, organization and use of knowledge. A complete account of human cognition and knowledge has yet to be provided by psychological theorists and researchers. Analogously, comprehensive theories of how to provide computer systems with knowledge and cognitive abilities has not been fully specified. To a large extent, therefore, artificial intelligence researchers, interested in the development of knowledgeable and intelligent computer systems, have employed pragmatic procedures. The consequence of this pragmatic approach has been the development of many ad hoc schemes for representing knowledge in computer systems. In this chapter, we attempt to organize the major methods of knowledge representation, provide examples, discuss general characteristics and compare advantages and disadvantages of the different approaches.

Types of Knowledge

Artificial intelligence researchers who desire to develop computer systems that behave intelligently may need to provide their systems with data structures and procedural operations for several types of knowledge. Representation schemes may need to include knowledge that is descriptive of objects and events and of interrelationships among them such as taxonomies, time lines and cause-effect sequences.

Processing Knowledge

Knowledge based computer systems that perform cognitive tasks (e.g., chess playing, understanding and responding to natural language, identifying and analyzing molecular compounds, comparing manuscripts to ascertain authorship) incorporate interrelated processes of learning (knowledge acquisition), memory (knowledge retrieval) and reasoning (knowledge derivation). In solving complex problems, computer systems deduce new knowledge from their data and procedural structures by a variety of reasoning formalisms such as rules of logical inference (e.g., the propositional calculus) and by reasoning methods such as reasoning by analogy, procedural reasoning (e.g., simulation), reasoning by generalization and reasoning by abstraction (Brachman, 1978; Flavell, 1979).

General Characteristics of Representation Methods

The selection of the optimal representation method for a particular knowledge-based computer system application is often guided by consideration of general characteristics of knowledge representation formalisms. In this section we shall discuss these general characteristics.

Scope of Representation Detail

In general, the amount of world knowledge detail that is to be paralleled in representation formalism detail depends upon the nature of the task, the detail necessary for the formalism to accomplish its reasoning processes and on the level or quality of the performance required of the computer system (McCarthy & Hayes, 1969). For example, specification of medical knowledge and reasoning about that knowledge for diagnostic and therapeutic purposes can be accomplished by a computer medical expert program only by representing extensive amounts of detail in its production system formalism.

Selection of Primitive Elements

In addition to the selection of a particular representation method (e.g., production system, mathematical logic), the selection of the primitive elements within the representation formalism will establish limits on the performance power of knowledge-based systems. For example, in the PARRY system (Colby, 1975) the primitive elements in its semantic network formalism compelled the paranoid system (described in chapter five) to the overly-vigilant detection of intimidating meanings in the statements of its interviewing psychiatrists.

Modularity in Knowledge Representation

Modularity refers to the extent to which changes can be introduced into an existing data structure without effecting the unmodified parts of the data structure. In knowledge representation systems characterized by non-modularity, the removal or addition of knowledge to the data base can not be accomplished without introducing interaction effects on the rest of the system that may be very difficult to understand and control. In general, knowledge representation schemes such as semantic networks tend to be non-modular, whereas logical production systems tend to represent knowledge in a modular way that makes them suitable for use in expert systems where updating portions of the knowledge base without serious interaction effects on the remainder of the knowledge base is an important consideration.

Procedural and Declarative Knowledge Representation

Researchers in knowledge representation methods frequently differ on the balance to be accorded to declarative and procedural methods (Brachman & Smith, 1980). It would appear that declarative methods such as those using logic formalisms (e.g., theorem proving) possess the advantages of precision and completeness in their reasoning operations, whereas procedural methods such as that used in the SHRDLU system (Winograd, 1972) possess the advantages of clear understanding of the design and performance of the system, since the reasoning operations are directly and relevantly embodied in domain restricted rules.

Representation Methods

At a fundamental level, the problem of artificial intelligence research is to discover methods by which knowledge can be introduced into a machine so that it can use the cognition represented in its data structures for knowledgeable and intelligent problem solving applications. In this section, we shall discuss a number of the most widely

used methods of representing knowledge in computer systems capable
of inferential behavior.

Logic-Based Representation

As much as the development of modern computers depended for
their hardware on advances in electronics, they depended even
more for the development of their programs on systems of logic that
could represent knowledge in their syntax and represent reasoning
in their rules of inference. Systems of logic and mathematical systems
of logic, in particular, are familiar in the theorem proving procedures
of Euclidean geometry and in the algebraic manipulation of equations.
These familiar logic systems have been greatly developed to more
advanced and powerful forms by philosophers of logic and mathematical researchers. From the point of view of artificial intelligence
research, these systems of logic (e.g., the propositional calculus, the
predicate calculus, first order logic) are extremely useful because
they have the power of generality of expression, systematic inferential
procedures, consistency and completeness that enable the computer
to use automatic theorem proving processes to test the validity of
new information as it is introduced into existing data structures
and to derive new information from systematically expanded data
structures.

Logic employs formal language. Logic's language is that of symbols
and formulas. Expressing ordinary sentences and relationships among
sentences as symbols and formulas provides logic with its power of
generality of application, clarity of expression, derivability of new
knowledge and criteria of knowledge validation.

In logic, propositions (sentences that are properly formed) are
evaluated with respect to their truth. A proposition has one of two
truth values, true or false (e.g., all planets rotate on their axes.).
Individual propositions can be built up into a system through the use
of logical connectives (e.g., all planets rotate on their axes and all
planets revolve around the sun; either the sun rotates on its own axis
or it does not revolve around the planets.). In the propositional
calculus, there are five logical connectives: and, not, or, equivalence,
implication. More generally, logic replaces the words with symbols
such as p and q or x and y and then employs a series of rules to test
the truth or falsity of relations among the propositions that are

created by the use of the logical connectives. The process of establishing validity of relations among propositions is often simplified by the use of a truth table (Wagman, 1984a, pg. 3–8) and by the use of rules of inference that determine the correctness of inferences derived from an initial proposition. The rules of inference (if correctly followed) ensure that the propositions derived from true propositions are true. This guarantee of truth lends a first level of power to logic. Levels of logical power are greatly augmented for computer application by employment of the methods of the predicate calculus, now to be briefly discussed.

The propositional calculus is a formalism for representing the truth value of sentences. The predicate calculus includes and extends the propositional calculus by formalisms for representing sentences about specific individuals, objects and their relationships. The predicate calculus thus increases the power of formalisms to represent knowledge with increasing specificity of description.

Predicates (e.g., is interesting, equals) are completed by arguments that represent variables (e.g., a range of individuals, a range of numbers) that can be applied to an individual constant value (e.g., Freud is interesting) or to a numerical constant value (e.g., sine 30° equals .5). As in the case of the propositional calculus, the predicate calculus employs symbols and formuli to express knowledge and rules of inference for reasoning with these formalisms.

In artificial intelligence systems, certain supplements to the predicate calculus are employed to facilitate expression of knowledge. The supplemented system constitutes first order logic that includes the concept of functions or operators. Functions advance the descriptive truth value status of predicates by producing the objects related to their arguments (e.g., the function father of assigned to the individual value Anna returns the value Sigmund Freud).

First order logic is employed in artificial intelligence problem solving systems in the form of axioms that represent conditions of the given problem and statements of the required goal or solution. Problem solving involves proving the theorem that given the logical premises of the problem, there exists a goal or solution state. The application of the symbols, formalisms and rules of inference of first order logic to problem solving is often executed in artificial intelligence systems by automated theorem proving procedures. Theorem provers are used by the artificial intelligence systems described in the following section.

Artificial Intelligence Applications of Logic

Green (1969) developed QA3, a question answering program that used theorem proving procedures to validate inferences about facts and problems in a variety of domains such as puzzles, simple automatic programming and robot movement and physical chemistry. Descriptive chemical facts about a compound, for example, were written in first order logic and theorem proving methods were applied to answer questions about the compound that could be logically derived from the logic representation of the chemical knowledge. A limitation of QA3 was that although it was capable of solving simple problems, it experienced difficulty with complex problems because the theorem resolution method tends to result in a combinatorial explosion when a very large number of facts are logically represented in the data base.

Fikes, Hart and Nilsson (1972) employed first order predicate calculus as a representation formalism in their development of the STRIPS system that controlled a robot as it moved and maneuvered among boxes. Theorem proving methods were used in the STRIPS system to determine facts about the robot's spatial location and means-ends search analysis was used to determine procedures for collecting boxes and bringing them to a common destination. Thus, STRIPS went beyond the theorem proving method of QA3 (Green, 1969) by its incorporation of appropriate search heuristics (Newell & Simon, 1972).

Advantages of Logic-Based Representation Methods

The formalisms of first order logic are characterized by lucidity and precision in expression (Hayes, 1977) and by powerful rules for stating and testing the truth of inferences. Logical representation has the characteristic of modularity. This is especially important in expert systems where new knowledge in the form of logical expression can be entered into the data base of the system without the introduction of potentionally negative interaction effects. The logical representation seems, in many ways, psychologically natural (McCarthy, 1977) and the development of new approaches for a difficult problem seems to be facilitated by its expression in clear logical terms (Green, 1969).

Procedural Representation

Procedural representations of knowledge are intended to provide program controls that govern theorem proving sequences and processes contained in the systems logic-based data structures. The significance of procedural representation is that it provides an efficient and directed way of utilizing the knowledge that has been encoded as logic or semantic net formalisms in the system.

Procedural representations contain many types of control information. For example, there are procedures for identifying the precise knowledge and sequence of knowledge applications required to achieve each of a series of sub-goals in a problem solving program.

Procedural Knowledge in PLANNER

The PLANNER programming language (Hewitt, 1972) has the ability to advise the use of theorems in a backward or forward direction and to specify the application of specific theorems in particular situations. To achieve these control functions, PLANNER (Hewitt, 1972) bases its inferential behavior on an integration of standard logic with various forms of intuitive logic and default reasoning (Reiter, 1978). The PLANNER logic, as exemplified in the SHRDLU system (see Chapter Five), enables the user to specify the essential procedural knowledge necessary for problem solution in a given domain.

Limitations and Advantages of Procedural Knowledge Representation

A strategic advantage of procedural representation over purely declarative representations is the efficiency gained by the application of specific heuristic information. While declarative procedures may apply all possible theorems to a given problem, the heuristics contained in procedural representations guide the application of those theorems that are most likely to prove useful in a given domain. These heuristic controls depend not only on formal deductive inferences, but, more importantly, on the use of informal plausible reasoning such as default reasoning and reasoning by analogy and metaphor that are so characteristic of human reasoning (McCarthy, 1977; Winograd, 1980a).

In comparing procedural representation with declarative representational formalisms the problem of consitency and the problem of modularity need to be considered. Purely theorem proving systems, in contrast to many procedural systems, possess the quality of consistency. A system is said to be consistent if all of its deductions necessarily follow from its premises. However, Hewitt (1975) points out that consistency is not always required or desirable, especially where we are interested in modeling human cognition, where in the face of incomplete knowledge and exceptions, though consistency is violated, empirically useful conclusions can be drawn.

Whereas declarative logical systems are modular, procedural representations because of their heuristic controls are necessarily non-modular. Changes in heuristic information have more far reaching interaction effects than do changes in the logic data base. However, this reduction in modularity accompanies the advantage of efficiency that is possessed by procedural representations.

Representation of Knowledge by Production Systems

The most general concept underlying production systems is that knowledge can be represented as rules that are composed of condition-action pairs. Knowledge encoded in the data base of such production systems is, usually, modular with minimal interaction effects. Examples of condition-action pairs are common place (if a tornado is imminent, then broadcast a warning siren). The explicitness of production rules facilitates their understanding and modification in expert systems such as MYCIN, DENDRAL, and PROSPECTOR. These expert systems seem to model the procedures that people say they use in solving problems. This computer representation of expert problem solving is known as knowledge engineering (Bernstein, 1977) and includes the capacity for explaining their problem solving reasoning to their human consultees, as well as for continuous adaptation by their aquisition of new knowledge, transferred to them by knowledge engineers (Feigenbaum, 1977).

Production systems contain several components and, typically, operate in cycles. The data base component contains the production rules. The context component is a memory data structure buffer. The interpreter component regulates the performance of the system. When the condition part of the production rule is satisfied (a tornado is indeed imminent.), the interpreter permits the action part of the production rule to fire (the warning siren is broadcast). However, the interpreter can act only if the condition part of the production rule is contained in the memory context. The context data structure can be modified by the action parts of the production rules (a warning siren is broadcast.), resulting in a state where the condition parts of other production rules can be met (if there is a warning siren, then ...). The interpreter selects the order of firing for each production rule and regulates the matching, conflict resolution and action phases of each operating production cycle.

In a large production system such as MYCIN, composed of hundreds of production rules, there is the problem of choosing the most appropriate production to be fired. It is necessary for the system to decide or resolve conflicts among the set of potentially applicable production rules. Conflict resolution has been approached by a variety of strategies (Davis & King, 1977). Examples of conflict resolution strategies are selecting (a) the rule whose condition part most precisely is a match of the present context, (b) the rule that matches the most up-to-date revision of the context and (c) all applicable rules in parallel exploration, a method used in the MYCIN system (Shortliffe, 1976; Davis, Buchanan & Shortliffe, 1977).

An Example of a Production System

One of the most successful applications of production system methodology is the MYCIN system (see Chapter Seven) that provides consultation to physicians regarding diagnostic evaluation and therapeutic recommendation for patients with various types of infections. Human expert level knowledge about this area of medicine is represented in MYCIN's data base of several hundred production rules. This rule base can be expanded or modified by expert physicians through a special sub-system that facilitates MYCIN's knowledge acquisition. As a medical consultant, MYCIN can conduct a dialogue with a physician about its medical evaluations and recommendations including an explanation of its reasoning in as much depth as the physician requires. Differential diagnoses are represented in the conclusion (action) part of each production, accompanied by a statement of the confidence limits within which each diagnosis and associated recommendation is offered.

Limitations and Advantages of Production Systems

A clear advantage of representing knowledge by production systems is that each production rule can be treated as a separate module of information. Production rule modules can thus be subtracted or added to a system, thereby facilitating both the development of the system and its adaptive application in a particular problem solving domain such as medical diagnosis or psychological testing (see Chapter Seven). There is, however, the possible limitation that, due to the strict modularity of production rules, inefficiencies can accumulate as data bases become extremely large and hierarchies of sub-routines for procedural control are not provided as components of the system (Barstow, 1979).

Knowledge Representation by Semantic Networks

The concept of semantic networks refers both to the structure of associations (nets) and to the ascribed meaning or interpretation of the net or portions of it (semantics). Each artificial intelligence researcher develops a procedure that provides the interpretation that the program will make of the knowledge encoded network. Quillian (1968) developed the concept of semantic nets as a research model of the structural meaning of associations in human memory.

The notation of semantic nets consists of nodes and links. As an illustrated notation, links are represented as arrows and nodes are drawn as boxes, circles or, simply as dots. The links connect the nodes and together with them, constitute the network. In illustrations of semantic networks, the nodes are labeled and can represent concepts, situations or objects in a given knowledge domain and the labeled links represent the relationships between the nodes. Salient facts and relationships are directly inferred in the network formalism by the labeled "sub-set" and "is a" links that form a property inheritance hierarchy; so that facts about objects or situations or concepts belonging to higher levels in the hierarchy are directly inherited by items lower in the hierarchy. For complex knowledge domains, in which facts can be deduced from the taxonomic structure, the choice of semantic networks as representational formalisms is especially suitable (e.g., the artificial intelligence PROSPECTOR program, based on geological and other earth science taxonomies).

Examples of Semantic Network Systems

As indicated above, Quillian (1968) originated the semantic net as a formalism that would model associative memory. In Quillian's semantic network, knowledge about a specific concept is represented by a cluster of nodes called planes. The concepts represented in the planes are interconnected by appropriate links that allow for combination, separation and modification of the meaning of concepts. In Quillian's (1968) spreading activation method, inferences are made about concepts by studying the pathways of inter-connecting nodes that represent each of them. As the original nodes activate other nodes and these still others, a spreading sphere of activation is created around each of the original nodes. The simultaneous activation of a particular concept from two directions registers the discovery of connecting relationships that are printed out by the program in a detailed description of the pathways taken by the spreading activation among the nodes and links in the network.

The question answering program SIR (Raphael, 1968) makes use of the general method of semantic networks to enable it to draw deductions concerning its particular domain of knowledge. For example, from the knowledge that a finger is part of a hand and a hand is a part of an arm, SIR (Raphael, 1968) could draw the inference that a finger is a part of an arm.

Another question answering program, though this time an interactive one, is SCHOLAR (Carbonell, 1970a; Carbonell & Collins, 1974). Knowledge about South American geography is represented in semantic networks. SCHOLAR (see Chapter Seven) is capable of performing as a tutor, posing questions to human students, giving hints, providing answers and suggesting appropriate reviews of portions of the system.

Advantages and Limitations of Semantic Network Representation

The link and node formalism, because of its simple, direct and transparent way of representing knowledge, is widely appreciated and used in artificial intelligence systems. However, researchers (Findler, 1979) have raised questions regarding the theoretical clarity and power of semantic network representation. Issues such as how to best represent complex ideas and beliefs in the node-link formalism are the subject of current research.

Knowledge Representation by Scripts and Frames

Among the newest methods of knowledge representation are frames (Minsky, 1975) and scripts (Schank & Abelson, 1977). Frames and scripts are still in the early stages of artificial intelligence research and many issues are unresolved. For example, researchers differ with respect to the exact meaning of the concept of frames.

The concept of frames was developed by Minsky (1975) as an aspect of his conviction that artificial intelligence research, in general, can best proceed by representing knowledge, especially everyday common sense knowledge, from a predominantly psychological perspective rather than from an exclusively logic based perspective that is favored by other researchers in artificial intelligence (Kolata, 1982). The psychological perspective recognizes that people, in reasoning about current situations, apply general knowledge and expectations acquired in the course of experience with previous similar situations. People, therefore, have a general framework, often with many specific details, that they can apply in a generic way for adaptation to expected or actual situations of the same type (e.g., arranging for a plane trip, attending a meeting, going to a dinner party). Minsky (1975) suggested that frames of such generic situations could be developed for application in artificial intelligence systems across such areas as regularly occuring types of dialogue or specific domains of problem solving (e.g., differential medical diagnosis).

Where frames (Minsky, 1975) might represent organized knowledge and expectations about objects, scripts (Schank & Abelson, 1977) represent organized knowledge and expectations about specific sequences of actions in given reoccuring situations. There might, for example, be a generic script for the sequence of actions to be taken by airline passengers as they interact with pre-flight and flight personnel (e.g., travel agents, reservation clerks, passenger agents, flight attendants).

Minsky (1975) suggested the concept of frame slots as a way of implementing the general knowledge and expectations contained in the frame. Thus, in the airline passenger frame, there might be an airline ticket slot in which there would be specific knowledge about cost, type of seat, type of food and drink service and expectations about intermediate arrival times, change of airline and final destination arrival time. The knowledge contained in the ticket slot allows airline passengers to check their expectations, plans and reasoning about their airline travel.

Frame and Script Prototypic Systems

As indicated earlier, research in frame and script systems is still at an early stage. Much of the developmental work has gone into the creation of special languages such as KRL (Knowledge Representation Language) used in the implementation of systems that process knowledge based on their organization of frames, slots and subslots that included procedures for determining specific situational constraints for their application or non-application (Bobrow & Winograd, 1977). As part of their KRL research project, Bobrow and Winograd (1977) developed a natural language understanding program based on frame processing and intended as a computerized airline reservation clerk that could expect and manage problems associated with responding effectively to typical inquiries made by airline passengers.

Schank and Abelson (1977) have applied script-based processing in their artificial intelligence system. For example, the SAM program can understand short stories, based on the assignment of a generic script to the story that enables the system to deduce answers to questions about events in the current story.

Summary

In this chapter, we discussed the problem of the representation of knowledge in computer systems. General characteristics and specific methods of knowledge representation were discussed.

It was indicated that in order for computer systems to perform cognitive tasks, knowledge about objects, events and processes need to be represented in appropriate data and procedural structures. Representational formalisms permit the encoding of data and processes necessary for computer systems to be capable of knowledge acquisition (learning), knowledge retrieval (memory) and knowledge derivation (reasoning).

Several general characteristics of knowledge representation formalisms were discussed. General characteristics of representational formalisms include the amount of real knowledge detail to be represented in the detail of the formalism, the amount of modularity in the formalism and the extent to which the formalism is declarative or procedural.

Logic-based representational methods (the propositional calculus, the predicate calculus, first order logic) are very useful in artificial intelligence research because they possess the characteristics of generality of expression, systematized inferential procedures, completeness and consistancy that permit automatic theorem proving processes. Several artificial intelligence applications that employ theorem provers were described. It was pointed out that logical representation has the characteristic of modularity, an important consideration in the development of expert systems where new knowledge can be introduced into the system without creating serious interaction effects on the existing data structures.

Procedural representations provide directed and efficient program controls that govern theorem proving sequences and the utilization of knowledge contained in the system's data structures. The PLANNER programming language was discussed with respect to the types of reasoning that it utilizes. In comparison with logic-based declarative representations which are modular, procedural representations, because of their heuristic controls, entail more interaction effects, but also entail more efficiency.

In production systems, knowledge is encoded as rules composed of condition-action pairs. Production systems operate in cycles and contain data base, context and interpreter components. Strategies of conflict resolution in the selection of production rules were discussed. Production systems were exemplified by the MYCIN system. It was indicated that production systems are modular.

Semantic networks consist of nodes that represent concepts, situations or objects in a given knowledge domain and links that represent relationships (e.g., sub-set) between the nodes. Examples and limitations of semantic networks were discussed.

The formalism of frames represents organized knowledge and expectations about familiar objects and the formalism of scripts represents organized knowledge and expectations about familiar actions in reoccurring situations. Examples of prototypic frame and script systems were described.

CHAPTER SEVEN

Expert Consultative and Tutorial Systems

Introduction

Expert systems are created by the transfer of domain specific knowledge from experts to computer scientists who, in turn, program computers with the knowledge and heuristic concepts of the experts, employing methods of knowledge representation that were discussed in the previous chapter. Expert systems may be designed to solve extremely difficult scientific problems that are beyond the scope of scientists or that are too time consuming and tedious for scientists. Expert systems can, sometimes, out-perform human scientists because they consider a larger number of possible solutions to problems. Expert systems, for example in chemical structure analysis, may out-perform chemists because the systems employ graph theoretical models that have been mathematically proven to be exhaustive of solutions for given problems. Thus, such expert systems utilize reasoning processes that are based on mathematical systems or algorithms that are represented within the computer in programming languages. These systems provide solutions to problems in chemistry, but do not explain their reasoning processes to the chemists interacting with the systems. There are, however, other expert systems which fulfill this consultation role. These consultation expert systems use a type of reasoning that is similar to the reasoning of professional practitioners and can, thus, explain and justify their solutions or recommendations during the course of consultative interactions. Thus, a physician interacting with a consultative expert system such as MYCIN may not only be advised regarding a differential diagnosis for a particular case, but may also be advised regarding the concepts and reasoning that MYCIN utilized to reach a determination of the final diagnosis.

In this chapter, we shall discuss a number of expert and consultative systems that constitute important applications of artificial intelligence research. Expert, consultative and tutorial systems in chemistry, mathematics, psychometrics, medicine and education will be discussed.

Expert Systems

DENDRAL

The DENDRAL programs are expert systems intended to assist chemists in the complex problem of molecular structure elucidation. Experience with DENDRAL indicates that for many chemical problems the program equals the performance of expert chemists and that for some problems DENDRAL is superior to expert chemists in the establishment of valid solutions (Smith et al., 1973). DENDRAL performs extremely well in molecular structure elucidation problems, not because it knows more chemistry than expert chemists know, but because DENDRAL makes extremely efficient and systematic use of its knowledge (Lindsay et al., 1980). DENDRAL has been widely applied in physiology and medicine to establish the structure of molecules (e.g., organic acids, metabolites, hormones, anti-biotics).

Originally, human experts in mass spectrometry transferred domain specific knowledge to DENDRAL. Subsequently, because of the expense and difficulty of the knowledge transfer process, automatic procedures were developed for the formation of new rules and constraints in structure elucidation that enabled DENDRAL to learn and, thereby, become increasingly expert in its task domain. The automatic generation of rules is an inductive process, somewhat analogous to human concept formation as it has been studied in cognitive psychology.

In its acquisition of new rules, DENDRAL's learning is facilitated by exposures to training instances composed of mass spectrometer produced input-output pairs that portray the corresponding molecular graph structure. DENDRAL learns the rules that are descriptive of the appropriate mass spectrometer fragmentations.

The DENDRAL programs have been valuable in the formation

of mass spectrometry rules for several classes of molecular structures. DENDRAL has re-discovered rules and significantly, from both a scientific and an epistemological perspective, has discovered previously unknown rules for a number of molecular structures (Buchanan, 1976; Lindsay et al., 1980).

MACSYMA

The MACSYMA system is an intelligent assistant to researchers in mathematics, science and engineering. MACSYMA aids in the solution of complex mathematical problems. MACSYMA comprises an extensive knowledge based system that can perform a wide variety of mathematical procedures such as solution of systems of equations, vector algebra, Taylor series expansions, differentiation, integration, order analysis and matrix operations.

In addition to MACSYMA's competence in performing mathematical operations, the system has stimulated research in the development of new algorithms previously unknown to mathematicians. MACSYMA researchers have discovered algorithms for asymptotic analysis (Norman, 1975; Zippel, 1976), symbolic integration (Moses, 1971) and factoring rational expressions (Wang & Rothschild, 1975).

The Computer Psychometrist

In recent years, computer applications of the diagnostic, interviewing, testing, test interpretation and report writing functions of the psychometrist, psychologist and psychiatrist (Erdmon, Klein, & Greist, 1985; Fowler, 1985) have been developed. These computer applications merit careful attention.

The Computer Diagnostician

Computer diagnostic and prognostic systems have been developed. Spitzer, Endicott, Cohen, and Fleiss (1974) have created a computer program that models the Diagnostic and Statistical Manual (DSM II). Greist, Klein, and Erdman (1976) developed a computer program that questions the clinician until the computer has obtained sufficient information to enable the computer's decision rules to yield a diagnosis. Lefkowitz (1973) developed a computer program to predict personal adjustment in marriage.

The Computer Interviewer

A wide range of computer interview programs have been developed (Byers, 1981; Byrnes & Johnson, 1981). Maulsby and Slack (1971) developed a computer interview system that yields data about a person's psychological, social, family, occupational, educational, marital, and financial problems. The computer's branching program permits a deepening and specifying of interview material. The computer prints out an organized report of the interview for the psychotherapist. Greist, Gustafson, Strauss, Rowse, Langren, and Chiles (1973) developed a computerized interview that assesses the likelihood of suicidal behavior. Lucas, Mullin, Luna, and McInroy (1977) developed a computer interview program focused on psychological problems associated with alcoholism.

The Computer Tester

A wide range of personality and intelligence tests have been computerized (Sampson, 1983). Hedl, O'Neil, and Hansen (1973) developed a computer administration of the Slosson Intelligence Test. Dunn, Lushene, and O'Neil (1972) computerized the administration and scoring of the Minnesota Multiphasic Personality Inventory (MMPI). Space and Hutzinger (1979) developed a computer-administered system for the Peabody Picture Vocabulary Test (PPVT). Space and Huntzinger (1979) programmed for computer-administered the Kelly Role Construct Repertory Test (KRCRT). Gilberstadt, Lushene, and Beugel (1976) have developed computer-administered and scoring of subtests of the Wechsler Adult Intelligence Scale (WAIS). Karson and O'Dell (1975) developed a computerized administration and scoring system for the 16 Personality Factor Test (16 PF). Scissons (1976) describes a computer-administered and scoring system for the California Psychological Inventory (CPI).

The Computer Report Writer

Computer-generated reports of test results have been based on either a single test (most frequently the MMPI) or on a combination of tests. Computer-generated report writing systems based on the MMPI have been developed by Finney (1966) and Fowler (1980). Paitich (1973) has developed a computer-based report writing system that integrates test findings from the Clarke-WAIS Vocabulary Test, the MMPI, the Raven Matrices, the 16 PF, and the Clarke Parent Child Relations Questionnaire. Gilberstadt et al. (1976) have developed a computer-generated report writing system based on results from the Raven Matrices, the digit symbol and digit span subtests of the WAIS. Computer report writing systems that integrate results from a large number of test scales as well as other information have been developed by Greist and Klein (1980) and Johnson and Williams (1980).

Advantages of the Computer Psychometrist

Computer-based test administration, scoring, interpretation and report documentation can dramatically facilitate the flow of mental health services by reducing time between test completion and report completion from 14 days to one hour. Johnson and Williams (1980) demonstrated that, excluding costs of equipment, computer evaluation costs half as much as traditional evaluation.

Computerized test administration permits the storage of data for simultaneous or later research analysis. Research data such as MMPI response latencies can be systematically recorded and analyzed by computer (Dunn et al., 1972).

In contrast to the human report writer, the computer report writer is rigorously reliable in that computer input of the same data inevitably yields the same psychological report. Also, the computer's interpretation rules can be readily modified to take account of new data and new research.

Criticism of the Computer Psychometrist

Criticism of computerized assessment is of two general types. The first general type represents attitudinal concerns. The second general type represents technical matters. The attitudinal type of criticism includes concerns that the person is an object in a computer-controlled situation, that the person's subsequent rapport with the psychotherapist is reduced, that neither the person nor the clinician feel that they are in control in a computerized assessment situation and that the person's privacy and text confidentiality may not be entirely secure.

Effectively trained clerks who introduce the person to the computer assessment situation in a supportive manner and who remain available during the computer testing and interviewing to answer questions and provide any necessary guidance can considerably alleviate the person's possible feeling of being an object in the computer assessment situation (Klinge & Rodziewicz, 1976). Regarding the relationship between computer interviewing and rapport with the psychotherapist or clinician, it has been demonstrated in several studies that there is no decrement in rapport when computerized medical history procedures rather than traditional procedures are used (Grossman, Barnett, McGuire, & Swedlow, 1979; Slack, Hicks, Reed, & VanCura, 1966; Stead, Heyman, Thompson, & Hammond, 1972). The pacing of computerized assessment can be regulated at the desire of the person (Kelley & Tuggle, 1981) so that possible feeling of computer control can be so mitigated that the person may feel less controlled than when traditional assessment procedures are used. The clinician's feeling that the computer controls the assessment situation and, by implication, that his/her professional role may be displaced may be modified by emphasizing that advancements (Hofer & Green, 1985) in computer assessment depend ultimately upon the information, discernment and decision-making abilities of the clinician and that, therefore, the combination of computer and clinician may advance the science of assessment more than either alone. The problems of confidentiality and privacy exist for both traditional assessment and computer assessment and as with computer applications in general (Wagman, 1983), there is a necessity for both ethical standards (Green, 1983; Matarazzo, 1983; Sampson & Pyle, 1983) and technological controls to insure confidentiality of computer data (Ford, 1976).

The technical type of criticism includes concerns that computerized assessment overlooks idiographic variables and emphasizes nomothetic variables, that the computer psychometrist is unable to differentiate normal response error from pathological response, that computer-based testing and interviewing can not make behavior observations and that computerized assessment does not adapt to the person's response style.

Computer programming to detect, quantify and extrapolate idiographic patterns can be developed as expert systems that model clinical inference processing (Space and Hutzinger, 1979). Distinctions among normal response error, malingering and pathological response are part of the computer's analysis of test data by specialized programs that model the test analysis logic of the MMPI lie and validity scales (Finney, 1966). Computer assessment procedures provide for behavior observation by the use of a trained clerk who may also type observations into the computer which then become part of the computerized psychological report (Gedye & Miller, 1969; Klinge & Rodziewicz, 1976). Computerized assessment procedures (Weiss, 1985) that allow for variations in style or content of response by adapting computer responses in a flexible pattern of encouragement or discouragement of selected aspects of interviewing by means of branching sequences have been developed (Greist & Klein, 1980; Stout, 1981; Vale, 1981).

Consultative Systems

MYCIN

MYCIN is a consultative medical system that advises physicians regarding problems in diagnosis and therapy for various types of infectious diseases (e.g., bacteremia, meningitis). The representation of medical knowledge in MYCIN is achieved through the use of production rules (see Chapter Six), encoded in the LISP programming language. The knowledge contained in the encoded representations is presented to the MYCIN user in ordinary English.

In determining a diagnosis and treatment recommendation, MYCIN systematically searches and evaluates all of its knowledge that bears upon the presenting problem and, after balancing positive evidence and negative evidence, presents to the clinician its conclusions, not in the form of sharp absolutes, but as probability statements or certainty factors (Shortliffe, 1976). This reasoning performance of MYCIN was designed to emulate human clinical reasoning as practice in medicine. The MYCIN program can explain its diagnostic reasoning as well as its anti-infection treatment regimen and can evaluate various treatment regimens that may be suggested by a physician consulting the system (Clancey, 1978).

MYCIN's capability can be augmented by new medical knowledge through revisions accomplished by a scientific medical expert interacting with the system. The modularity of its production rules and its capacity for explaining and justifying its reasoning facilitate the process of knowledge revision. MYCIN, thereby, increases its value as a consultative resource in its domain of medical diagnosis and treatment.

INTERNIST

INTERNIST is a diagnostic consultative program in the area of internal medicine. In the consultative process with INTERNIST, a physician enters patient manifestations, (e.g., symptoms, laboratory test results) in response to a series of questions, the answers to which are evaluated by INTERNIST in order to narrow the search along the many nodes of the "disease tree" that is stored in its memory. INTERNIST (Pople, 1977) is an expert system that contains large bodies of medical knowledge concerning manifestations and diseases (e.g., lung, heart, liver) and that models the ways in which clinicians reason with sets of hypotheses in reaching a diagnostic conclusion from the interrelationships of sets of manifestations and sets of possible diseases. INTERNIST processes patient manifestations by beginning with an overall "disease tree" and partitioning it into smaller and smaller sub-disease trees, culminating in the smallest set of terminal nodes that can explain the entire set of patient manifestations (qualitative, quantitative, temporal).

INTERNIST contains comprehensive knowledge of diseases in internal medicine and is capable of acquiring new knowledge that results from medical research. INTERNIST has been especially useful as a consultant to physicians confronted with difficult cases characterized by the simultaneous presence of several diseases (Pople, 1977).

Tutorial Systems

SCHOLAR

SCHOLAR (Carbonell, 1970b) is an interactive tutorial system concerned with facts about South American geography. As a tutoring system, SCHOLAR can pose questions and follow up on responses. In addition, the student can initiate conversation with SCHOLAR by asking questions. Natural language capacity permits the understanding and production of simple English sentences.

The SCHOLAR program is written in the LISP programming language and its geographical knowledge is represented in the form of semantic nets (see Chapter Six). SCHOLAR, as an intelligent tutor, employs the Socratic method of teaching wherein material is presented that results in self-contradiction or otherwise encourages the student to become aware of his/her own miscomprehensions.

An interesting aspect of SCHOLAR is that it is not restricted to mechanical answers, but can reason with its limited data base as a human tutor might when questions are posed to it that are beyond its direct knowledge representation. In such cases, SCHOLAR's inferential structures permit it to engage in plausible reasoning (Collins, 1978) that leads to conclusions of the type "I am not completely certain, but it seems quite resonable from what I know that ... ".

WHY

In contrast to the SCHOLAR system which offers tutorial guidance in the acquisition of *facts* about geography, the WHY system (Stevens, Collins, & Goldin, 1978) provides tutorial guidance, in an interactive mode, concerning interrelationships among complex sequential and causative factors involved in understanding the natural process of rainfall. As a tutor, WHY is closely directed toward the modification of student's misconceptions about the necessary and sufficient conditions for the production of rainfall. The WHY system is a Socratic tutor that uses counter-examples to challenge and correct students' misconceptions of what constitutes a necessary factor or a sufficient cause in the process of rainfall production.

The WHY system represents knowledge about rainfall through the use of scripts (see Chapter Six) and employs a series of heuristics that locate, challenge and correct students' misconceptions. Stevens and Collins (1977) describe two general misconceptions that are applicable not only to an understanding of rainfall, but that might be applied to understanding any complex process. In over-generalization, the student uses a restricted set of factors or data to produce a generic rule. In over-differentiation, the student includes factors or data that are not strictly necessary for an explanation of a process and the WHY system, in its Socratic mode, will pose counter-examples to demonstrate the lack of necessity of such factors or data.

Although research in the tutorial dialogue of the WHY system has used the process of rainfall as its content area, it seems clear that other content could be used. In particular, types of psychological counseling that are cognitive and psycho-educational in their content might be developed into useful tutorial systems. The topic of computer counseling is discussed in the next part of this book.

Summary

In this chapter, we discussed a number of expert, consultative and tutorial systems. The DENDRAL, MACSYMA and computer psychometrist expert systems were described. An account was presented of the MYCIN and INTERNIST consultative systems. The SCHOLAR and WHY tutorial systems were discussed.

The DENDRAL systems are expert systems that determine the structure of molecules and that have general applications in biochemical, physiological and medical research. DENDRAL has the capacity to become increasingly expert in its task domain through the use of automatic procedures for the generation of mass spectrometry rules that guide elucidation of molecular structures.

The MACSYMA system assists researchers in mathematics, engineering and science in the solution of complex mathematical problems. MACSYMA can perform advanced mathematical procedures that include solution of systems of equations, asymptotic analysis, symbolic integration and vector algebra.

Computer psychometrist systems that perform traditional psychologist and psychiatrist functions of diagnostic testing, interviewing and report writing were described. The advantages and disadvantages of these systems were discussed with respect to technical and attitudinal considerations.

MYCIN is a consultative medical system that assists physicians in the diagnosis and therapy of infectious diseases. MYCIN can explain and justify the medical reasoning processes it employed in reaching its diagnostic conclusions and therapeutic recommendations.

INTERNIST is a consultative system in internal medicine that models human clinical reasoning in establishing diagnoses for a wide variety of medical problems. INTERNIST has proven especially valuable for complex cases characterized by the simultaneous presence of several diseases.

The SCHOLAR system is an intelligent tutor that utilizes the Socratic method in teaching facts about geography. SCHOLAR's inferential structures permit it to make use of plausible reasoning when questions are posed to it by students that are beyond its limited knowledge representation.

The WHY system is a Socratic tutor that employs counter-examples to challenge and modify students' misconceptions about necessary factors and sufficient causes that account for the natural process of rainfall production. Over-generalization and over-differentiation were discussed as examples of student misconceptions for which WHY provides tutorial guidance. It was suggested that general Socratic tutorial strategies of the WHY system might possibly be extended to the development of cognitive and psycho-educational computer counseling systems.

PART III

Computer Counseling

CHAPTER EIGHT

Computer Models of Personality

Introduction

In this chapter, we shall discuss two computer models of personality. The Neurotic Program (Colby, 1963, 1964, 1965; Colby & Gilbert, 1964) derives from the paradigm of psychoanalysis and was designed to simulate the analysand in psychoanalytic therapy. The theory guiding the construction of the Neurotic Program included psychoanalytic concepts of free association, mechanisms of defense and levels of consciousness.

CLIENT 1 (Lichtenberg, Hummel & Shaffer, 1984) was designed as a computer model of a counselor involved in general counseling interviews. CLIENT 1 was directed primarily toward the facilitation of counselor training and supervision.

Neurotic Program

Colby (1963, 1964) considered three general goals in the development of his Neurotic Program. The major goal was the contribution that the computer program might make to the clarification of the theory of psychoanalysis and psychoanalytic therapy. Theoretical contradictions, latent assumptions, unknown conceptual linkages and unrecognized lacunae in the theoretical structure would be lucidly revealed as a consequence of the simulation of a neurotic process because methods of knowledge representation generally require clear, complete and consistent data structures and procedural operations (see chapter six). A second general goal was the achievement of a better

85

understanding of the therapeutic process that might result from
studying the ways in which the neurotic process produces defensive
reactions to therapeutic interpretations that arouse anxiety and the
ways in which subsequent therapeutic interpretations bring about a
reduction in anxiety and an amelioration in the neurotic process. A
third general goal was the use of the Neurotic Program in psychoanalytic therapy training. Colby (1963) indicated that training with a
computer model of neurotic personality might have advantages over
the usual training procedures because the Neurotic Program provided
a standard condition and because the inevitable blunders of psychoanalytic neophytes could not have harmful effects on the neurotic
computer personality.

The Model of Neurosis

The Neurotic Program was designed as a theoretical model of a
neurotic woman who had been in psychoanalytic therapy for a series
of several hundred interview hours over a period of three years
(Colby, 1963). The woman was troubled by a compulsive need to
get married and by an equally compulsive need to find something
significantly unacceptable about every potential husband. The compulsive intensity of her conflict was related to a complex of conflicting
beliefs concerning her father. Through a content analysis procedure
applied to therapy interview tapes and notes, Colby (the woman's
psychoanalyst) determined a set of major themes that represented
the predominant issues in her lengthy psychoanalytic therapy. The
set of major themes was programmed as complexes or groups of
belief statements with each belief accompanied by a number that
represented its emotional cathexis or charge.

   In neurosis, the free expression of beliefs is interfered with by the
presence of conflicts among beliefs that stimulate anxiety which the
system avoids by the use of mechanisms of defense that, without
solving the conflict, produce distorted beliefs and a temporary reduction in anxiety. In the Neurotic Program, beliefs are organized
into complexes. A belief is randomly chosen from a complex and is
designated as the regnant belief. The system searches the complex
for any beliefs that may be in conflict with the regnant belief. For
example, the regnant belief "I hate father" is in conflict with the
belief "I must love Father" and, therefore, the danger monitor in
the system is alerted and defense mechanisms or transforms are

surveyed from a list of stored transforms to determine the most suitable defense to protect the system against the free and undistorted expression of the regnant belief.

The list of transforms in the model is as follows (Colby, 1963, p. 172):

1. Deflection: Shift Object (Not Self)
2. Substitution: Cascade Verb
3. Displacement: Combine (1) and (2)
4. Neutralization: Neutralize Verb
5. Reversal: Reverse Verb
6. Negation: Insert *Not* Before Verb and Do (5)
7. Reflexion: Shift Object to Self
8. Projection: Switch Subject (Self) and Object (Not Self)

Each transform has a specified numerical capacity to reduce the charge on a belief and to reduce the level of the system's numerical anxiety monitor. In the above list, the transforms are rank ordered with respect to their effectiveness in reducing charges and inversely rank ordered with respect to their effectiveness in reducing anxiety. Transform 1 (Deflection) is most effective in reducing charges and least effective in reducing anxiety. Transform 8 (Projection) is least effective in reducing charges and most effective in reducing anxiety. Depending on quantitative algorithmic relationships (Colby & Gilbert, 1964) a transform will be selected that results in a derivative and distorted belief that is printed out by the system. The distorted belief, itself, may produce further conflict and anxiety in the system and a series of additional transforms may have to be selected in the neurotic system's vain attempt to resolve its conflicts. Colby (1963, p. 173) provides an example of how transforms succeeded each other during a crises in the neurotic system:

Let us follow the details of an actual run which generated the output statement "I want to help father." In a random search of the complex list, the complex D_3 was selected. A random search for D_3 produced the belief B_1 which stands for "I want to hurt Father." Matching B_1 as the regnant against all others in the complex a conflict was found with B_2 standing for "I must not hurt father." B_1 and B_2 each had a charge of 300 which drove the anxiety level up to 400. At this time, the transform handling anxiety of degree 400 was No. (4), Neutralization. Hence, a derivative of B_1, B_{22}, was created to assert "I am indifferent to father." In matching B_{22} against others in the complex D_3, however, it ran into conflict with B_{19}, "I must not be indifferent to father." Failure of this operation raised the anxiety level another 100 units to 500. At this time, No. (5), Reversal, was attempted, producing the derivative B_{23}, "I want to help father." B_{23} was passed through the complex and, since it found no conflict, it was output as an expressible belief. Reversal was promoted as a transform, the charge on B_1 and B_2 was reduced by the percentage the transform of Reversal handles, the charge of B_{23} was reduced to zero, B_{23} was added to the complex D_3, the charge on the complex was reduced but not sufficiently so the next cycle began by random searching D_3 for the next regnant belief.

The Neurotic Program contains several monitors in addition to the anxiety or danger monitor whose bearing on the selection of trans-forms was discussed above. The self-esteem numerical monitor is raised or lowered according to whether a belief is executed that satisfies a moral imperative (supergo). A lowered level of the self-esteem monitor raises the emotional charges on many beliefs and results in repeated neurotic concern with these beliefs until a transform can be located that produces a satisfactory (though distorted) belief that the system can out-put, with an accompanying numerical index that registers the extent and intensity of non-verbal behavior (body language) that clinicians regularly observe during psychotherapy with their human neurotics. The well-being numerical monitor indicates the extent to which the system, as a whole, is being threatened with intense disruption or dissolution under the impact of extremely severe conflict. Since a basic postulate of the Neurotic Program (Colby & Gilbert, 1964) is that the system, at all costs, must survive, the well-being monitor in response to pre-set numerical readings, causes the system to replace (repress) the complex of beliefs that is causing the stress with a new complex of beliefs derived from the system's belief matrix memory (Colby & Gilbert, 1964). This cycle of replacement of belief complexes, each involving different beliefs, rationalizations, danger monitors, transforms, etc., can continue endlessly as the distorted beliefs created by the transforms are added to the system's belief matrix memory and the reasons that the system gives (rationalization, denial, isolation) to support and justify these beliefs are added to the system's reason matrix memory (Colby & Gilbert, 1964). The Neurotic Program, therefore, is a dynamic, evolving, self-renewing and self-extending symbol producing system that meets the postulate of self- survival, at the cost of chronic pathological thought and emotion.

Commentary

A computer program that attempts to model the human neurotic process represents a unique research approach to the study of pathological cognitive and affective processes. The special characteristics, advantages and limitations of this approach will be briefly discussed.

Colby (1963, 1964) asserts the insufficiency of traditional research methods (statistical measures and comparisons of mean group performance) to represent adequately the semantic (and particularly the emotional aspects of meaning) nature of thought, in general, and of neurotic thought, in particular. More precisely, in Colby's attempt (1963) to represent free association productions of his neurotic analysand, he had to steer a clear course between reproduction, for computer processing, of the complete complex of subtle, multilevel, idiosyncratic and evanescent verbal and emotional products and a representation by number and quantity that would simplify the problem of knowledge representation. It would appear that Colby's chosen compromise course was to represent the complete record of analysand productions by persistent and pervasive emotional themes (beliefs) that would have attached to them numerical and quantitative indices that could be processed through the application of mathematical algorithms. It is of interest that Freud (1926), long before the era of computers, had referred to the predominant mental content of neurosis as consiting of emotional complexes with associated quantitative cathexes. Computerization, of course, would add dimensions of numerical precision, quantification, speed, memory and general information processing capability far beyond what Freud or later researchers could achieve relying solely on their own intellectual powers.

A distinct advantage of computerization, in general, is that the governing mathematical algorithms require exact specification of variables, values, definitions and relationships. This requirement for precision had resulted in the clarification of theories in other scientific fields such as mass spectrometry, as in the DENDRAL computer programs (see Chapter Seven). For example, the theory of the mechanisms of defense that is the heart of the understanding of the neurotic process (Freud, 1926) must inevitably be clarified and strenghthened as a result of the type of quantitative definitions and measurements that are present in the Neurotic Program (Colby & Gilbert, 1964). Mathematical indices of transforms, anxiety, well-being, etc., can be modified in experiments conducted with the

Neurotic Program to take account of corresponding vicissitudes in the human neurotic personality that result from the interplay of idiosyncratic experience and general defense mechanisms or from the specific and general effects of psychotherapeutic communications made to the system (human or computer). Experiments that involve varying interpretations made to the standard Neurotic Program or standard interpretations made to varying Neurotic Programs can be conducted with almost instantaneous registration of effects displayed on the computer screen. These experimental simulations have the advantages of safety, control, speed and reproducibility. The interpretation of experimental results can be immediately applied to the adjustment of mathematical algorithms and to revisions in concepts that strengthen the scope and precision of the theory of psychoneurosis and its psychotherapy.

The limitations of the Neurotic Program (Colby, 1963, 1964; Colby & Gilbert, 1964) derive from several sources. First, theories of human psychoneurosis and its amelioration from Freud to the present are neither complete nor consistent nor precise. Second, as a frontier of scientific research, the development of the Neurotic Program was confronted with all the difficulties of pioneering investigation. Third, the attempt at computer representation of the neurotic process and its therapy took for its scope the complex and, perhaps, intractable field of psychoanalysis rather than beginning with a more constrained and simple psychological theory. A different research strategy, with its own advantages and limitations, will be discussed in the following section.

CLIENT 1

CLIENT 1 simulates the behavior of a client in an initial counseling interview. As an interactive program, CLIENT 1 provides a standard situation in which the counseling behavior of counselors and supervisees can be studied in an effort to advance knowledge about the conditions that facilitate client movement.

Unlike Colby's Neurotic Program which models a person with intensive, chronic and complex psychological difficulties, CLIENT 1 (Hummel, Lichtenberg, & Shaffer, 1975; Lichtenberg, Hummel & Shaffer, 1984) models a person with moderate problems. In addition, it does not appear that CLIENT 1 contains a representation of the complex dynamics and concepts that are characteristic of psycho-analytic theory and psychotherapy that was modeled in the neurotic Program.

The theory guiding CLIENT 1 would appear to be that CLIENT 1 (the person model) feels threatened by certain topics and would prefer to discuss them at a general level and that the counselor and supervisee need to use techniques that will reduce the threatening connotations of these topics so that CLIENT 1 can express its concern with greater and greater specification and definition of its particular problem. Thus, the fulcrum of the counseling interview and a significant measure of client movement is the mastery of those counseling processes by which CLIENT 1's expression of its problems becomes, progressively, less general and vague and more specific and defined; so that CLIENT 1 is progressively enabled to express, explicitly, increasingly precise and threatening versions of its problem.

Description of Program

Although CLIENT 1 is, potentially, capable of modeling a wide variety of clients by changes in its data and procedural variables, the person actually simulated is a thirty year old married businessman who is experiencing career difficulties and who appears to be suitably communicative and motivated for participation in an initial counseling interview. CLIENT 1's data structure for the topic of career diffi-culties contains a graded series of statements that are numerically calibrated from low degrees of threat for general statements to high degrees of threat for specific, direct and fully disclosed accounts of its problem. The problem of natural language communication (see Chapter Five) between counselors and CLIENT 1 is managed by coded data lists from which, under procedural rules, CLIENT 1 selects responses and by lists of sentence fragments, menus and prompts on the computer display screen from which the counselors select elements that enable them to construct responses that permit different modes (e.g., direct question, qualified statement) and con-tent (e.g., factual, affective). Hummel, Lichtenberg and Shaffer (1975, p. 165) provide the following detailed description of the mode and mechanism of interaction between counselors and CLIENT 1:

A human counselor sits at a cathode ray tube computer terminal (CRT) and responds using the terminal's keyboard to the natural language state-ments made by the simulated client. After each client statement or series of statements, the counselor constructs his response and sends it to the client. The counselor's message is constructed by selecting and typing in the various numerical codes which refer to the counselor's lead, the affect, the content area, and the person reference which he wishes to include, plus several prepositions which are used as connectives in message construction. A tentative statement can be constructed by selecting a qualifying phrase to preface the counselor's statement. The program takes the coded information and displays the equivalent verbal message on the CRT. For instance, the counselor's displayed response to a client statement might be, "You feel tense about relationship with boss." *You feel* is the lead, *tense* is the affect, *relationship* is the content, and *boss* is the person referenced in the statement. Qualified, the statement would read: "I'm not sure but I think you feel tense about relationship with boss." The message is processed by the client, a response determined and returned to the counselor, and the cycle begins again. The variety of affects, content areas, and persons, along with qualifiers and counselor leads, permits the counselor to construct more than 30,000 different statements which could affect the client program.

Lichtenberg, Hummel and Shaffer (1984, p. 161) provide the following sample interviews between counselors and CLIENT 1:

Sample Interview I

Cl: Work seems to be going ok for me most of the time, but sometimes I have trouble coping with it.

Co: You feel a sense of uncertainty about work situation.

Cl: The trouble is that I am caught in the work situation and I do not know what to do.

Co: I am not sure, but I think you feel anxiety about work situation.

Cl: I especially feel this way when I work around the secretaries.

Co: You feel tense with secretaries.

Cl: When I am around the secretaries, I am uncertain of just how to act ... what to do.

Co: You are telling me about a sense of uncertainty about behavior with secretaries.

Cl: I guess it is not all the secretaries though ... I feel most tense around my own secretary.

Co: I think it would be a good idea if you could tell me about anxiety about secretary.

Cl: I really feel wound up when I have to work around my secretary.

Cl: It is not that she is a bad secretary ... in fact, in some ways she makes me feel kind of secure at work.

Co: I am not sure, but I think you feel affection for secretary.

Cl: You know, it is strange but I want to be around her more and more of the time.

Cl: It is when I get to feeling those things about my secretary that I get all wound up inside.

Sample Interview II

Cl: Work seems to be going ok for me most of the time, but sometimes I have some trouble coping with it.
Co: I am not sure, but I think you feel wound up inside.
Cl: Generally, work is all right. Sometimes I have trouble with it.
Co: I think it would be a good idea if you could tell me about frustration with work situation.
Cl: My job does have its problems.
Co: Tell me about problem(s).
Cl: My work has been causing me some problems.
Co: Tell me about work situation.
Cl: My job presents some difficulties.
Co: You feel frustration about work situation.
Cl: Sometimes I feel kind of trapped by my work.
Co: You are telling me about a sense of being trapped by work situation.
Cl: Like, for instance, work does not pay as I would like it to, and financially things are getting out of proportion for me.

Note. Sample Interview I is from "CLIENT 1: A computer program which simulates client behavior in an initial interview" by T. J. Hummel, J. W. Lichtenberg and W. F. Shaffer, 1975, *Journal of Counseling Psychology,* 22, p. 166. Copyright 1975 by the American Psychological Association. Reprinted by permission.

Client Trust and Counselor Evaluation

CLIENT 1 adjusts its level of trust in the counselor as a function of the counselor's ability to employ the techniques of reflection and interpretation. Reflections that are inaccurate and interpretations that are wide of the mark or too deep raise threat levels in CLIENT 1 and reduce its trust in the counselor, perhaps to the point of terminating the relationship. Effective counselor use of the techniques of reflection and interpretation will increase CLIENT 1's trust in the counselor and permit it to tolerate increased threat as it moves toward a more specific and complete account of its problem.

CLIENT 1 evaluates how effectively the counselor employs the techniques of reflection and interpretation. CLIENT 1 contains a set of computer routines and templates that compare the completeness of counselor statements with CLIENT 1 statements (evaluation of reflection technique) and calculate the quantity and specificity of new material produced (evaluation of interpretation statements). CLIENT 1 can provide feedback information to counselors regarding their over-all performance in the form of a good counselor index, as well as concise and quantitative data concerning level of trust (in effect, the strength and quality of the counseling relationship). Through this information feedback, in association with a printed protocol of counselor statements and CLIENT 1 responses during the interview, counselor education and training can be facilitated as strengths, weaknesses and progress are objectively identified.

Commentary

CLIENT 1 appears to be, simultaneously, a computer model of a specific person with a specific problem, a tutorial expert system (see Chapter Seven) that guides and evaluates student performance and a natural language understanding system (see Chapter Five) that participates in an initial interview with a human counselor. These theoretical, educational and research aspects of CLIENT 1 will be briefly discussed.

As a computer model of personality, CLIENT 1 may be usefully compared with neurotic (Colby & Gilbert, 1964) and psychotic (Colby, 1975) models of personality. As discussed in this chapter and in Chapter Five, the neurotic and psychotic models of personality represent complex psychoanalytic theories of anxiety and defense. As models of personality, the Neurotic Program and the psychotic program encapsulate significant aspects of the history and experience of persons that they model in a representation that takes account of significant dynamic and structural personality themes (neurotic beliefs, paranoid beliefs). On the other hand, CLIENT 1 is clearly not created in the image of psychoanalytic theory and the developers of CLIENT 1 make little reference to theory, other than a brief reference to Rogerian theory (Rogers, 1951) and, in addition, appear to identify the complex psychology of human personality with the information processing concept of a problem space, as in the research of Newell and Simon (1972). Thus, the person modeled in CLIENT 1 is not a neurotic or psychotic personality or even a normal personality, but, rather, a "person" whose existence consists of a series of statements (with associated threat values) arranged in a hierarchy from general to specific that defines the problem space and solution goal that the counselor is expected to reach by techniques of reflection and interpretation that manuever the system through the problem space. The issue is a more general one, in that the use of artificial intelligence methods, especially in the area of human personality and beliefs, operate in such a way as to abstract (and, perhaps, distort) the knowledge and theory that are being represented and processed (see Chapter Six).

From the perspective of CLIENT 1 as a tutorial expert system, the choice of information processing concepts of problem, problem space, problem-solving sequences (Newell & Simon, 1972) to represent the model of the personality and its concerns, the model of the counseling process and the model of counselor education may be seen as consonant with general education practice in which the complexities of a given knowledge domain are intentionally oversimplified for didactic purposes. The counseling student, thus, in interacting with CLIENT 1, can safely view this artificial situation as one in which he/she has the technical problem of acquiring and practicing technical skills on a technical instrument. To what extent technical skills (e.g., reflection, interpretation) are significantly improved through tutorial with CLIENT 1 and to what extent transfer of learning occurs with human clients (whose personality and behavior are more complex and different from the specific problem statement definition of CLIENT 1) are deserving of comparative research with traditional didactic methods of counselor education. It is of interest that Hummel and Shaffer (1979), focusing on the specific goal of teaching empathic responses, found CLIENT 1 training, in certain respects, to be superior to traditional training.

As a system of natural language understanding, CLIENT 1 may have certain advantages when compared with other systems. As compared with the ELIZA system (see Chapter Five), CLIENT 1 has the advantage of accurate "understanding". In CLIENT 1, counselors construct their natural language responses from a computer controlled menu, so that CLIENT 1's "understanding" of counselors' statements simply represents the processing of numerical codes associated with sentence components and phrases that counselors use to construct their responses. In the ELIZA system, the use of pattern recognition methods permit unrestricted input. However, many possible "misunderstandings" on the part of ELIZA arise from its use of pattern recognition procedures in its natural language "understanding". In the case of CLIENT 1, its research and educational purposes are, perhaps, best served by the method of restricted selection from a computer listing of possible response segments. In the case of the ELIZA system and also the PARRY system (see Chapter Five), their purposes of modeling client centered psychotherapy or psychiatric interviewing are, perhaps, best served by a method that permits normal, flexible and unrestricted expression in communicating with the computer model.

Summary

In this chapter, we discussed two computer models of personality, Neurotic Program and CLIENT 1. For each system, major features were described and a general commentary was presented.

Designed to simulate the analysand in psychoanalytic therapy, research with the Neurotic Program had three general goals. These goals included the clarification of the theory of psychoanalysis, the achievement of a better understanding of the processes of psychoanalytic therapy and the improvement of training in psychoanalytic psychotherapy.

The Neurotic Program models an analysand with respect to major emotional beliefs and neurotic process including mechanisms of defense or transforms that reduce conflict and anxiety in the system by expression of distorted beliefs. The eight transforms vary with respect to their effectiveness in reducing emotional charges associated with the beliefs and in reducing general levels of anxiety in the system. Among the transforms, deflection is most effective in reducing charges and least effective in reducing anxiety, whereas projection is least effective in reducing charges and most effective in reducing anxiety. An example is provided of how the transforms are serially selected and applied during a crisis in the neurotic process.

The Neurotic Program contains several general monitors that influence general tension in the system and emotional charges on specific beliefs or complexes of beliefs. Among these monitors are the anxiety monitor that signals changes in psychological danger, the self-esteem monitor that signals the violation of a moral standard (super ego) and the well-being monitor that signals the imminent threat of intense disruption or dissolution of the system. The well-being monitor insures the survival of the system by replacing (repressing) complexes with new belief complexes that, temporarily raise the general level of psychological integration in the system. It was pointed out that the cycle of replacement of belief complexes is interminable as newly created and distorted beliefs are added to the systems's belief matrix memory and justifications to support beliefs (rationalization, isolation, denial) are added to the system's reason matrix memory.

In a commentary, it was indicated that the Neurotic Program, in attempting to model the human neurotic process, constitutes a unique research approach to the study of pathological affective and cognitive processes. The particular strategies, advantages and limitations of this research approach were discussed.

CLIENT 1 is an interactive computer model of a client involved in an initial counseling interview. CLIENT 1 has several general goals. These goals include the clarification of theories of counseling, the specification of the techniques of counseling and improvement in the training of counselors.

The personality problems of CLIENT 1 and counseling goals in working with CLIENT 1 were discussed. Since CLIENT 1 simulates only an initial interview, personality structure is represented as a data base consisting of a series of statements calibrated from a general and vague description of CLIENT 1's problem to a specific and exact statement. The expression of CLIENT 1's problem as a general statement carries little threat, whereas a specific statement of CLIENT 1's problem carries high threat. Counselors' goals are to use effective techniques that will move CLIENT 1 from a general statement of its problem to a specific statement.

A detailed description of CLIENT 1 was presented. The means by which counselors construct responses from computer displayed menus of phrases, affects, situations, persons and leads were explained. Sample interviews between CLIENT 1 and counselors were presented.

CLIENT 1 provides means of studying trust in the counselor and of evaluating counselor performance. It was pointed out that CLIENT 1's trust in the counselor is increased by the counselor's effective employment of the techniques of reflection and interpretation. CLIENT 1 contains algorithms that evaluate counselors' performance with respect to their adequacy in employing the techniques of reflection and interpretation. Quantitative evaluations can be presented by CLIENT 1 to counselors in the form of a good counselor index.

In a commentary, it was indicated that CLIENT 1 represents a model of personality, a tutorial expert system that guides and evaluates counselor performance and a natural language understanding system that permits interaction with a human counselor. These conceptual, research and educational characteristics of CLIENT 1 were discussed.

CHAPTER NINE

Examples of Computer Counseling

Introduction

In this chapter, four examples of computer counseling systems are discussed. Characteristics of each system are described and a brief illustrative protocol is presented.

Each system is historically conditioned. The DOCTOR program and the Psychotherapy Interview program represent early attempts to simulate counselor behavior by the use of pattern recognition methods of natural language understanding and communication. The MORTON and PLATO DCS programs place less emphasis on simulation of counselor behavior with respect to modeling a psychotherapist's communicative style and more emphasis on the capability of the computer to execute specific reeducative counseling procedures.

The presentation of the computer counseling programs is organized with respect to general theories or systems of counseling or psychotherapy. Four systems will be discussed: client-centered system (DOCTOR), psychoanalytic system (Psychotherapy Interview program), cognitive behavior system (MORTON) and problem-solving system (PLATO DCS).

Client-Centered System

Perhaps the earliest attempt to develop a personal computer program based on a recognized technique of counseling was the development of the computer program ELIZA (Weizenbaum, 1965). As the first attempt, not surprisingly, the background and subsequent history of the ELIZA program are somewhat curious.

ELIZA was developed by a computer scientist (Weizenbaum, 1965) as a generic program that would accommodate natural language conversation in a variety of settings. Named for Eliza Doolittle, the main character in the play Pygmalion, the computer program was taught to mimic human speech and conversation. In an application of ELIZA, a program titled DOCTOR was developed that mimicked client-centered counseling and, more specifically, the technique of recognition and reflection of client feelings. It is important to understand several perspectives that enter into the interaction between DOCTOR and the client.

First, the computer program DOCTOR merely translates the client's typed input into a set of numerical codes. One such code is based on position and sequence of words in a clients's sentence. Another translates, automatically, first person phrases (e.g., "I feel") into second person phrases (e.g., "Does it bother you that" or "Would it please you if"). Thus, the client statement "I slept late today" would be translated by DOCTOR through its set of codes into "You slept late today" and then into "Does it bother you that you slept late today?". This question would appear on the display screen.

Second, the client may have the distinct impression that the computer is indeed recognizing reflecting feelings. He or she may thus be encouraged to type in additional self-statements stimulating further DOCTOR responses. A typed protocol of client and DOCTOR responses might, if not labeled as a computer-client interaction, be read and understood as an extract from a client-centered counseling interview.

The DOCTOR program stimulated lively interest and discussion in general scientific and professional circles. Weizenbaum (1976) insisted that despite the belief of many psychiatrists and psychologists in the efficacy of DOCTOR as a client-centered counselor, DOCTOR was only an exercise in the generic language ELIZA. He also stated that DOCTOR is not a therapist and that its responses are not therapeutic, because the machine can have no feelings when it produces on the display screen responses such as "I understand."

The problems of personifying or anthropomorphizing the computer and modeling the computer as a counselor were discussed earlier in this book. The following extracts from Holden (1977) and Palmen (1978) are very pertinent. Holden (1977) gives an example of the

DOCTOR program and discusses the emotional effects of the computer on the user and the issue of the empathic ability of the computer:

Men are all alike. IN WHAT WAY They're always bugging us about something or other. CAN YOU THINK OF A SPECIFIC EXAMPLE Well, my boyfriend made me come here. YOUR BOYFRIEND MADE YOU COME HERE He says I'm depressed much of the time. I AM SORRY TO HEAR YOU ARE DEPRESSED It's true. I am unhappy. DO YOU THINK COMING HERE WILL HELP YOU NOT TO BE UNHAPPY I need some help, that much seems certain. WHAT WOULD IT MEAN TO YOU IF YOU GOT SOME HELP Perhaps I could learn to get along with my mother TELL ME MORE ABOUT YOUR FAMILY My mother takes care of me. WHO ELSE IN YOUR FAMILY TAKES CARE OF YOU My father. YOUR FATHER You are like my father in some ways. WHAT RESEMBLANCE DO YOU SEE You are not very aggressive but I think you don't want me to notice that. WHAT MAKES YOU THINK I AM NOT VERY AGGRESSIVE You don't argue with me. WHY DO YOU THINK I DON'T ARGUE WITH YOU You are afraid of me. DOES IT PLEASE YOU TO BELIEVE I AM AFRAID OF YOU My father is afraid of everybody. WHAT ELSE COMES TO MIND WHEN YOU THINK OF YOUR FATHER Bullies. DOES THAT HAVE ANYTHING TO DO WITH THE FACT THAT YOUR BOYFRIEND MADE YOU COME HERE

Weizenbaum reported that he was "startled to see how quickly and how very deeply people conversing with DOCTOR became emotionally involved with the computer and how unequivocally they anthropomorphized it." People did not want him to examine the conversations, "clear evidence that people were conversing with the computer as if it were a person who could be appropriately and usefully addressed in intimate terms."

Many lessons could be drawn from this, one of which is that even the appearance of empathy (combined, of course, with the computer's quite genuine nonjudgmentalism) can be extraordinarily powerful. (Holden, 1977, p. 32; Copyright 1977 by AAAS, reprinted by permission)

Palmen (1978) develops the issue of the empathic ability of the computer by distinguishing between the empathy of the computer program and the empathy of the programmer. He makes the following interesting comments:

Of what help could it possibly be to anyone to know that he is worthy of being liked by a computer? asks Joseph Weizenbaum (Letters, 28, Oct. 1977, p. 354). It should be remembered that any sympathetic response provided by the machine results from the programming made by a human being. So it is not really the machine which is talking to the patient, it is in fact the programmer, who considered many possible responses in advance.... The medium should not be confused with the message, which was originally devised by a real person. When I get a love letter, I don't think that the letter has fallen in love with me. (Palmen, 1978, p. 934; Copyright 1978 by AAAS, reprinted by permission)

Weizenbaum (1977) is critical of the notion that computerized personal counseling can serve the therapeutic function of the client-therapist relationship. He argues on rational ground that the non-judgmental and empathic communication of a computer are very impoverished insofar as helping a client develop feelings of self-worth based on emotional interchange. In reaction to Weizenbaum, both Gaschnig (1977) and Vanderplas (1977) point out that the therapeutic function of computerized personal counseling is an em-pirical question and not one that can be settled with rational argument. Vanderplas also points out that along with *feelings* of self-worth, "the *realization* of the possibility of being worthy may depend more on cognitive processes than on emotional ones" (Vanderplas, 1977, p. 880; Copyright 1977 by AAAS, reprinted by permission). Weizenbaum's DOCTOR program has never been tested in a clinical setting (Selmi, Klein, Greist, Johnson, & Harris, 1982).

Psychoanalytic System

The problem of developing a computer program that might be capable of psychotherapeutic responses such as questioning, clarify-ing, focusing, rephrasing, interpreting, and managing resistance and transference was investigated by Colby, Watt, and Gilbert (1966). They developed a computer program containing over 500 keys, each of which recognizes a specific type of user input. The keys are circuited to a set of responses that contain standard phrases linked to the operation of keys that, for example, change "my" into "your". An example, given by Colby et al., is: PERSON-MY MOTHER DISLIKES ME. PROGRAM-WHY DO YOU FEEL YOUR MOTHER DISLIKES YOU (Colby et al., 1966, p. 148; Copyright 1966 by The Williams and Wilkins Co., reprinted by permission).

Colby et al. (1966) indicated that their program can perform as would a human therapist only for the opening first or second session and that it is not capable, therefore, of handling deep interpretations of transference and resistance typical of the middle and final stages of a course of psychoanalytic psychotherapy. The following is an example of the computer's ability in the initial interview with a man in his 50s:

PROGRAM-HOW CAN I HELP YOU. PERSON-I DON'T KNOW. PROGRAM-TRY TO TELL ME SOMETHING ABOUT IT. PERSON-NO. PROGRAM-CAN YOU ELABORATE. PERSON-I AM SICK AND TIRED TODAY. PROGRAM-DO YOU HAVE ANY IDEA WHY. PERSON-YES, I'M OLD. PROGRAM-PLEASE GO ON. PERSON-I SEEM TO HAVE LOST INTEREST IN EVERYTHING. PROGRAM-TELL ME MORE ABOUT SUCH FEELING. PERSON-I HAVE SOME IDEA WHY I FEEL THIS WAY TOO. PROGRAM-YOU HAVE. PERSON-IT SEEMS THAT I MISS HAVING A FAMILY. PROGRAM-WHAT MAKES YOU FEEL YOU MISS HAVING A FAMILY. PERSON-THERE IS A CHALLENGE ABOUT IT. PROGRAM-WHY IS THAT IMPORTANT TO YOU. (Colby et al., 1966, p. 150; Copyright 1966 by The Williams and Wilkins Co., reprinted by permission)

According to Colby et al., the program's greatest weakness is its "inability to offer interpretations based on the cognitive model of the person" (Colby et al., 1966, p. 151; Copyright 1966 by The Williams and Wilkins Co., reprinted by permission). A human therapist, they point out, constructs a cognitive model of the person, built up over a series of interviews, that permits the therapist to make inferences regarding the suitability or unsuitability of a given type of interpretation. The authors recognize that incorporation of such a cognitive model for each individual client into the computer program constitutes a very formidable problem. Apparently, further development of the program and extensive clinical trials will be needed (Selmi et al., 1982).

Cognitive Behavior System

In contrast to client-centered and psychoanalytic methods, cognitive behavior methods have well-defined strategies that should make computer application more feasible. Selmi et al. (1982) developed a computer program that uses cognitive behavior strategies in the treatment of mild and moderate depression. The authors indicate that their computer version of Beck's (1976) cognitive methods for the treatment of depression requires, instead of the usual 20 sessions with a therapist, six to eight sessions with the computer "because the computerized techniques are experimental and 'psycho-educational' in nature" (Selmi et al., 1982, p. 183; Copyright 1982 by Psychonomic Society, Inc., reprinted by permission).

The program, entitled MORTON, is limited in its ability to interpret free-formed responses made by the user. Therefore, greater reliance is placed on the use of multiple-choice formats, brief case histories, and general forms of identifying and managing dysphoric thoughts (Selmi et al., 1982).

MORTON uses the first person in relating to the user, whom MORTON addresses by first name. After establishing rapport, MORTON elicits the user's complaints and expectations about therapy and uses information about the complaints to make homework assignments to the user. MORTON explains the theory of cognitive therapy and tests user knowledge and understanding by a series of multiple-choice questions. MORTON provides feedback for the user's answers.

In the second session, MORTON and the user review the homework assignment, including reactions, questions, and clarifications. MORTON then reviews and tests, through multiple-choice items, the principles of cognitive behavior therapy that were presented in the initial session. Homework assignments are given in each session and reviewed in the following session. These assignments consist of the user writing down specific situations that lead to feelings of depression in his or her life. In the remaining sessions, MORTON assists the user in the identification of automatic thoughts of a dysphoric character, explaining the cognitive misunderstanding or distortions contained in these thoughts and teaching the person more reasonable and more realistic responses to automatic thoughts. In the final session, MORTON provides guidance to the person for managing future depressions.

The following is an example of interaction in a therapy session between MORTON and user:

MORTON: Last week, we talked about the principles of Cognitive Therapy. If you recall, Principle No. 1 stated that feelings are caused by cognitions or thoughts. Today, I want for us to examine this principle in great detail. How does this sound to you? 1. Sounds fine. Let's continue. 2. I would like a brief review of the major points you made last week, before continuing. SUBJECT: 1. MORTON: Good. Let's try a few examples ... If a person were to think to him or herself "I am inferior" what is likely to occur? 1. The person would compare himself to others and find faults in himself and feel bad. 2. Probably would feel real low about himself. 3. He would get angry. (choose the best answer(s)) SUBJECT: 1, 2. MORTON: You're right, John. By saying to himself, "I'm inferior," he would compare himself to others, be very critical of himself, and probably get depressed. Let's try another.... Suppose a boss gets upset and starts yelling at the employee and the employee thinks: "That guy has got the nerve! I won't stand for this!" How will the employee feel? 1. Anxious. 2. Depressed/low. 3. Angry. SUBJECT: 2. MORTON: No, he wouldn't feel depressed, John. He would be angry, because the employer has put him down and the employee won't stand for that. Perhaps the employee has thought that the "put down" was unjustified. Can you see from this example that different thoughts about the same situation can produce different feelings? (Selmi et al., 1982 p. 184; Copyright by Psychonomic Society, Inc., reprinted by permission)

The authors of MORTON plan to conduct future research to determine the differential effectiveness of MORTON and a human cognitive behavior therapist (Selmi, 1983) in the treatment of mild or moderate depression. They believe that computer-assisted packaged therapies such as MORTON can assist in providing mental health services to persons who cannot now afford such services.

Problem-Solving System

The comprehensive PLATO® Computer-based Dilemma Counselling System (PLATO DCS) provides counseling for personal problems and teaches a generic method of problem solving. (PLATO® is a service mark of Control Data Corporation. The PLATO® system is a development of the University of Illionois.) PLATO DCS treats moderately difficult psychological problems.

The PLATO Dilemma Counseling System (Wagman, 1979, 1980a, 1984a; Wagman & Kerber, 1980) is a generic problem-solving method for psychological dilemmas. Dilemma Counselling was designed for treatment of avoidance-avoidance problems.

Application of Dilemma Counselling to an avoidance-avoidance problem first involves the formulation of the problem as a psychological dilemma (see Chapter Ten). Once formulated, the problem is resolved by use of the generalized dilemma matrix (see Chapter Ten).

PLATO DCS (Wagman & Kerber, 1978) teaches Systematic Dilemma counseling and provides counseling for a psychological dilemma through individualized interaction with the PLATO computer system. The PLATO DCS is comprised of three components:

Dilemma Counseling, Specific Dilemma Solutions, and Structural Dilemma Solutions (see Chapters Ten and Eleven). Wagman & Kerber (1979) present a detailed description of displays that users encounter as they interact with the computer.

The Dilemma Counseling component contains six parts (see Chapter Ten). Users who are unfamiliar with Dilemma Counseling would begin with part one and proceed to part six. Users who know the method could proceed directly to part six, in which they work on their own psychological dilemma. Because it requires approximately two hours on PLATO to learn Dilemma Counseling and approximately one hour to apply the method to a personal problem, users may stop working upon completion of any section and return to PLATO DCS at the point where they ended a previous session. It is also possible to skip sections or to study them out of sequence (e.g., if a review of a particular part were necessary).

Part one of the Dilemma Counseling component introduces the meaning of psychological dilemmas. Directions are given regarding the general format of avoidance-avoidance problems.

Parts two and three give practice in phrasing problems as dilemmas. In part two, PLATO provides examples of psychological problems and demonstrates how to formulate these problems as dilemmas. Poor dilemma formulations are contrasted with better formulations of the same problems, and explanations are presented. In part three, PLATO encourages the user to formulate practice problems as dilemmas. The computer judges the correctness of the response by searching for important keywords. The user is encouraged to formulate each phrase of the dilemma correctly and is rewarded when the attempt is successful.

Parts four and five give practice in generating solutions. In part four, PLATO demonstrates examples of the application of the dilemma matrix (see Chapter Ten) to several psychological problems. In a series of displays, each row of the completed dilemma matrix is presented along with commentary that explains the different parts of the matrix. Potential solutions to the example problems are also given, and the user is encouraged to compare the solutions and rank their quality. In part five, the user completes the dilemma matrix for several practice problems and generates potential solutions. He or she completes the dilemma matrix one row at a time, with the corresponding row of the generalized dilemma matrix as a model. The user also must find a solution for each row of the matrix before proceeding to the next row. In this way, the user has practiced every step of the Dilemma Counseling method, including the generation of solutions, before working on his or her own problem.

A user applies Dilemma Counseling to his or her own problem by using the techniques learned in parts one through five of the Dilemma Counseling component. Thus, in part six, the user formulates his or her problem as a dilemma, completes the dilemma matrix for the problem, and generates possible solutions. On the final display, all solutions generated by the user are presented simultaneously on the display screen. The user ranks solutions from best to worst and is encouraged to consider the adequacy of the best solution.

If the user needs help in thinking of solutions, instructions in part six of the Dilemma Counseling component explain how to access the Specific or the Structural Dilemma Solutions components (see chapter eleven). These components contain 69 representative problems and over 400 specific and general solutions to assist the user in creatively solving his or her problem.

The purpose of the Specific Dilemma Solutions component is to provide examples of how Dilemma Counseling has been used to help people with various kinds of problems. Users are instructed to search for specific cases similar to theirs and to consider the usefulness of the solutions generated by other people.

The purpose of the Structural Dilemma Solutions component is to provide assistance for those people unable to find cases in the Specific Dilemma Solutions component that are relevant for them. Structural solutions convey useful strategies for generating solutions to problems of a general type, regardless of specific content of the problem.

The following is an example of the application of PLATO DCS to a psychological problem (Wagman & Kerber, 1979, p. 65):

Original Wording of the Problem
I find I get depressed very easily and quite often. I know how to get myself down by thinking about past painful experiences. I seem to be changing so rapidly that my life is completely separate from what it was two years ago. I feel I cannot talk to parents or friends. I feel very lonely. Music, which is my major, seems to frustrate me because I become very competitive. I need someone to be with me, yet I fear I will become too dependent and be hurt again. As a result, I have many acquaintances but no one really cares.

Dilemma Formulation:

If I think about past experiences, then I become depressed and lonely. If I don't think about the past, then I must look toward the unknown in the future which frightens me. But I must either think about the past, or look to the future. Therefore, I will either become depressed and lonely or become frightened.

Dilemma matrix

Dilemma component	Extrication route	Creative inquiry
1. If I think about past experiences, then I become depressed and lonely.	Thinking about the past does not necessarily lead to depression and loneliness.	How can it be that thinking about the past will not lead to depression and loneliness?
2. It is bad to be lonely and depressed.	Loneliness and depression are not necessarily bad.	How can this be the case?
3. If I do not think about the past then I must look to the future which is uncertain and frightening.	Not thinking about the past and looking ahead will not necessarily be uncertain or frightening.	How can this be true?
4. Being afraid and uncertain is bad.	This is not necessarily bad.	How can this be?
5. Either I think about the past or I do not think about the past.	There are other alternatives available.	What other alternatives are there?

Solutions

1. Think about the happy past experiences and do not allow yourself to become depressed.
2. This period may be a time to sort things out and pull yourself together trying to teach yourself to look at the more positive side of life.
3. Look ahead to the future as an adventure. Think in positive terms and think about the assets you already have and the possibilities for learning and experiencing life.
4. Everyone has fears. That is what makes life a challenge. If everything were planned out, you would have nothing to learn from or look forward to.
5. Don't worry so much about being in the past or in the future.

Concepts, methods and evaluation of PLATO DCS are presented in Chapters Ten and Eleven. Research comparing PLATO DCS with human counselors is presented in Chapter Twelve.

Published by Control Data Corporation (Wagman & Kerber, 1978), PLATO DCS has been used, internationally, in colleges and universities and business and government organizations.

Summary

In this chapter, characteristics and protocols of four computer counseling systems were presented. The computer programs were DOCTOR (client-centered system), Psychotherapy Interview program (psychoanalytic system), MORTON (cognitive behavior system) and PLATO DCS (problem-solving system).

It was indicated that the DOCTOR program was a specific application of the generic ELIZA natural language understanding system. Technical codes underlying communication between DOCTOR and clients were briefly described. The role of DOCTOR as client-centered counselor was described and viewpoints concerning the issues of its effectiveness and empathic capability were discussed. A protocol of an interview between DOCTOR and a young woman was presented.

It was indicated that the Psychotherapy Interview program was directed primarily to the initial sessions of a course of psychoanalytic psychotherapy. The technical mode of its operation was described. A protocol of a therapeutic interview between the program and a middle-aged man was presented. Limitations were discussed including the program's inability to construct a cognitive model of each patient that could guide the application of appropriate decision rules for the content and timing of therapeutic interpretations and other techniques.

The MORTON program uses cognitive behavior strategies in the treatment of mild and moderate depression. MORTON has only limited ability to understand natural language and relies upon multiple choice formats, case history summaries and didactic cognitive therapy information to guide the identification and management of dysphoric cognition. The sequence and content of sessions as conducted by MORTON was described. A detailed protocol of a cognitive behavior therapy interview between MORTON and a young man was presented.

The PLATO computer-based Dilemma Counseling System (PLATO DCS) is a generic problem solving program that provides counseling for moderately difficult psychological dilemmas. PLATO DCS has three components. The dilemma counseling component teaches the dilemma counseling method. The specific dilemma solutions component provides a wide range of detailed cases and solutions. The structural dilemma solutions component provides general strategies and solutions that are broadly applicable. A protocol of solutions to a psychological dilemma generated through interaction with PLATO DCS was presented.

CHAPTER TEN

PLATO DCS: An Expert Computer System for Personal Counseling

Introduction

Part of the difficulty in accomplishing the goal of developing a computer as a personal counselor has been that research has proceeded much too directly without due attention to the problems of match between computer communication logic and psychotherapy communications. Thus, Colby et al. (1966) found it very difficult to assimilate into the binary logic of computers the multilogic or non-logic of free association in psychoanalytic communication. A second difficulty was that researchers began the difficult process of developing computer-based personal counseling with the most complex and sophisticated forms of psychotherapy rather than with the simplest forms. A third difficulty was that predominantly affective (Colby et al., 1966; Weizenbaum, 1965) rather than predominantly cognitive types of counseling or psychotherapy were chosen. A fourth difficulty was that the computer technology of the 1960s was not sufficiently sophisticated with respect to speed, flexibility, memory, and individuated interaction capability to be used effectively in personal counseling.

In planning for the development of what ultimately came to be the PLATO Dilemma Counseling System (PLATO DCS)*, a careful rationale was employed to approach and overcome these difficulties.

---

*The PLATO system is a development of the University of Illinois. PLATO is a service mark of Control Data Corporation.

A method of simple interactive cognitive counseling was invented in which communication logic was commensurate with the computer's logic. A sophisticated computer system and computer network was fortunately available at the University of Illinois Urbana-Champaign campus.

The PLATO computer system at the University of Illinois at Urbana-Champaign (Alpert & Bitzer, 1970; Holt, 1983; Smith & Sherwood, 1976) links over 2,000 graphical display terminals to Control Data Corporation Cyber 73 computers. The terminals are located at various colleges, universities, and community, government and business organizations in the United States, United Kingdoms, Canada and other countries. Therefore, thousands of clients could potentially be served by a personal counseling procedure developed and made available over the PLATO system.

PLATO DCS Display and Terminal

Each terminal is composed of a keyset that transmits the user's input to the central computer and to a display screen that shows computer-generated information. The keyset is composed of the standard typewriter characters plus special function keys by which the user controls the flow of PLATO DCS materials. The display screen shows letters, figures, drawings, graphs, and other information typed by the user or produced by the central computer. Writing speed on the display screen is 180 characters per sec with a display capacity of 2,048 characters. Response time from user input to computer response is .2 sec.

Dialogue with PLATO DCS

In their simplest form, materials presented on the PLATO DCS display screen consist of a repeating sequence, that is, a display on the user's screen followed by the user's response to that display. The user reacts to each display by pressing a single key in order to move on to new material or by typing a word, sentence, or other expression. A user's response might also be a question or a command to PLATO DCS to respond with a particular type of display. Authors of PLATO DCS materials provide enough details about possible user responses so that PLATO DCS can maintain a dialogue with each user. Thus, the PLATO DCS system allows for individualized interaction sequences between the user and the computer.

Systematic Dilemma Counseling

Concepts of Dilemma Counseling

Unpleasant dilemmas usually have the quality of inevitability or necessity. The person feels driven, blocked, and helpless, between, if-not-on-the horns of the dilemma. The person feels trapped between what he/she believes are necessary evils. The emotional state of conflict, puzzlement, and tension of the person experiencing a personal dilemma is further intensified and complicated by the difficulty of reasoning competently with dilemmas (Leahey & Wagman, 1974; Wagman, 1978, 1984a; Wason, 1964).

Counselors and psychotherapists see many clients who are involved in personal choice problems, which can be considered avoidance-avoidance problems according to topological theory. In general, the problems read as follows: If I make a decision for action p, then unhappy consequence r will occur; and if I make a decision for action q, then unhappy consequence s will occur. But, I must do either p or q, and so one of these unhappy consequences, r or s, must occur.

Techniques of Dilemma Counseling

Application of the dilemma counseling method to a psychological case problem requires (a) the careful formulation of the case as a psychological dilemma and (b) the resolution of the dilemma through the dilemma matrix method.

Dilemma counseling techniques can be grouped into five sequenced and interrelated processes. These processes may be listed as (a) formulating the original case problem as a psychological dilemma, (b) formulating the extrication route for each dilemma component, (c) formulating the creative inquiry for each extrication route, (d) generating solutions for each creative inquiry, and (e) ranking and evaluating solutions.

Originally developed and shown to be effective (Wagman, 1979) in a counselor-treated mode, dilemma counseling in two successive experiments was modified to a semiautonomous treatment mode (Wagman, 1980b) and then to a fully autonomous form that was shown to be effective (Wagman, 1981). The autonomous form of systematic dilemma counseling consisted of (a) a self-help booklet that provided examples, practice, and guidance in learning how to solve psychological dilemmas and (b) an accompanying set of cassette recordings that contained a running text of supportive counselor commentary. Following this experiment, it was felt that autonomous dilemma counseling could be greatly improved through the use of a personal interactive computer that would provide a more vivid and self-paced method for solving a current psychological dilemma and for learning how to solve future psychological dilemmas.

Integrating Systematic Dilemma Counseling and the PLATO Computer System

Rationale

Computer-based counseling is a frontier of scientific thought. Previous attempts to develop computerized client-centered counseling (Weizenbaum, 1965) or computerized psychoanalytic counseling (Colby et al., 1966) have floundered because of the incommensurability of the precise logic of the computer and the free-flowing associations of counseling. Computer-based dilemma counseling has solved this problem by developing a highly structured set of strategies based on the logic of implication, which is also the logic of computers in their "if-then" operation sequencing (Wagman, 1984a).

The functions of a computer-based education system that provides a medium for presenting a method of self-help counseling can be explored by viewing PLATO DCS in three different roles: that of teacher, counselor, and researcher.

PLATO DCS as Teacher of the Dilemma Counseling Method

PLATO DCS allows for individualized teaching whereby students can work at their own pace, review material of their own choosing, and seek help when the necessity arises. Also, the judging capabilities of PLATO DCS allow for a continuous monitoring of student responses, with instantaneous feedback regarding appropriate or inappropriate student input.

PLATO DCS as Counselor for Psychological Dilemmas

In individualized counseling, each person can tailor the use of PLATO DCS materials to his/her own problems. Persons can work at their own pace and can seek help when needed. PLATO DCS can provide praise and encouragement contingent on specific responses, much as a human counselor might do. Also PLATO DCS could potentially make suggestions regarding specific and generalized solutions to psychological problems via a wealth of material that could be stored in the memory of the computer.

PLATO DCS can be instructed to remember all or part of any interaction with an individual for reference at a later time by the individual or by a counselor. Finally, the accessibility of material on PLATO DCS would allow persons who are already familiar with PLATO DCS to return on later occasions to solve minor psychological problems and perhaps more serious ones, thereby relieving counselors and psychotherapists for work on more serious cases.

PLATO DCS as a Researcher in Dilemma Counseling

All types of PLATO DCS parameters, such as number of attempts to answer a particular question, number of requests for additional materials, amount of review, time spent in a particular portion of PLATO DCS, and so on, can be stored simultaneously for many users and can be referenced on-line or via hard-copy printouts. Such PLATO DCS parameters can be utilized to improve materials in light of PLATO DCS effectiveness. It would also be possible to change the structure of PLATO DCS for research purposes to test the effectiveness of different methods of presenting the same material.

Description of PLATO DCS

To convey an adequate description of the development and use of PLATO DCS, displays similar to the actual display prints of the system will be included in the textual discussion. The following is a display of the six main parts of PLATO DCS. As the student finishes reading each paragraph, he/she merely presses the NEXT key on the PLATO DCS keyset to move to sequential displays.

Dilemma Counseling System

This system has six major parts. The first part is a general introduction to the dilemma counseling method. The second and third parts give you practice in phrasing problems as dilemmas. The fourth and fifth parts give you practice in generating solutions to these dilemmas. The final part allows you to apply the dilemma counseling method to a problem of your own.

Select the appropriate number for the part of the Dilemma Counseling System that you wish to see.

A final press of the NEXT key on this initial display erases the introductory material and presents a new display entitled Dilemma Phrasing Checklist. This checklist provides criteria for constructing the dilemma phrasing for various example, practice and personal problems:

Dilemma Phrasing Checklist

1. Have you determined the central theme of the problem? That is, have you determined the two choices that must be made and the unhappy or aversive consequences for this problem?

2. Does the dilemma formulation contain two choices, i.e., choice p and choice q?

3. Do the two choices result in two unhappy or aversive consequences?

4. Are the two choices and their consequences in the "if-then" and "either-or" phrasing?

5. Are any inferences that you have made about the choices or about the unhappy consequences that are present consistent with the problem as stated by the person?

For each of the dilemma phrasing example problems, the process is as follows: (a) The original wording of a problem is written on the screen, (b) a press of the NEXT key displays a poor dilemma phrasing comment below the poor dilemma phrasing, (c) a third NEXT instruction to the computer erases the poor dilemma phrasing and the instructional comment while retaining the original wording of the problem, and (e) displays a better dilemma formulation. The following is the initial display for dilemma phrasing Example Problem 1. Notice that the directive at the end of the display reminds the client that he/she can again see the dilemma phrasing checklist by simply pressing the HELP key on the PLATO DCS keyset.

Example 1

This is the way the person wrote the problem originally:

I just don't know what to do. I have to choose a major and I can't decide whether to go into business or into some branch of science. There are some good and bad things about both fields. I can make more money being a businessman but there's nothing very intellectually rewarding about it. On

the other hand, a scientist does have an intellectually rewarding job, but he doesn't make very much money. So, what do I do?
A poor dilemma phrasing might be:
   If I have a limited income, then I will be unhappy. And if I have limited intellectual satisfaction, then I'll also be unahppy. But either I have to have a limited income or limited intellectual satisfaction and therefore I will be unhappy.
Comment: While this is probably true as far as the subject is concerned, it doesn't take into account the choices that he is trying to make, i.e., being a scientist or businessman. Consequently, the trapped choice situation is not captured in the formulation above. The phrasing does not meet Criteria 1 and 2 in the Dilemma Phrasing Checklist.
   Press HELP to see the Dilemma Phrasing Checklist

   The next display is also from dilemma phrasing Example Problem 1. In this display, the poor dilemma phrasing and the comment from the previous display, have been replaced by a better phrasing formulation and by an appropriate comment. Reference to the dilemma phrasing checklist is still possible. Dilemma phrasing Example Problems 2 and 3 consist of displays that are similar (similar structure, different content) to those for Example Problem 1.

Example 1

This is the way the person wrote the problem originally:
   I just don't know what to do. I have to choose a major and I can't decide whether to go into business or into some branch of science. There are some good and bad things about both fields. I can make more money being a businessman but there's nothing very intellectually rewarding about it. On the other hand, a scientist does have an intellectually rewarding job, but he doesn't make very much money. So, what do I do?
A better formulation would be:
   If I become a scientist, then I will have a limited income, and if I become a businessman, then I will have limited intellectual satisfaction. But I must either become a scientist or become a businessman, and therefore, I will either have a limited income or I will have limited intellectual satisfaction.
Comment: Now we have the trapped choice situation with the person having a clear idea of what choices he sees and the unhappy consequences of each. Press HELP to see the Dilemma Phrasing Checklist.

   Thus, a student practices the formation of the dilemma phrasing for each of three problems in the following manner. An arrow appears on the display screen for each dilemma part, one at a time and in sequence. For each arrow, the student must type in the appropriate phrasing by referring to the original wording of the problem, which is also displayed on the screen. On completion of his/her response for each dilemma part, the student's phrasing is examined by the computer for the presence of a specific key word or of several key words. If the words are present, the student moves on to the next dilemma part; if the words are not present, the student is asked to retype his/her response to include the specified key words. As each dilemma part for a particular problem is completed, it remains on the screen for later reference. The following display from dilemma phrasing Practice Problem 1 demonstrates what happens if a client does *not* include the appropriate key word for one of the dilemma parts.

Original Wording
I have a very domineering mother. She interferes with my life constantly. She says that since I am still at home, she can tell me to do anything and I have to obey. If I say I don't want to, she threatens to stop paying for my education and kick me out of the house. She won't let me buy a motorcycle or car with my own money. She won't let me visit my girlfriend's parents, at their invitation. She even bosses my stepfather around. He may agree with me on some matters but will not cross my mother.
Dilemma Phrasing
   If I obey my mother *then* I will not be able to do what I want
   If I do not obey my mother then she will stop paying for my education
   But *either* I obey my mother or not>do what I want
      therefore *either*
or
Press NEXT and try this phrase again.
Use the keyword *obey* in your answer.
Press LAB to start over the dilemma phrasing for this problem.
Press NEXT to continue.

When the student has successfully filled in all of the eight dilemma parts for a specific problem, he/she is then asked a series of five questions based on the dilemma phrasing checklist. Each of the questions deals with a specific criterion for the formulation of a good dilemma phrasing.

Finally, the student can compare his/her dilemma formulation to a previously prepared good dilemma formulation for each problem. The original wording of each problem is erased from the screen and is replaced by the good dilemma phrasing while the student's phrasing remains on the screen. A comment is also displayed at this time to point out any characteristics of the process of formulating the dilemma for this particular problem, which might generalize to the formulation of other dilemmas.

The student is now introduced to the components of the dilemma matrix by an example problem. The following is the dilemma phrasing and first matrix row for Example Problem 1. A comment is displayed with an arrow pointing to the center cell of the matrix row. Successive displays that are similar to this one review each row of the dilemma matrix for this problem. A comment is given about *each* cell of *each* matrix row. After the comment for the third cell of each row of the matrix, a sample solution is displayed that is appropriate for the creative inquiry in that row of the matrix.

Example 1

If I become a scientist, then I will have a limited income, and if I become a businessman, then I will have limited intellectual satisfaction. But I must either become a scientist or become a businessman, and therefore, I will either have a limited income or I will have limited intellectual satisfaction.

Dilemma	Route of extrication	Creative inquiry
If I become a scientist, then I will have a limited income.	Becoming a scientist will not necessarily lead to having a limited income.	How is it that I can become a scientist and yet not have a limited income?

We can phrase this a little more positively by adding key words such as *not necessarily lead to*. The extrication route here takes the general form: Doing action p won't necessarily lead to unhappy consequence r.

The following is a display of all five of the sample solutions for matrix Example Problem 1. On this display, clients are asked to rank the quality of the solutions from 1 (best) to 5 (worst). In a succeeding display the student is shown his/her ranking of the five solutions and must respond to the display by rating how adequate the best solution is on a scale from 1 (not at all adequate) to 8 (completely adequate).

Example 1

Rank 2

While many scientists are on a limited salary, many also derive income from industrial and technical consultations and from writing and publishing.

Rank 1

Though your income as a scientist may be limited, it would still enable you to live quite comfortably, since scientific incomes are in the top 10% of general population income.

Rank 3
Intellectual satisfaction is derivable from intellectual activities and participation outside of business hours. Also, many aspects of business make great demands on intellectual imagination and acumen.

Rank __
A person seeking unlimited intellectual satisfaction in his business may soon find that the necessary, practical everyday business activities are being neglected.

Rank __
You could combine business and science as in director of research, director of scientific personnel, marketing and advertising of scientific technology and products, pharmaceutical sales manager, etc.

Please rank the solutions from 1 (best) to 5 (worst).

The student is next introduced to the structural components of the generalized dilemma matrix.

The user is instructed how to make use of the structural components as a general guide when working with specific problems.

Dilemma Matrix Table
If I do action p, then unhappy consequence r will occur. And if I do action q, then unhappy consequence s will occur. But I must either do action p or action q, and therefore unhappy consequence r or s will occur.

Dilemma	Route of extrication	Creative inquiry
1. If I do action p, then unhappy consequence r will occur.	Doing action p will not necessarily lead to unhappy consequence r.	How can it be that doing action p will not necessarily lead to unhappy consequence r?
2. Unhappy consequence r is bad.	Unhappy consequence r is not necessarily bad.	How can it be that this is the case?
3. If I do action q, then unhappy consequence s will occur.	Doing action q will not necessarily lead to unhappy consequence s.	How can it be that this is true?

Dilemma	Route of extrication	Creative inquiry
4. Unhappy consequence s is bad.	Unhappy consequence s is not necessarily bad.	How can it be that unhappy consequence s isn't necessarily bad?
5. I must do either action p or action q.	There are other alternatives besides action p or action q.	What other alternatives are there?

The following is a display from the dilemma matrix Practice Problem 1. This shows that when the student correctly completes the matrix row (as judged by PLATO DCS), the row from the generalized dilemma matrix table is erased. It is replaced by (a) the completed row of the matrix for the current problem as filled out by a dilemma counselor and (b) a space for the student's solution for this row of the matrix. Thus, a student can compare his/her version of the matrix row with that of an expert in the dilemma counseling method and he/she can gain experience in generating creative solutions for the dilemma-type problems. The other four rows of the matrix for Practice Problem 1 are completed by using displays that are analogous to those of the first matrix row. Dilemma matrix Practice Problem 2 consists of displays that are very similar (similar structure, different content) to those for Practice Problem 1.

Practice Problem

If I stay in finance, then I may continue having trouble. If I don't stay in finance, then it might take a longer period of time to graduate and upset my parents. But I must either stay in finance or not stay in finance, and therefore I may either continue having trouble or take a longer period of time to graduate and upset my parents.

Dilemma	Route of extrication	Creative inquiry
If I stay in finance, then I will continue having trouble.	Staying in finance will not necessarily lead to having trouble.	How can it be that staying in finance will not necessarily lead to having trouble?

Dilemma	Route of extrication	Creative inquiry
If I stay in finance, I may continue having trouble.	Staying in finance will not necessarily lead to continuing to have trouble.	How can it be that this is not necessarily the case?

Now type in a solution for this row of the matrix table.

It may be that other finance courses will be much less difficult for me.

In summary, a client learns the dilemma counseling method on PLATO DCS by constructing the dilemma formulation and the dilemma matrix for several sample problems. The client is also required to generate possible solutions to the sample problems. The computer provides feedback to the client regarding the appropriateness of his or her work.

A client applies the dilemma counseling method to his or her own problem by using the techniques that were learned in the first portion of the material on PLATO DCS. The first step in applying the method is for the client to type a description of his or her problem onto PLATO DCS. This initial description is in paragraph form.

Next, the client is asked to generate the dilemma formulation for his or her problem. The original wording of the problem remains on the PLATO DCS screen while the client formulates the dilemma. Instructions on the screen remind the client that he or she may redo the formulation, if necessary, to make changes or corrections.

On completion of the dilemma formulation, the original wording of the client's problem is erased from the screen. The dilemma formulation is retained on PLATO DCS while the client completes each row of the dilemma matrix. The dilemma component, route of extrication, and creative inquiry are completed with regard to the client's specific problem by referring to the corresponding row of the generalized dilemma matrix shown at the bottom of the screen.

On completion of each row of the matrix, the client is asked to generate answers to the creative inquiry. The dilemma formulation and the current row of the matrix for the client's problem remain on the screen while the client responds to the creative inquiry. As mentioned earlier, responses to the creative inquiry represent possible solutions to the client's problem.

The final display on PLATO DCS presents the solutions generated by the client for his/her problem. The client ranks these solutions from best to worst and then considers the adequacy of the best solution.

A more complete description of PLATO DCS can be found in Wagman and Kerber (1979, 1980).

Exploratory Research: Method

Exploration of reactions to PLATO DCS concerns user's evaluations regarding (a) personal acceptance of computer counseling, (b) effectiveness of PLATO DCS as a teacher of a method of solving psychological problems, and (c) effectiveness of PLATO DCS as a counselor for a current troubling psychological dilemma. The method for carrying out this exploratory study of users' attitudes and evaluations of PLATO DCS will now be described.

Students who were experiencing troublesome psychological dilemmas were randomly assigned to a PLATO DCS group or to a no-contact control group. After two sessions on the computer, subjects in the PLATO DCS group completed a questionnaire in which they evaluated PLATO DCS. Subjects in both groups responded to a series of self-report measures of problem improvement at a 1-week follow-up session.

Subjects

Seventy-seven male and female undergraduate students at the University of Illinois at Urbana-Champaign served as subjects in connection with course requirements. These participants were selected from a larger group of 160 students on the basis of the following criteria.

Procedure

In an initial large group session, 160 subjects first responded to the Maudsley Personality Inventory (MPI; Eysenck, 1959). Subjects then read a booklet which contained a series of eight typical psychological problems faced by university students. Next, subjects were asked to write in the booklet at least four of their own personally troubling psychological problems. They also rated each problem on an 8-point problem troublesomeness scale.

The problems written by subjects were typed and then evaluated by two research assistants to determine whether they met specified selection criteria. To be selected, a problem had to be sufficiently detailed and conflictful to be dilemma formulable. The second criterion was that the problem was rated by the subject at or above 6 on the problem troublesomeness scale, where 1 meant not at all troublesome and 8 meant extremely troublesome, interfering with my life. The reliability coefficient between the two research assistants was $r = .92$. Ninety subjects, each of whom had one problem meeting both criteria, were selected for further participation in the study.

Each participant was randomly assigned either to the PLATO DCS condition or to the control condition. Scheduling problems reduced the number of subjects in the PLATO DCS ($n = 41$) and control ($n = 36$) groups. Participants in the PLATO DCS condition interacted individually with the computer system during two sessions. There was a 3-day interval between the two sessions. In the first session, participants spent up to two hours learning the dilemma counseling method. In the second session, participants spent up to 1 hour applying the learned method to their own psychological dilemmas. At the conclusion of the second session, subjects rated on an 8-point scale the adequacy of the best solution they generated for their problem (1 = completely inadequate for solving this dilemma and 8 = perfectly adequate for solving this dilemma) and responded to a questionnaire in which they evaluated PLATO DCS. During a one-week follow-up session, problem improvement was assessed with several self-report scales.

Participants in the control condition had no contact with PLATO DCS. In addition to participating in the initial group session, these subjects responded during a follow-up session to the same problem improvement scales taken by participants in the PLATO DCS condition. The amount of time from the initial group session to the follow-up session was matched for PLATO DCS and control subjects.

Evaluation Measures

After completing their interaction with PLATO DCS, subjects responded to a nine-page questionnaire in which they evaluated the system. There were 22 items. Eight items related to personal acceptance of the computer system. Each of these items (e.g., "too impersonal") was rated on a 5-point scale, in which 1 meant strongly disagree and 5 meant strongly agree. These personal acceptance items are further described in the Results section of the present study.

Eight items related to the teaching effectiveness of PLATO DCS. Each of these items (e.g., "applying the method to my own problem") was rated on a 5-point scale, in which 1 meant not at all helpful and 5 meant extremely helpful. Examples of specific items concerned with PLATO DCS counseling and teaching effectiveness as well as several global evaluation items are given in the Results section.

Performance Measure

In addition to its role as counselor and teacher, PLATO DCS functioned as a researcher by collecting data on each subject's performance as he/she worked through the practice problems and his/her own problem. Such performance data as time to complete own problem versus time to complete practice problems for both dilemma formulation and dilemma matrix were registered by the computer as objective measures of subjects' learning.

Correctness of Dilemma Formulation and Dilemma Matrix

Each subject's input for his/her own problems and practice problems was printed out in hard copy. A trained rater then scored the accuracy with which each subject completed the dilemma formulation and dilemma matrix for his/her own problem and for one practice problem. The rater was trained by use of the PLATO DCS dilemma phrasing checklist and by conferences with the author. Further description of rater training is given in Wagman and Kerber (1979).

Follow-Up Measures

The PLATO DCS participants and the control participants were assessed on two measures of problem improvement for the 1-week follow-up session. On the first scale, participants rated the overall degree of improvement in their problems (1 = extremely improved and 8 = extremely worse). On the second scale, participants rated the troublesomeness of the problem (1 = not at all troublesome and 8 = extremely troublesome, interfering with my life). The solutions that had been generated a week earlier during computer interaction were also rated by PLATO DCS participants as to how the solutions applied to their problems (1 = extremely helpful and 8 = extremely harmful).

Results

Forty-two subjects completed the PLATO DCS Evaluation Questionnaire. With respect to the global item, 21% of the subjects felt
that PLATO DCS was considerably or extremely helpful in finding
solutions to their problems: 69% thought that PLATO DCS was
slightly or somewhat helpful. Only 10% of the subjects thought that
PLATO DCS was not at all helpful in finding solutions to their
problems. Table 10.1 summarizes the responses of the subjects to
additional items that pertain to PLATO DCS.

Subjects in the PLATO DCS group responded to 22 items concerning their evaluation of the dilemma counseling system. A principal components analysis was performed on the responses to these
items. On the basis of a plot of the eigenvalues and on the basis of
interpretability, three components were extracted that accounted for
55% of the variance. A varimax rotation was employed to yield
three orthogonal components. Each item was identified with the
component on which it loaded most highly.

Component 1 (30% of the variance) dealt with the evaluation of
PLATO DCS as a teacher. Items that loaded highly on this component included questions about specific parts of the dilemma
counseling system (e.g., the dilemma phrasing problems and the
generalized dilemma matrix). Subjects with high scores on this

TABLE 10.1. Evaluation of PLATO Dilemma Counseling System (PLATO
DCS)

Item	%		
	Disagree	Neutral	Agree
Interesting to work on	10	29	62
Rather use a printed booklet	83	7	10
Learned the method quite well	2	12	86
Would use lesson again	40	21	38
Too impersonal	56	15	29
Feel more at ease on PLATO DCS than if I saw a counselor	34	24	42
Useful to see counselor *and* use PLATO DCS	14	21	64
Feel more satisfaction in solving my problem on PLATO DCS than if I saw a counselor	21	33	45

Note: The disagree category consists of ratings of 1 or 2 and the agree category of ratings of 4 or 5
on a scale in which 1 meant "disagree" and 5 meant "agree". Values in the table are rounded to
the nearest whole percentage.

component thought that the various parts of the system were useful when learning the dilemma counseling method. They also indicated that they learned the method quite well by using PLATO DCS.

Component 2 (15% of the variance) dealt with the evaluation of PLATO DCS as a counselor. Subjects with high scores on this component thought that PLATO DCS was helpful in solving their problems, desired to use PLATO DCS again in order to solve a problem, and felt that PLATO DCS was not too impersonal. They also felt that they were more at ease and that they experienced greater satisfaction when they used PLATO DCS to solve a problem as opposed to when they saw a counselor.

Finally, Component 3 (9% of the variance) dealt with satisfaction in the use of PLATO DCS. Subjects with high scores on this component thought that PLATO DCS was interesting to work on and stated that they would rather not use a printed booklet in place of PLATO DCS in order to learn the dilemma counseling method. They also felt that it did not take too much time to complete PLATO DCS and that there was not too much typing to do in PLATO DCS.

Perfomance Measures

Reductions in the amount of time to complete successive dilemma phrasing problems, dilemma matrix problems, and solutions for the matrix problems may in part be an indication of the teaching effectiveness of PLATO DCS. Therefore, several analyses were conducted on the amount of time (Table 10.2) required for each subject to complete his/her problems. Findings indicated that subjects improved in their ability as they progressed from practice problems to their own problems.[1] Complete analyses for all performance variables are given in Wagman and Kerber (1979).

---

[1] It seems plausible that the time to complete various parts of PLATO DCS would be related to typing ability. However, all correlations between each subject's estimate of his/her typing ability and the times to complete designated parts of PLATO DCS were non-significant. For example, the correlation between typing ability and the total time to complete PLATO DCS was -.13. These results indicate that typing speed was probably *not* an important factor influencing progress through PLATO DCS.

TABLE 10.2. Performance variables: PLATO Dilemma Counseling System (PLATO DCS)

Variable	N	M	SD
Number of keywords			
Dilemma phrasing practice	43	3.47	2.01
Dilemma matrix practice	42	3.21	2.65
Dilemma matrix own problem	43	1.77	1.85
Time			
3 Dilemma phrasing practice problems	43	18.02	7.33
Dilemma phrasing practice problem: Finance	43	6.22	4.76
Dilemma phrasing practice problem: Obey	43	5.39	2.44
Dilemma phrasing practice problem: Drinking	43	6.40	3.65
Dilemma phrasing own problem	43	3.04	1.22
Dilemma matrix own problem	43	9.93	5.95
Solutions own problem	43	5.88	2.92
Entire dilemma counseling system	43	136.03	24.21

Note. Time is expressed in minutes.

Correctness of Dilemma Formulation and Dilemma Matrix

The dilemma formulation and the dilemma matrix for one practice problem and for the subject's own problem were stored on PLATO DCS for each subject. The dilemma formulations were rated by a trained rater on six criteria of a correct dilemma formulation. If the formulation met a particular criterion, it was given a score of 1; if it did not meet the criterion, it was given a score of 0. Therefore, scores for each formulation could range from 0 to 6. The mean rating for the practice problem was 4.28, and the mean rating for the subject's own problem was 4.75, $t(39) = 1.29$, *ns.*

Each cell of both dilemma matrices was rated for correctness by the same rater. If the dilemma part, extrication route, or creative inquiry for a particular cell of the matrix was correct, it was given a score of 1; if it was incorrect, it was given a score of 0. Therefore, scores for each matrix could range from 0 to 15. The mean rating for the practice problem was 13.58, and the mean rating for the subject's own problem was 14.00, $t(30) = .82$, *ns.*

A correlational analysis indicated that the correctness of the dilemma formulation problems and the dilemma matrix problems was unrelated to the time to complete those problems.

Follow-Up Measures

The PLATO DCS group and the control group were assessed on two measures of problem improvement at the one-week follow-up session. For each subject, the measures of improvement were self-ratings of troublesomeness and degree of improvement. An analysis of covariance was conducted on the troublesomeness rating for the one-week follow-up, with the rating of troublesomeness for the first session of the study as the covariate. Results indicated that the PLATO DCS group showed a greater reduction in problem troublesomeness as compared with the control group, $F(1,74) = 5.87$, $p<.01$. Adjusted means for the two groups were 2.22 (PLATO DCS) and 4.97 (control).

A t test was conducted on the rating of degree of improvement for the one-week follow-up. Results indicated that the PLATO DCS group showed significantly greater improvement in their problems as compared with the control group, $t(75) = 4.40$, $p<.01$. Means for the two groups were 1.95 (PLATO DCS) and 4.12 (control).

Intercorrelation of Personality, Performance, Evaluation, and Follow-up Measures

Correlations were computed among the Neuroticism and Extroversion scores from the MPI, the performance variables, the evaluation component scores, and the measures taken during the one-week follow-up session.[2] Subjects with higher neuroticism scores (a) spent more time completing their own dilemma matrix, $r(38) = .34$, $p<.05$, (b) spent more time generating solutions to their own problems, $r(38) = .35$, $p<.05$, (c) spent more total time in PLATO DCS, $r(38) = .52$, $p<.05$, (d) gave more positive evaluations of PLATO DCS as a counselor, $r(38) = .33$, $p<.05$, and (e) indicated greater improvement in their problems at the one-week follow-up $r(36) = .42$, $p<.05$.

Subjects who spent more time generating solutions to their problems gave more positive evaluations of PLATO DCS as a counselor, $r(39) = .36$, $p<.05$, and experienced greater satisfaction in their use

---

[2]Of the 148 possible correlations among these measures, approximately 8 would be significant by chance at the .05 level. Results indicated that 19 of the correlations were significant at the .05 level.

of PLATO DCS, $r(39) = .33$, $p<.05$. Subjects who spent more time working on the dilemma phrasing for their own problems also gave more positive evaluations of PLATO DCS as counselor, $r(39) = .41$, $p<.05$, as did those subjects who spent more total time in PLATO DCS, $r(39) = .34$, $p<.05$.

Subjects with more positive evaluations of PLATO DCS as a teacher rated their best solutions as more adequate to solve their problems, $r(39) = .32$, $p<.05$. Subjects with more positive evaluations of PLATO DCS as a counselor also rated their best solutions as more adequate, $r(39) = .31$, $p<.05$. Finally, subjects who experienced greater satisfaction in their use of PLATO DCS found the solutions that they applied to their problems more helpful at the one-week follow-up, $r(33) = .34$, $p<.05$.

Discussion

The results of this exploratory research generally tend to be quite supportive of PLATO DCS and its various functions. Students find the experience of interacting with a sophisticated computer counseling system highly stimulating and interesting. Such user enthusiasm probably serves as a strong motivater for acceptance of PLATO DCS in both its teaching and counseling functions.

Critics of personal computer counseling (Weizenbaum, 1976, 1977) present concerns about the supposedly impersonal nature of solving psychological dilemmas on a computer. However, a majority (56%) of the participants in the present study felt that PLATO DCS was not too impersonal. In addition, a substantial proportion of the participants actually felt more at ease (42%) and more independent (45%) on the computer than if they saw a counselor. It is evident, however, that for most subjects the computer is a professional resource to be sought in addition to the professional skills of the counselor. Sixty-four percent of the current sample felt that it would be helpful to use PLATO DCS and to see a counselor to solve a personal problem.

These positive findings need to be balanced by several observations pointing to the need for additional research beyond this exploratory investigation. First, it would be desirable to test for placebo effects by a group of subjects who interact with the PLATO computer system but who did not use the procedures of systematic dilemma counseling. Second, it would be useful to expand the types of follow-up measures to include behavioral observations and ratings and possibly standardized personality tests. However, one obstacle in the way of such expansion of follow-up measures is the great diversity in the range, complexity, and malleability of psychological dilemmas. Third, a comparative study of PLATO DCS alone, personal counseling alone, and PLATO DCS plus personal counseling would be useful. Fourth, the comparative study might involved clients drawn randomly from the many university campuses where PLATO DCS is available.

Generating and Judging Self-Help Dilemma Solutions

It should be noted that experimental research with PLATO DCS made certain demands on the participants. Clients were asked to interact with an experimental procedure that was at once novel in using a computer for personal counseling and unusual in expecting clients to teach and counsel themselves to generate solutions to their psychological problems.

It is of interest therefore that approximately two thirds of the clients succeeded in generating solutions to their troubling psychological dilemmas. Futhermore, the adequacy of these solutions as judged by the clients themselves was quite high (M = 5.76, SD = 1.85; 8.00 = perfectly adequate for solving this dilemma). Judgment of the adequacy of solutions to psychological problems suggests an interesting area for research (Wagman, 1979), especially when the problems are cognitively complex (as is true of psychological dilemmas) and when the process of comparing, ranking, and judging quality of solutions involves idiosyncratic personal values.

Correlational Findings

The correlational findings involving evaluation of PLATO DCS functions, adequacy of subjects' best solutions, and helpfulness of these solutions when actually applied to the subjects' problems are provocative. Although correlation coefficients are not reliably interpreted in general, they seem to be highly illuminating in terms of directions of causation in this first exploratory investigation of the effects of PLATO DCS.

Among the various correlational findings, the following pattern seems quite significant. Subjects who gave more positive evaluations to PLATO DCS as a counselor also spent more time generating solutions to their problems and rated their best solutions as more adequate. In turn, subjects who rated their best solutions as more adequate to solve their problems also expressed more positive evaluations of PLATO DCS as a teacher of the dilemma problem-solving method. This pattern taken as a whole suggests that subjects who experienced greater satisfaction in their use of PLATO DCS found the solutions that they applied to their problems more helpful at the 1-week follow-up.

The above analyses and interpretations were based on the entire research sample. It is of interest that the Neuroticism-Stability factor of the MPI (Eysenck, 1959) was related to some of these evaluation performance and outcome variables. Thus, persons with higher Neuroticism scores spent more time generating solutions to their problems, spent more total time in PLATO DCS, gave more positive evaluations of PLATO DCS as a counselor, and indicated greater improvement in their problems at the one-week follow-up. Taken together, these findings might suggest that persons who need counseling more (i.e., maladjusted persons), respond positively to a computer by staying involved. They spend more time interacting with the computer and working on solving their personal dilemmas, resulting in stronger evaluations of the computer as a counselor and, significantly, greater improvement in their problems at the one-week follow-up. These findings will require cross validation in future research, but it is of interest that Greist et al (1973) found that suicidal patients preferred interacting with a computer to a counselor (psychiatrist) and that the computer was more accurate in predicting suicidal attempts.

Finally, it should be pointed out that PLATO DCS participants rated the adequacy of their solutions to their problems prior to their evaluation of PLATO DCS, which, in turn, preceded the ratings of problem improvement by a week. Thus, it may be that the quality of the solutions created by interaction with PLATO DCS influenced the evaluation and the perceived usefulness of the system. In the present study, the mean value for the adequacy ratings was 5.76 (*SD* = 1.85) on an 8-point scale, in which 8 meant perfectly adequate for solving this dilemma. Thus, solutions generated by PLATO DCS were generally of high quality as rated by the subjects.

Future Research in Computer-Based Counseling

Computerized self-help counseling offers advantages to both client and counselor that could be explored by the computerization of other counseling techniques. From the point of view of the client, computer counseling prevents the buildup of dependency on a counselor for solving moderately difficult psychological problems. In addition, the computer can teach a method for solving future problems; this will further increase the autonomy of the client. Research on the use of problem-solving techniques for teaching and maintaining self-help or self-control procedures is very relevant (Goldfried & Davidson, 1976; Mahoney, 1974; Richards & Perri, 1978).

From the point of view of the counselor, computerization of counseling procedures could result in significant advances because techniques must be very clearly and concisely articulated to make computer applications feasible. The computer could be used to model various counseling techniques. Counselors could then use the techniques as clients to achieve new perspectives in their work. In addition, research on counseling could be improved as a result of the stardardization of procedures (Lang, 1969). The process of computerization could therefore result in significant theoretical and practical advances.

Conclusion

As in the case of dilemma counseling, it would appear that cognitive counseling approaches (Cochran, Hoffman, Strand, & Warren, 1977; Dilley, 1967; Krumboltz, 1965; Mahoney, 1977; Wilson & Franks, 1982) are most appropriate for computer applications. The particular advantage of the dilemma counseling technique for computer presentation is that the logic of the method is the logic of the computer; that is, the logic of conditionals that forms the basis for dilemma counseling (Wagman, 1979) is also the logic of the computer (Wagman, 1984a). Future attempts at computerized counseling should be preceded by serious consideration of the match between the technique and the medium of presentation.

The flexibility, objectivity, and speed of the computer present admirable qualifications for any counselor (Kleinmuntz, 1975; Sagan, 1977). These qualifications summarize the potential of a modern computer system to aid clients in the solution of psychological problems. However, the actualization of this potential for the purpose of computer-based counseling depends on the skills of the counselors who construct the materials (Holden, 1977; Palmen, 1978) for use on the computer.

The logical structures and processes of PLATO DCS would permit applications to populations other than university students. The type of population would define the specific content of the system (e.g., the common dilemmas of managers, executives, and supervisors; the career dilemmas of women; the practical and existential dilemmas of retired persons; dilemmas in medical practice and genetic counseling. PLATO DCS has recently been published by Control Data Corporation (Wagman & Kerber, 1978). PLATO DCS can also be used with IBM, Apple and other personal computers. As a result, PLATO DCS is currently available at a large number of colleges and universities throughout the United States and Canada.

Finally, the counseling service provided by PLATO DCS to university students and to other types of populations implies the use of the system for research, whereby data are collected and program content is devised and enlarged as knowledge and experience accumulate.

CHAPTER ELEVEN

PLATO DCS: Further Development and Evaluation

Introduction

People often face life-choice problems that involve two possible actions and two corresponding aversive consequences. In general, these avoidance problems can be phrased: If I make a decision for action p, then unhappy consequence r will occur. If I make a decision for action q, then unhappy consequence s will occur. But I must either do action p or action q. Therefore, unhappy consequence r or unhappy consequence s must occur.

The resolution of avoidance-avoidance problems involves reasoning with implication, that is, "if-then" sequences (Inhelder & Piaget, 1958). Unfortunately, a number of studies have shown that people have difficulty with such reasoning (Johnson-Laird & Wason, 1970; Leahey & Wagman, 1974; Roberge, 1971; Wagman, 1978; Wason, 1964; Wason & Johnson-Laird, 1972). In addition, the logical structure of the avoidance-avoidance problem seems to impose the inescapable necessity of enduring aversive consequences. The person feels trapped in the dilemma and helpless in the face of the negative outcomes. These difficulties are often intensified by the confused emotional state of the person who experiences the conflict. The dilemma counseling method (Wagman, 1979) represents a systematic approach to the formulation and solution of avoidance-avoidance problems.

AUTHOR'S NOTE: This research project was supported by a grant from the University of Illinois Research Board.

Application of the dilemma counseling method to an avoidance-avoidance problem first involves the careful formulation of the problem as a psychological dilemma. The dilemma is then resolved by use of the generalized dilemma matrix as shown in the following display. The first column of the matrix presents five components of the dilemma formulation, which restate the basic assumptions of the problem. The second column of the matrix presents five extrication routes corresponding to the five dilemma components. The extrication routes encourage the client to negate the various assumptions of the problem. The third column of the matrix presents five creative inquiries that challenge the client to develop alternatives or new perspectives that are more realistic and more optimistic with respect to the consequences of the problem. These alternatives represent solutions to the original dilemma by eliminating the necessity of enduring aversive consequences.

Generalized Dilemma Matrix

If I do action p, then unhappy consequence r will occur. And if I do action q, then unhappy consequence s will occur. But I must either do action p or action q, and therefore unhappy consequence r or s will occur.

Dilemma	Route of extrication	Creative inquiry
1. If I do action p, then unhappy consequence r will occur.	Doing action p won't necessarily lead to unhappy consequence r.	How is it that doing action p won't necessarily lead to unhappy consequence r?
2. R is bad (aversive).	R isn't necessarily bad (aversive).	How is it that r isn't necessarily bad (aversive)?
3. If I do action q, then unhappy consequence s will occur.	Doing action q won't necessarily lead to unhappy consequence s.	How is it that doing action q won't necessarily lead to unhappy consequence s?
4. S is bad (aversive).	S isn't necessarily bad (aversive).	How is it that s isn't necessarily bad (aversive)?

Dilemma	Route of extrication	Creative inquiry
5. I must do either action p or action q.	There are other alternatives besides action p or action q.	What other alternatives are there besides action p or action q.

The dilemma counseling method was originally shown to be effective for use by clients with the help of a counselor (Wagman, 1979) and was later shown to be effective for use in a self-help form (Wagman, 1981). The availability of the PLATO computer system at the University of Illinois at Urbana-Champaign allowed for computer presentation of self-help dilemma counseling.

The PLATO computer system at the University of Illinois at Urbana-Champaign (Alpert & Bitzer, 1970; Holt, 1983; Smith & Sherwood, 1976) links hundreds of graphical display terminals to a central computer. Each terminal is composed of a keyset that transmits the user's input to the computer and then to a display screen that shows computer-generated information. In their simplest form, materials presented on PLATO DCS consist of a display on the user's screen followed by the user's response to that display. The user reacts to each display by pressing a single key to move on to new material or by typing a word, sentence, or other expression. A user's response might also be a question or a command to PLATO DCS to respond with a particular type of display. Thus, the PLATO DCS system allows for individualized interaction sequences between the user and the computer.

A client learns the dilemma counseling method on PLATO DCS by constructing the dilemma formulation and the dilemma matrix for several sample problems. The client is also required to generate possible solutions for the sample problems. The computer provides feedback to the client regarding the appropriateness of his or her work. A client applies the dilemma counseling method to his or her own problem by using the techniques that were learned by working on the sample problems. A more complete description of PLATO DCS and the dilemma counseling system can be found in Chapter Ten and in Wagman and Kerber (1979).

In Chapter Ten the effectiveness of PLATO DCS was compared to a no-contact control condition. Improvement that resulted from the use of PLATO DCS exceeded that obtained in the no-contact control condition (i.e., spontaneous remission). In addition, favorable reactions to the teaching and counseling functions of PLATO DCS suggested that many clients found the computer to be helpful in solving psychological dilemmas.

In the present study, the effectiveness of computer-based dilemma counseling was examined by assessing self-reported problem improvement in a group of undergraduate students treated in PLATO DCS and in a no-contact control group. The study differed in three important respects from the previous assessment of PLATO DCS. First, to assist clients in finding solutions for their problems, two solution sources were created on PLATO DCS: The Specific Dilemma Solutions component and the Structural Dilemma Solutions component. Second, problem improvement was evaluated on five scales designed to reflect over-all improvement in addition to cognitive and affective aspects of improvement. As in the preceding study (Chapter Ten), the assessment of improvement was based on self-ratings by each client; however, multiple measures of improvement were used as a more adequate assessment procedure. Finally, the present study included a 1-month follow-up session in addition to the one-week session in the preceeding study.

Method

Students who were experiencing troublesome psychological dilemmas were randomly assigned to a PLATO DCS group or to a no-contact control group. After two sessions on the computer, subjects in the PLATO DCS group completed a questionnaire on which they evaluated PLATO DCS. Subjects in both groups responded to a series of self-report measures of problem improvement at a one-week and a one-month follow-up session.

Subjects

There were 110 male and female introductory psychology students at the University of Illinois at Urbana-Champaign who served as subjects in connection with course requirements. These subjects were selected from a larger group of 200 students on the basis of the criteria to be described.

Procedure

Subjects initially met in large group sessions during which they wrote descriptions of several personal problems that were currently troubling them. They also rated the problems on several scales designed to assess the severity of the problems. To participate in subsequent sessions of the study, one of each subject's problems had to meet the following criteria: First, the problem was rated by the subject at or above 6 on a scale in which 1 meant "not at all troublesome" and 8 meant "extremely troublesome, interfering with my life." Second, the problem could be formulated as a dilemma.

Due to limitations on the availability of computer terminals for research, only 48 subjects could be accomodated on PLATO DCS. These subjects were randomly selected from the 110 students who met the criteria for this study. The remaining 62 subjects were assigned to the control condition.

Subjects in the experimental condition interacted with PLATO DCS during two sessions. Subjects initially spent up to two hours learning the dilemma counseling method. Two days later, subjects spent up to one hour applying the method to their dilemmas. At the conclusion of the second session, subjects rated the adequacy of the best solution they generated for their problem (1 = completely inadequate for solving this dilemma; 8 = perfectly adequate for solving this dilemma) and responded to a questionnaire on which they evaluated PLATO DCS.

All subjects participated in two follow-up sessions during which problem improvement was assessed on several self-report scales. The amount of time from the group sessions to the follow-up sessions was matched for PLATO DCS subjects and for control subjects. The follow-up sessions occurred at one-week and at one-month after the final session of PLATO DCS.

Treatment

PLATO DCS consists of three interrelated components. The components are mutually accessible. The Dilemma Counseling component teaches users how to use the dilemma counseling method and how to apply the method to their own dilemmas (see Chapter Ten). The Specific Dilemma Solutions component and the Structural Dilemma Solutions component provide suggested solutions to a wide variety of psychological dilemmas. If the user needs help in thinking of solutions to his or her problem, instructions in part six of the Dilemma Counseling component explain how to access the Specific and the Structural Dilemma Solutions components. These components contain 69 representative problems and over 400 specific and general solutions designed to assist the user in creatively solving his or her problem.

Over 800 dilemmas of undergraduate students were collected in connection with an earlier project dealing with Systematic Dilemma Counseling (Wagman, 1979, 1980b). Through content analysis, these dilemmas were grouped into 17 categories as follows: curriculum (6), dating (8), drop out (4), drugs and smoking (3), extracurricular activities (2), family relationships (3), financial (3), fraternity-sorority (3), intimate relationships (6), interpersonal relationships (6), living accomodations (4), marriage (2), miscellaneous (7), occupational choice (2), study habits (5), summer (3), and transfer (2). These 69 cases are contained in the Specific Dilemma Solutions component. Each of the 17 categories has an index that lists all the cases within a category; each case within a category is composed of five creative inquiries and at least five suggested solutions to the dilemma.

The purpose of the Specific Dilemma Solutions component is to provide the user with examples of how dilemma counseling has been used to help people with various kinds of problems (Wagman & Kerber, 1979). Users are instructed to search for specific cases that are similar to their problems and to consider the usefulness of the solutions generated by other people.

The Structural Dilemma Solutions component of PLATO DCS was developed through a process of abstracting from the cases and solutions within each category of the Specific Dilemma Solutions component (Wagman & Kerber, 1979). Typical problems were constructed to represent the general features of different types of problems. In addition, the general strategies and common features of the specific solutions within each category were abstracted as structural or general solutions. Each structural solution is clarified by providing two specific examples relevant to the category.

The purpose of the Structural Dilemma Solutions component is to provide assistance for those people who are unable to find cases in the Specific Dilemma Solutions component that are similar to their problems (Wagman & Kerber, 1979). Structural solutions are designed to convey useful strategies for generating solutions to problems of a general type, regardless of the specific content of the problem.

To maintain confidentiality, users are instructed *not* to identify themselves by name when working on PLATO DCS (Wagman & Kerber, 1979). The data for each person are identified with randomly assigned code numbers and with code words constructed by and known only to each user.

Evaluation Measures

Subjects in the PLATO DCS group responded to a questionnaire that was designed to evaluate PLATO DCS. There were 18 items that referred to the Dilemma Counseling component, 12 items that referred to the Specific Dilemma Solutions component, and 12 items that referred to the Structural Dilemma Solutions component. There were three types of items. First, the subject rated the helpfulness of each component in finding solutions to his or her problem (1 = not at all helpful; 5 = extremely helpful). Second, the subject rated the usefulness of specific features of each component when working on PLATO DCS (1 = not at all useful; 5 = extremely useful). Finally, the subject agreed or disagreed with each of a series of statements referring to the particular components (1 = disagree; 5 = agree). Items of each type are discussed in the Results section of this study.

Follow-up Measures

The PLATO DCS group and the control group were assessed on five measures of problem improvement for both the one-week and the one-month follow-up. Subjects rated the overall degree of improvement in their problems (1 = extremely improved; 8 = extremely worse). Subjects also rated the troublesomeness of the problem (1 = not at all troublesome; 8 = extremely troublesome, interferring with my life) and the manageableness of the problem (1 = extremely manageable, I can fully deal with it myself; 8 = extremely unmanageable, I must have considerable help to deal with it). Finally, subjects rated their affective reaction to the problems in terms of pleasant versus unpleasant feelings (1 = extremely pleasant; 8 = extremely unpleasant) and good versus bad feelings (1 = extremely good; 8 = extremely bad).

Subjects in the PLATO DCS group also responded to four additional items at both folow-up sessions. Subjects were asked how much free time they spent actively trying to solve their problems (1 = no time at all; 8 = a great deal of time) and how much effort they expended actively applying some solution to their problems (1 = no effort at all; 8 = a great deal of effort). Subjects also rated the helpfulness of the solution that they applied to their problems (1 = extremely helpful; 8 = extremely harmful) and any change in the severity of their problems as a result of applying the solution (1 = extemely improved; 8 = extremely worse).

Results

Evaluation Measures

Subjects evaluated each of the three PLATO DCS components with respect to their helpfulness in solving the subject's dilemmas. Twenty-five percent of the subjects stated that the dilemma counseling component was extremely or considerably helpful in solving their dilemmas. This component was judged as being helpful by 71% of the subjects, and only 4% of the subjects stated that the component was not at all helpful.

Of the 48 subjects in the PLATO DCS group, 22 used the Specific Dilemma Solutions Component, and 8 used the Structural Dilemma Solutions Component. Of those subjects who used the specific component, 27% felt that it was extremely or considerably helpful in solving their dilemmas. This component was judged to be helpful by 46% of the subjects, and 27% felt that it was not at all helpful. Of those subjects who used the Structural Component, responses were distributed as follows: extremely or considerably helpful, 26%; helpful, 74%; not at all helpful, 0%.

Subjects also responded in an agree/disagree format to a series of statements about each component. Table 11.1 summarizes responses to 12 items pertaining to the three components on PLATO DCS.

A principal components analysis was performed on the responses to 18 items concerning the dilemma counseling component. On the basis of the eigenvalues and interpretability, three components were extracted that accounted for 49% of the variance. A varimax rotation yielded three orthogonal components. Each item was identified with the component on which it loaded most highly.

Component 1 (26% of the variance) dealt with the evaluation of PLATO DCS as a teacher. Items that loaded highly on this component included questions about specific parts of the dilemma counseling component (e.g., the dilemma phrasing problems and the dilemma matrix problems). Subjects with high scores on this component thought that the various parts of PLATO DCS were

TABLE 11.1. Evaluation of PLATO DCS

Component	n	Disagree	Neutral	% Agree
Dilemma	48			
Interesting to work on		2	29	69
Rather use a printed booklet		73	10	17
Could independently apply the method		13	21	67
Would use lesson again		21	27	52
Too impersonal		54	25	21
Feel more at ease on PLATO DCS then if				
I saw a counselor		31	29	40
Useful to see counselor *and* use PLATO				
DCS		15	13	73
Feel more independent on PLATO DCS				
than if I saw a counselor		31	25	44
Specific	22			
Could find a similar problem		55	5	41
Solutions are helpful		41	18	41
Structural				
Could find a similar problem	8	38	38	25
Solutions were helpful	7	57	29	14

Note. PLATO DCS = PLATO Computer-Based Dilemma Counseling system. The disagree category consists of ratings 1 or 2 and the agree category consists of ratings of 4 or 5 on a scale in which 1 means "disagree" and 5 means "agree". Values are rounded to the nearest whole percentage.

useful when learning the dilemma counseling method. They also favored using PLATO DCS as opposed to a printed booklet to learn the method, and they believed that they could independently apply the dilemma method on completion of PLATO DCS.

Component 2 (13% of the variance) dealt with the global evaluation of PLATO DCS. Subjects with high scores on this component thought that PLATO DCS was helpful in solving their problems, found PLATO DCS to be interesting to work on, desired to use PLATO DCS again to solve a problem and thought it would be useful to see a counselor and use the materials on PLATO DCS.

Finally, Component 3 (11% of the variance) dealt with the evaluation of PLATO DCS as a counselor. Subjects with high scores on this component felt that PLATO DCS was not too impersonal. They also felt that they were more at ease and more independent when they used PLATO DCS to solve a problem as opposed to when they saw counselors.

Follow-up Measures

Table 11.2 shows the intercorrelations of the five follow-up measures at both the one-week and the one-month follow-up session. With respect to the over-all improvement rating, the PLATO DCS group tended to report greater improvement than the control group at the 1-week follow-up session, $t(108) = 1.62$, $p<.11$, and at the one-month follow-up session, $t(107) = 1.71$, $p<.09$. Means and standard deviations for these analyses are shown in Table 11.3.

TABLE 11.2. Intercorrelations of Measures of Improvement: One-Week and One-Month Follow-up Sessions

Variables	1	2	3	4	5
1. Improve	–	.72	.76	.69	.75
2. Trouble	.66	–	.79	.77	.81
3. Manage	.53	.70	–	.68	.72
4. Pleasant	.54	.68	.53	–	.92
5. Good	.51	.64	.52	.92	–

Note. Correlations for the one-week session are below the diagonal. All correlations are significant at the .01 level.

TABLE 11.3. Means and standard deviations for measures of improvement in the control group and the PLATO DCS group: Pretest, One-Week, and One-Month Follow-up Session

Variable	Pretest M	Pretest SD	One-week M	One-week SD	One-month M	One-month SD
	Control group (62)					
Improve	–	–	3.65	1.42	3.27	1.44
Trouble	6.79	.81	4.58	1.85	3.98	1.91
Manage	5.50	1.30	3.90	1.82	3.44	1.83
Pleasant	6.71	.91	5.82	1.27	4.61	1.57
Good	6.37	.93	5.42	1.19	4.29	1.83
	PLATO DCS group (48)					
Improve	–	–	3.25	1.04	2.83	1.20
Trouble	6.21	.99	3.69	1.78	3.30	1.80
Manage	4.81	1.66	3.15	1.56	2.96	1.55
Pleasant	6.17	1.14	4.46	1.69	3.51	1.84
Good	5.81	1.16	4.35	1.59	3.38	1.87

Note. PLATO DCS = PLATO Computer-Based Dilemma Counseling system. Number in parentheses are *ns*.

For the four self-ratings of improvement, multivariate analyses of covariance (MANCOVA) were conducted for each follow-up session.[1] For these analyses, the covariates were the ratings on the four measures of improvement taken from the first session of the study. Unadjusted means and standard deviations for these analyses are shown in Table 11.3.

The PLATO DCS group showed significantly greater improvement in their problems than the control group at the one-week follow-up, $F(4,101) = 3.80$, p<.01. Univariate analyses on the adjusted group means indicated that the PLATO DCS group (4.64) felt more pleasant than the control group (5.68) at the one-week follow-up, $F(1,104) = 13.69$, p<.01. Also, the PLATO DCS group ($M = 4.52$) experienced more good feelings than the control group ($M = 5.29$) at the one-week session, $F(1, 104) = 8.09$, p<.01.

At the one-month follow-up, the PLATO DCS group tended to show greater improvement than the control group, $F(4, 101) = 2.23$, p<.08. Univariate analyses on the adjusted means indicated that the PLATO DCS group (3.62) felt significantly more pleasant than the control group (4.47) at the one-month follow-up, $F(1,104) = 6.39$, p <.05.

Intercorrelation of Follow-up and Evaluation Measures

Correlations were computed among the evaluation component scores and the follow-up measures taken during the one-week and the one-month follow-up sessions. The component that represented a global evaluation of PLATO DCS was related to several measures taken during the follow-up sessions. Subjects with more positive evaluations of the dilemma counseling component stated that during the first week they (a) spent more free time trying to solve their problems, $r(46) = .41$, p<.01, (b) exerted more effort trying to apply some solution to their problems, $r(46) = .44$, p<.05, (c) found the solution that they applied to their problems more helpful, $r(43) = .31$, p<.05, and (d) found the solution that they applied to their problems led to greater improvement, $r(43) = .36$, p<.05. Subjects with more positive evaluations also stated that during the first month

---

[1]The multivariate analyses of variance reported here were conducted with the multi-variance statistical program (Finn, 1972).

they exerted more effort trying to apply some solution to their problems, $r(45) = .32$, $p<.05$.

Subjects who rated their best solutions as more adequate to solve their problems gave more positive global evaluations of the dilemma counseling component, $r(46) = .36$, $p<.05$, and gave more positive evaluations of PLATO DCS as a counselor, $r(46) = .47$, $p<.01$. Also, at the one-week follow-up session, subjects who rated their best solutions as more adequate to solve their problems found the solutions that they applied to their problems more helpful, $r(43) = .30$, $p<.05$, and found the solutions that they applied led to greater improvement in their problems, $r(43) = .37$, $p<.05$. In turn, subjects who found the solutions that they applied to be more helpful showed a greater reduction in (a) the troublesomeness of their problems at the one-week follow-up session, $r(43) = .42$, $p<.01$, (b) the unpleasant feelings generated by their problems at the one-week follow-up, $r(43) = .36$, $p<.05$, (c) the bad feelings generated by their problems at the one-week follow-up, $r(43) = .35$, $p<.05$, (d) the troublesomeness of their problems at the one-month follow-up, $r(42) = .36$, $p<.05$, and (e) the bad feelings generated by their problems at the one-month follow-up, $r(42) = .34$, $p<.05$. Subjects who found the solutions that they applied led to greater improvement showed a greater reduction in (a) troublesomeness of their problems at the one-week follow-up, $r(43) = .44$, $p<.01$, (b) the unpleasant feelings generated by their problems at the one-week follow-up, $r(43) = .31$, $p<.05$, and (c) the troublesomeness of their problems at the one-month follow-up, $r(42) = .30$, $p<.05$.

Computer-Assisted Versus Self-Generated Solutions

Two supplementary components were availabe on PLATO DCS for those subjects in the PLATO DCS group who desired additional help in solving their problems. Of the 48 subjects in the PLATO DCS group, 26 made use of one or both of these lessons (computer-assisted solutions group), and the remainder did not access the supplementary material (self-generated solutions group). These two PLATO DCS groups did not differ in overall improvement at either the one-week follow-up session, $t(46) = .69$, or the one-month follow-up session, $t(45) = 1.33$. A MANCOVA on the four measures of improvement for the one-week follow-up, $F(4, 39) = 2.09$, and for the one-month follow-up, $F(4, 38) = .88$, indicated that the two PLATO

DCS groups did not differ in problem improvement. Unadjusted means and standard deviations for these analyses are shown in Table 11.4.

A series of t tests indicated that the computer-assisted solutions group and the self-generated solutions group did not differ on the evaluation component scores, solution adequacy, or the additional follow-up measures.

Finally, separate correlation matrices involving the evaluation component scores, solution adequacy, and the follow-up measures were computed for the two PLATO DCS groups. One interesting difference was that the adequacy of the best solution was related to the evaluation of PLATO DCS as a teacher in the self-generated solution group, $r(20) = .69$, $p<.01$, whereas adequacy was related to the evaluation of PLATO DCS as a counselor in the computer-assisted solution group, $r(24) = .54$, $p<.01$.

Discussion

In support of previous research (see Chapter Ten), this study indicated that PLATO DCS is an effective counselor for psychological dilemmas and is an effective teacher of the dilemma counseling

TABLE 11.4 Means and standard deviations for measures of improvements in the computer-assisted solutions group and the self-generated solutions group: Pretest, One-Week, and One-Month Follow-up Sessions

Variable	Pretest		One-week		One-month	
	M	SD	M	SD	M	SD
Computer-assisted solutions group (26)						
Improve	—	—	3.15	1.01	3.04	1.18
Trouble	6.04	.96	3.62	1.83	3.27	1.99
Manage	4.62	1.75	3.42	1.75	3.08	1.62
Pleasant	6.08	1.06	4.35	1.57	3.69	1.85
Good	5.73	1.12	4.31	1.57	3.54	1.98
Self-generated solutions group (22)[a]						
Improve	—	—	3.36	1.09	2.57	1.21
Trouble	6.41	1.01	3.77	1.74	3.33	1.59
Manage	5.05	1.56	2.82	1.26	2.81	1.47
Pleasant	6.27	1.24	4.59	1.84	3.29	1.85
Good	5.91	1.23	4.41	1.65	3.19	1.75

Note. Numbers in parentheses are ns.
[a] For the self-generated solutions group at the 1-month follow-up session, $n = 21$.

method. Students who used PLATO DCS showed significantly greater improvement in their problems than students in a no-contact control group. Also, the majority of students who used PLATO DCS agreed that they learned the dilemma counselling method well enough to independently apply the technique to a personal problem.

The present study included several changes from the previous assessment of PLATO DCS. First, the Specific and Structural Dilemma Solutions Components were programmed on PLATO DCS to assist clients in finding solutions to their problems. Over half of the students in the PLATO DCS group accessed one or both of these components. Subjects in the self-generated solutions group appeared to view PLATO DCS as a teacher who would instruct them in a problem-solving technique that the subjects could apply without additional help. For these students, the Specific and Structural Components were not necessary. Subjects in the computer-assisted solutions group appeared to view PLATO DCS as a counselor who would make suggestions about how to solve their dilemmas. For these students, the Specific and Structural Components were a valuable source of possible solutions. It would be of interest to investigate whether such personality factors as dependency-autonomy (Gough, 1976) or such intellectual factors as cognitive complexity (Harvey, Hunt, & Schroeder, 1969) can distinguish students who self-generate solutions from students who access computer-generated solutions. The major difficulty with the two components was the range of problems: 55% of the students using the Specific Component and 38% of those using the Structural Component could not find sample problems that were similar to their own problems. These components should be expanded to cover additional problem categories.

A second change in the present study involved the use of five self-report measures of problem improvement. These measures were intended to assess overall improvement in addition to cognitive and affective aspects of improvement. As shown in Table 11.2, the various measures of improvement were highly intercorrelated, suggesting that an independent assessment of different components of improvement was not achieved. However, several analyses indicated that the ratings of pleasant versus unpleasant and good versus bad feelings were more sensitive to the effects of treatment than the troublesomeness or manageableness ratings. It is interesting that measures of affect are the most sensitive measures of the effects of such a highly cognitive and rational procedure as dilemma counseling.

A major problem with the current evaluation procedure was that all measures of improvement were self-report scales and, thus, were subject to problems of reactivity. In future research, it would be important to include additional measures of improvement (e.g., behavioral assessments or peer reports). In addition, it would be desirable to control for a possible placebo effect through the inclusion of an experimental group in which subjects interacted with the PLATO Computer System, but did not use PLATO DCS. PLATO DCS (Wagman & Kerber, 1978) is available on many university PLATO systems (e.g., the University of Illinois at Urbana-Champaign), and may also be used with IBM, Apple, and other personal computers. The availability of computer-based dilemma counseling will allow for additional research, perhaps with actual clients rather than with introductory psychology students. The additional research could contain clients drawn randomly from campuses where PLATO DCS is available and could compare treatment by PLATO DCS only, PLATO DCS and counselor, and counselor only.

As an expert system, PLATO DCS, in addition to providing direct service to clients, can provide an educational function to counselors and counselor-trainees interested in learning the dilemma counseling method. In addition to this tutorial service, PLATO DCS, by means of its Specific and Structural Dilemma Solutions Components, could provide a consultative service to professional counselors and counselor-trainees confronted by especially difficult client dilemma situations. This consultation function of PLATO DCS would be analogous to the consultation function that is provided by the MYCIN system (see Chapter Seven) to physicians confronted with problems in medical diagnosis.

The third change in the present study was the addition of a one-month follow-up session. After one-month, the effects of treatment by PLATO DCS were approximately equaled by the rate of spontaneous remission (except for the pleasant-unpleasant improvement measure). The high rate of spontaneous remission probably was due to the moderate severity of the problems reported by the students. With these types of problems, the value of PLATO DCS is not that improvement remains higher across time for treated as opposed to untreated problems, but rather that improvement occurs more rapidly for treated problems.

The correlational findings in this study highlight the importance of solution adequacy as it related to the evaluation of PLATO DCS and to problem improvement. More adequate solutions (as rated by the subjects) were associated with more positive evaluations of PLATO DCS and with greater problem improvement at the one-week follow-up session. Ratings of solution adequacy preceded the evaluation of PLATO DCS and the ratings of problem improvement. Thus, it may be that the quality of the solutions generated on PLATO DCS influenced the evaluation and the perceived usefulness of the system. The mean value for the adequacy ratings in the present study was 6.04 (SD = 1.44) on an 8-point scale, where 8 meant "perfectly adequate for solving this dilemma." Thus, solutions generated on PLATO DCS were generally of high quality as rated by the subjects.

Some psychologists may be concerned about the supposedly impersonal nature of solving psychological problems on a computer (Weizenbaum, 1976, 1977). However, a majority (54%) of the subjects in this study felt that PLATO DCS was not too impersonal. In addition, a substantial percentage of the subjects actually felt more at ease (40%) and more independent (44%) on the computer than if they saw a counselor. On the other hand, for most subjects the computer is a resource to be sought in addition to the skills of a counselor. Of the current sample, 73% felt that it would be helpful to use PLATO DCS and see a counselor to solve a personal problem.

Perhaps the most important finding in this study is that students reacted very favorably to the teaching and counseling functions of a modern computer system. In addition to the attractiveness of PLATO DCS as a medium of presentation, the particular advantage of the dilemma counseling method for computer presentation is that the logic of the method is the logic of the computer (see Chapter Ten). Future attempts at computerized counseling should be preceded by serious consideration of the match between the technique and the medium of presentation. It would appear that cognitive approaches (Mahoney, 1977; Wilson & Franks, 1982) and problem-solving approaches to counseling (Heppner, 1978) rather than affective approaches to counseling (Colby, Watt, & Gilbert, 1966; Weizenbaum, 1965) are most appropriate for computer application.

CHAPTER TWELVE

Experimental Comparison of the PLATO DCS Expert System and Human Counselors as Methods of Psychological Counseling

Introduction

Background

Several lines of theory and research were involved in the development of PLATO DCS. Beginning around 1969, the author conducted gradute seminars (Department of Psychology, University of Illinois, Urbana-Champaign) in reasoning and cognition with particular attention to fallacious reasoning and its modification. Research, growing out of these seminars, inquired as to whether there might be cognitive methods of modifying fallacious reasoning that would be applicable across both scientific and personal domains of knowledge. At this time, the focus was not on programming computers to identify and correct fallacious reasoning, but on providing people with effective methods. The demonstration of fallacious reasoning through reductial ad absurdum procedures and other methods of demonstrating logical inconsistency have a long history in

Author's Note: The research was supported by a grant from the University of Illinois Research Board. I wish to thank Deborah Freco, David White, and Nancy Rotchford for their assistance in conducting the experiment and in analysis of the data. I wish to thank Deborah Allen, Barbara Bremmer, Helaine Moody, Ralph Trimble, and Marie Zimmerman, Clinical and Counseling Psychologists at the University of Illinois Counseling Center for their participation in the experiment.

the philosophy of logic and, in the form of theorem proving programs, have been employed in computer problem solving algorithms.

The results of research (Wagman, 1978) concerned with comparative methods of modifying fallacious reasoning indicated that people had great difficulty in applying self-contradiction methods (reductial ad absurdum), but could effectively apply cognitive information feed-back procedures, based on a teaching machine metaphor. Moreover, whereas the former method was uniformly ineffective, the latter method was effective across both scientific and personal domains of knowledge. The implication was drawn that a teaching machine or a computer program might be used to teach or counsel people regarding their reasoning fallaciously about personal problems.

A second line of theory and research involved in the development of PLATO DCS proceeded from the concepts and methods of systematic dilemma counseling (Wagman, 1979). The concepts of systematic dilemma counseling embraced the nature of psychological dilemmas as pervasive in human behavior and the stress resulting from the failure to apply effective methods of resolving personal dilemmas. It was demonstrated that the logic of conditionals provided a universal structure for psychological dilemmas and that a general logical structure for the resolution of dilemmas could be developed and effectively applied. The methods of systematic dilemma counseling were demonstrated to be effective when used by a counselor (Wagman, 1979) and in a semi-autonomous form (Wagman, 1980b) and in a fully autonomous form (Wagman, 1981). However, in all of these forms of application, the structure of the logic of conditionals and the structure of reasoning with dilemmas was constant. It soon became apparent that since computers also employ the logic of conditionals in their processing of information, a computer form of systematic dilemma counseling would be feasible. A theoretical congruence was thus established between counseling method and computer presentation. The idea of a computer counselor was created and several crucial problems ensued.

It was early decided that a computer counselor should not attempt to emulate the professional human counselor, but rather, to emulate the techniques of counseling, capitalizing on the specific competencies of personal computers. Once programmed, a computer would perform with precision and completeness and would not be subject to the universal professional human counselor characteristic of not always performing at the most optimal level. A computer counselor can be programmed with an indefinitely large number of possible solutions to psychological dilemmas. In addition, the types of solutions can range across an extensive variety of theoretical perspectives that would allow for maximization of the client's freedom in selecting and applying appropriate solutions.

Purpose

Computer Counseling represents a frontier of scientific research. In previous studies (Wagman, 1980a; Wagman & Kerber, 1980), PLATO DCS (Dilemma Counseling System) was demonstrated to be effective when compared with a no-treatment control condition.

The purpose of the present research is to explore the characteristics and effectiveness of PLATO DCS, by comparing it with human counselors. The comparisons concern effectiveness, reactions, methods, personality and demographic variables.

In studying effectiveness, comparisons are made among PLATO DCS, professional clinical and counseling psychologists and a no-treatment control condition. In studying client reactions, comparisons are made between clients treated by PLATO DCS and clients treated by the counselors. In studying treatment methods, the standard method of dilemma counseling used in PLATO DCS is compared with a wide variety of techniques of counseling used by professional counselors. In studying client personality and demographic variables, comparisons are made with respect to relationships between each of these variables and the effectiveness, reactions and methods variables.

Method

Subjects

Research subjects were undergraduate and graduate students at the University of Illinois and were payed for their participation in the experiment.

Materials

DEPENDENT MEASURES

In this experiment, both general dependent measures and specific research dependent measures were used. The general dependent measures were: Brief Symptom Inventory, State Trait Anxiety Inventory, and Coopersmith Self-Esteem Inventory. The specific research dependent measures consisted of a series of ratings of problem characteristics.

1. Brief Symptom Inventory (Derogatis, 1975) consisted of 22 problems and complaints people sometimes have that cause discomfort. Subjects were asked to indicate how much discomfort each problem had caused them in the past week on a scale from 0 (not at all) to 4 (extremely). Total scores could range from 0 to 88.

2 and 3. State Trait Anxiety Inventory (Speilberger, Gorsuch, & Lushene, 1970) was employed as a measure of anxiety. The State Anxiety Inventory is composed of twenty items, as is the Trait Anxiety Inventory. Responses are made on a 4-point scale (1 = not at all; 4 = very much so). Separate scores were computed for the State Anxiety Inventory and for the Trait Anxiety Inventory. Scores could range from 20 to 80 on each scale, with a high score indicating high levels of anxiety.

4. Coopersmith Self-Esteem Inventory (Coopersmith, 1967) consists of 58 items describing feelings people may have. The required response to each item is either "Like me" or "Unlike me". Scores can range from 0 to 58, with high scores indicating high self-eteem.

5. Subjects rated their life-choice problems on several dimensions. On 8-point scales the following dimensions were rated: 1) frequency (1 = never; 8 = all the time), 2) condition (1 = best condition; 8 = worst condition), 3) troublesomeness (1 = not troublesome at all, 8 = extremely troublesome—interfering with my life), 4) manageableness (1 = extremely manageable—can fully deal with it myself; 8 = extremely unmanageable—I must have considerable help to deal with it), 5) feelings of pleasantness (1 = pleasant; 8 = unpleasant), 6) good versus bad feelings (1 = good; 8 = bad), and 7) effort or time put into solving the problem (1 = no time or effort at all; 8 = an extreme amount of time or effort).

6. On a 5-point scale (1 = not at all; 5 = extremely), subjects rated how much certain feelings had bothered them in the past seven days with respect to the problem. The feelings were: 1) being trapped, 2) dejection or discouragement, 3) being confused, 4) anxiety or apprehension, 5) preoccupation with the problem, and 6) physical upset.

EVALUATION MEASURES

Subjects in the counselor condition and in the PLATO DCS condition evaluated the counseling they received on the basis of seven items which were rated on a 7-point scale (1 = not at all; 7 = very much). Subjects in the PLATO DCS condition also responded to ten items about PLATO DCS on a 5-point scale (1 = strongly agree; 5 = strongly disagree).

Both groups filled out a second evaluation form consisting of seven items which were the same for both groups and differing only in the word "counselor" or " PLATO". The items were rated on a 7-point scale (1 = very stongly disagree; 7 = very strongly agree).

Subjects in the PLATO DCS group also responded to another questionnaire that was designed to evaluate PLATO DCS or its components. There were three items that referred to the Dilemma Counseling component (see Chapter Ten), seven items that referred to the Specific Dilemma Solutions component (see Chapter Eleven). and nine items that referred to the Structural Dilemma Solutions component (see Chapter Eleven). There were six items that referred to PLATO DCS in its entirety. There were two types of items. First, the subject rated the helpfulness of each component in finding solutions to his or her problem (1 = not at all helpful; 5 = extremely helpful). Second, the subject agreed or disagreed with each of a series of statements referring to PLATO DCS or its components (1 = disagree; 5 = agree). Items of each type are presented in the Results section of the study.

PERSONALITY MEASURES

Four measures of personality characteristics were used in this experiment.

1. The introversion-extroversion scale of the Eysenck Personality Inventory (Eysenck, 1959) was employed as a measure of extroversion. The scale consists of 24 items, with a yes-no response. Scores could range from 1 to 24, with a high score indicating extroversion.
2. Authoritarianism was measured by 22 items taken from the California F Scale (Adorno, Frenkel-Brunswik, Levinson & Sanford, 1950). Eleven of the items were from the original F-Scale and were chosen on the basis of their high discriminatory power (as reported in Byrne, 1974, pp. 93–94). The remaining eleven

items were reversed items which correlated best with scores on the original text. These eleven reversed items (Byrne, 1974, pp. 123–124) were alternated with the eleven original items. Items were answered on a 7-point Likert Scale (1 = strongly agree). A person's score was the total of the eleven original items plus the eleven reversed items, and could range from 22 to 154. A high score indicates high authoritarianism.

3. Locus of control was measured with the Rotter I-E scale (Rotter, 1966). The I-E scale consists of 25 scored items and 4 filler (unscored) items. The 29 items are forced-choice questions with two alternatives. Scores could range from 0 to 25, with a high score indicating an external locus of control.

4. Six subscales of the Personality Research Form (Jackson, 1967) were used. Each of the subscales consists of 20 true-false items. The score for each subscale is separately computed, and can range from 0 to 20.

Subscale	A high score indicates
Cognitive Structures	Accurate, precise, meticulous
Order	Organized, systematic, methodical
Understanding	Analytical, logical, rational
Affiliation	Sociable, friendly, relationship seeking
Succorance	Sympathy, advice and reassurance seeking
Change	Adapts readily to change, open to new experiences

PROBLEM SOLUTIONS FORM

Subjects in all groups responded to a Problem Solutions Form on which they described up to five solutions they had generated for their problem either with the help of PLATO, the counselor, or on their own. They also ranked these solutions and rated the adequacy of the solution they ranked as the best. This rating was done on an 8-point scale (1 = completely inadequate for solving my problem; 8 = perfectly adequate for solving my problem).

FOLLOW-UP QUESTIONNAIRE

The Follow-up Questionnaire measured the status of subjects' problems after applying their solutions. On this measure, subjects rated the over-all improvement in their problems (1 = extremely improved; 8 = extemely worse). Subjects also rated the troublesomeness of the problem (1 = not at all troublesome; 8 = extremely troublesome, interfering with my life) and the manageableness of the problem (1 = extremely manageable, I can fully deal with it myself; 8 = extremely unmanageable, I must have considerable help to deal with it). In addition, subjects rated their affective reaction to the problems in terms of pleasant versus unpleasant feelings (1 = extremely pleasant; 8 = extremely unpleasant) and good versus bad feelings (1 = extremely good; 8 = extremely bad).

Subjects were also asked how much free time they spent actively trying to solve their problems (1 = no time at all; 8 = a great deal of time) and how much effort they expended actively applying some solution to their problems (1 = no effort at all; 8 = a great deal of effort).

CONCURRENT TREATMENT MEASURE

All subjects indicated whether or not they had received any outside counseling during the course of experiment. This concurrent treatment question presented six possible sources of treatment: private professional counselor, religious counselor, family physician, family, friends, and other.

MEASURE OF TECHNIQUES USED

The measure of techniques used consisted of a series of rating scales on which the counselor, following the final counseling session, indicated the frequency of use of a particular technique during the course of the counseling with the client. The rating was done on a 5-point scale (1 = not at all; 5 = predominantly). The measure of techniques used is presented in its entirety in the discussion section of this chapter.

DEMOGRAPHIC MEASURE

All subjects responded to the demographic measure which contained questions concerning: age, gender, year in college or graduate school, major, career goal, grade-point average, amount of contact with computers.

Procedure

INITIAL SESSION

For the initial session, subjects met in groups of 10−25. Subjects responded to the demographic measure and to the general dependent measures. Subjects wrote descriptions of four personal problems they were presently experiencing. Subjects rated all four of their personal problems on the specific research dependent measures.

To participate further in the study, subjects had to have at least one problem which was rated 6 or higher on the troublesomeness scale and could be formulated as a dilemma. Subjects (n = 102) with appropriate problems were randomly assigned among the experimental treatments: PLATO DCS condition, counselor condition, control condition.

COUNSELOR CONDITION

Subjects in the counselor condition were randomly assigned among five counselors at the University of Illinois Counseling Center. Each counselor decided the number of hours a subject would be seen for counseling depending on progress made in counseling sessions. Subjects were seen by counselors for one, two or three fifty minute weekly sessions. Following the final counseling session, subjects responded to the specific research dependent measures and to the general dependent measures. In addition, subjects responded to the counselor evaluation measure, the Problem Solutions Form and the concurrent treatment measure.

Following the final session with each client, the counselor responded to the measure of techniques used.

PLATO DCS CONDITION

Each subject in the PLATO DCS condition interacted with the computer during two sessions. During the first session, subjects spent up to two hours learning the dilemma counseling method (see Chapters Ten and Eleven).

There was a two or three day interval between the first session and the second session with PLATO DCS. In this second session, subjects used PLATO DCS to work out solutions to their own problems. They could access both the General and Specific Dilemma

Solution components for help in generating solutions. The second session lasted one hour. Upon completion of the second session, subjects responded to the specific research dependent measures and to the general dependent measures. In addition, subjects responded to the PLATO DCS evaluation measures and to the concurrent treatment measure.

All interaction of subjects with PLATO DCS during the second session was stored by the computer and print-outs of this information were obtained.

CONTROL CONDITION

Subjects in the control group met for a one-hour session in groups of 5 −15 and were simply asked to fill out some forms. These forms included the specific research dependent measures, the general dependent measures, the problem solutions form and the concurrent treatment measure.

FOLLOW-UP SESSION

Approximately one week after the final treatment session or control group session, subjects returned for a one-hour follow-up session. All subjects responded to the specific research dependent measures, the general dependent measures, the follow-up questionnaire, the concurrent treatment measure and the personality measures.

This session completed the subjects' participation in the experiment, and subjects were given a written debriefing upon completion.

Results

Differences Between Treatment Groups

DEPENDENT MEASURES

A series of multiple analyses of covariance (MANCOVA)[2] was conducted to determine the relative effectiveness of PLATO counseling, standard counseling, and no counseling in terms of the various dependent measures. The first MANCOVA compared the

---

[2] All analyses were conducted with the Statistical Package for the Social Sciences. (Nie, et al, 1975)

post scores of the PLATO counseling, standard counseling, and control groups on the Brief Symptom Inventory, State Anxiety, Trait Anxiety and Coopersmith's Self-Esteem measures. The pre scores on these same measures were used as covariates. The second MANCOVA compared the follow-up scores of the three groups on the Brief Symptom Inventory, State Anxiety, Trait Anxiety and Coopersmith's Self-Esteem dependent measures, again using the pre scores as covariates. Both of the MANCOVAs were followed by analysis of variance (ANOVA) F tests on the post scores and the follow-up scores, respectively, after adjusting for the co-variates. The adjusted means for the three groups are reported in Table 12.1.

The over-all multivariate analyses and the univariate tests were followed by specific comparisons to determine the effectiveness of PLATO counseling relative to no counseling and PLATO counseling relative to standard counseling.

The F statistics and associated p values indicate that the scores of the PLATO counseling, standard counseling, and control group participants differ significantly at both the post session, $F (16, 284) = 9.31$, $p<.001$, and the follow-up session, $F (16, 224) = 6.42$, $p<.001$. The subsequent ANOVAs on the adjusted post scores show that the Brief Symptom Inventory, $F (4, 80) = 15.05$, the State Anxiety Inventory, $F (4, 80) = 9.80$, the Trait Anxiety Inventory, $F (4, 80) = 29.46$, and Coopersmith's Self-Esteem measures, $F (4, 80) = 34.06$, are all significant ($p<.001$). The ANOVAs on the adjusted follow-up scores indicate that the same four dependent measures, $F (4, 64) = 12.41$, $F (4, 64) = 6.32$, $F (4, 64) = 29.67$, $F (4, 64) = 23.49$, all significant at $p<.001$, are responsible for the significant multivariate F.

The specific comparisons indicate that there is a significant difference between the PLATO counseling and control group scores on

TABLE 12.1. Adjusted means-dependent measures

	PLATO DCS		Standard Counseling		Control	
	Post	Follow-up	Post	Follow-up	Post	Follow-up
Brief Symptom Inventory	24.92	22.68	20.52	14.01	26.12	22.79
State Anxiety Inventory	41.41	38.56	38.32	36.57	40.61	43.72
Trait Anxiety Inventory	41.27	41.87	39.51	36.24	44.92	43.20
Coopersmith Self-Esteem Inventory	36.10	35.44	38.01	41.29	34.42	35.35

the four dependent measures at the post session, $F (4, 76) = 2.66$, $p < .05$. Table 12.1 shows that the PLATO counseling group scores are lower than the control group on the Brief Symptom and Trait Anxiety measures, but higher than the control group on the State Anxiety and Coopersmith's Self-Esteem measures. There is no significant difference $F (4, 60) = 1.16$, between the PLATO counseling and control groups at the follow-up session, but differences on three of the measures are in the expected direction: the PLATO counseling group is lower than the control group on the State Anxiety and Trait anxiety measures and higher on the Coopersmith Self-Esteem measure. The PLATO counseling and standard counseling groups show significant differences at the follow-up session, $F (4, 60) = 2.84$, $p < .05$, but not at the post session, $F (4, 76) = 1.91$. The standard counseling group has higher scores than the PLATO counseling group on the Coopersmith Self-Esteem measure at both the post and follow-up session and lower scores on the other three measures at the two sessions.

The third MANCOVA compared the PLATO counseling, standard counseling, and control groups with respect to the post scores on the frequency, condition and feelings of pleasantness dependent measures. Pre scores on these same measures were used as covariates. The fourth MANCOVA compared the follow-up scores on the frequency, condition, and feelings of pleasantness dependent measures, using the pre scores as covariates.

The results indicate no significant multivariate difference, $F (9, 93) = 1.69$, between the PLATO counseling, standard counseling, and control group post-scores. However, there is a significant multivariate F for the session scores, $F (9, 99) = 2.97$, $p < .05$. The ANOVA results indicate that the frequency dependent measure, $F (3, 43) = 3.08$, $p < .05$, is responsible for this significant difference. None of the specific comparisons between the PLATO counseling and no counseling or the PLATO counseling and standard counseling are significant. However, the PLATO counseling group (2.91) as compared with the control group (3.65) and the PLATO counseling group (2.91) as compared with the standard counseling group (3.28) has lower scores on the frequency dependent measure.

The fifth and sixth MANCOVAs compared the post scores and follow-up scores, respectively, on the troublesomeness, manageableness, and good versus bad feelings dependent measures. There is a significant difference between the scores of the three groups on all three dependent measures at the post session, F (9, 107) = 2.52, p<.05, but none of the post-sessions univariate tests are significant. The multivariate F test is not significant at the follow-up session.

The seventh and eight MANCOVAs compared scores of the PLATO counseling, standard counseling, and control groups at the post and follow-up sessions, respectively, on six dependent measures: feelings of being trapped, feelings of discouragement or dejection, feelings of confusion, feelings of anxiety or apprehension, preoccupation with the problem, and feelings of physical upset.

The results indicate a significant difference at the post session between the three groups across the six dependent variables, F (36, 160) = 1.98, p<.01. Of the univariate tests, scores on the feelings of dejection or discouragement, F (6, 41) = 2.60, p<.05, and the feelings of physical upset, F (6, 41) = 5.47, p<.001, measures are significantly different for the three groups. None of the specific contrasts between the PLATO counseling versus control and PLATO counseling versus standard counseling are significant. For the follow-up session, the MANCOVA is not significant, F (36, 165) = 1.31.

Evaluation Measures

The means and standard deviations of items dealing with reactions of PLATO counseling and standard counseling group participants to their respective programs are given in Table 12.2. The means and standard deviations for additional reaction items answered by PLATO counseling participants are given in Table 12.3.

TABLE 12.2. Means and standard deviations-reaction items for PLATO DCS Group and Standard Counseling Group

	PLATO DCS (N=31)		Standard Counseling (N=31)	
	M	SD	M	SD
How useful was the PLATO program/counseling in general?[a]	4.32	1.25	4.61	1.54
How useful were the solutions that PLATO/counseling generated?[a]	4.71	1.16	4.61	1.73

TABLE 12.2. *(Cont.)*

	PLATO DCS (N=31)		Standard Counseling (N=31)	
	M	SD	M	SD
To what extent will you use the solutions from PLATO/counseling?[a]	4.94	1.34	4.94	1.84
Can you apply things learned in PLATO/counseling to future problems?[a]	5.58	1.09	5.32	1.38
How interesting was the PLATO/counseling to work with?[a]	4.61	1.76	5.36	1.56
How much did you like PLATO/the counselor as a teacher?[a]	4.68	1.73	4.59	1.77
Over-all liking of the counseling you received from PLATO/the counselor?[a]	5.48	1.52	5.12	1.49
PLATO/the counselor has encyclopedic knowledge.[b]	4.26	1.34	3.67	1.16
I felt very dependent while working with PLATO/the counselor.[b]	3.45	1.65	3.39	1.16
PLATO/the counselor intruded too much into my personal privacy.[b]	2.39	1.26	2.00	.97
PLATO/the counselor taught a problem solving method which can apply to future psychological problems.[b]	5.48	1.26	4.06	1.90
PLATO/the counselor is objective.[b]	5.13	1.48	5.06	1.32
PLATO/the counselor has a problem solving orientation.[b]	4.64	1.47	4.90	1.11
PLATO/the counselor hurried me too much.[b]	2.64	1.08	2.39	1.14

[a] These statements use the scale:

Not at all						very much
1	2	3	4	5	6	7

[b] These statements use the scale:

Very strongly disagree						Very strongly agree
1	2	3	4	5	6	7

TABLE 12.3. Reaction items responded to by PLATO DCS participants

	PLATO DCS (N=31)	
	M	SD
It is important to me that PLATO DCS has been researched and is effective.[a]	2.45	1.09
I like the fact that PLATO DCS keeps no records when I use it.[a]	1.90	.94
I like the objectivity of PLATO DCS in working on my problems.[a]	2.23	1.06
It is advantageous to use my own values in solving problems on PLATO DCS.[a]	1.68	.70
I would not like to use PLATO DCS without also seeing a counselor at same time.[a]	1.58	1.26
As compared with seeing a counselor, PLATO DCS is more convenient for me to use.[a]	2.36	.88
As compared with seeing a counselor, PLATO DCS allows more freedom to choose my own solution to my problem.[a]	1.68	1.22
As compared with seeing a counselor, PLATO DCS is more reliable.[a]	3.45	.85
As compared with seeing a counselor, PLATO DCS allows me to spend as much time as I need on my problem.[a]	2.61	1.26
As compared with seeing a counselor, PLATO DCS allows more control over the direction my counseling will take.[a]	1.52	1.22
Was the Dilemma Counseling Component helpful in solving your problem?[b]	3.03	.95
Were Dilemma phrasing problems helpful to you?[b]	3.61	.96
Was the generalized dilemma matrix helpful to you?[b]	3.74	.96
PLATO DCS was very interesting to work on.[c]	3.39	1.20
After using PLATO DCS, I could apply dilemma counseling to my problems without further instruction.[c]	3.94	1.00
Using PLATO DCS in order to solve a problem is not too impersonal.[c]	3.61	1.14
I would feel more at ease using PLATO DCS for a personal problem than going to a counselor.[c]	2.71	1.42

TABLE 12.3. *(Cont.)*

	PLATO DCS (N=31)	
	M	SD
I would feel more independent in solving my problems with PLATO DCS than with a counselor.[c]	3.00	1.37
Was the Specific Dilemma Solutions component helpful in finding solutions to your problem?[b]	2.65	1.31
It was easy to move between my problem and the Specific Dilemma Solutions component.[c]	3.21	1.32
The case descriptions in the Specific Dilemma Solutions component were not very clear.[c]	2.42	1.17
I was able to find a problem in the Specific Dilemma Solutions component that was similar to my own.[c]	3.21	1.48
In general, the solutions to the problems in the Specific Dilemma Solutions component were too long.[c]	2.21	1.08
Moving from problem to problem in the Specific Dilemma Solutions component was easy.[c]	4.05	1.22
Solutions contained in the Specific Dilemma Solutions component were helpful in generating solutions to my problem.[c]	3.37	1.50
Was the Structural Dilemma Solutions component helpful in finding solutions to your problem?[b]	3.09	1.14
It would be helpful to see a counselor and use PLATO to work on a problem.[c]	3.90	1.61
Were Structural Dilemma Solutions component instructions helpful?[b]	3.91	.70
Were dilemma matrices for typical problem types helpful?[b]	4.00	.76
Were examples of structural solutions helpful?[b]	3.91	.54
The structural solutions contained in the component were helpful in generating solutions to my problems.[c]	3.91	.83
It was easy to move between my own problem and the Structural Dilemma Solutions component.[c]	4.30	.48
Typical problem types in the Structural Dilemma Solutions component were too general to apply to my own problem.[c]	2.90	1.10

TABLE 12.3. *(Cont.)*

	PLATO DCS (N=31)	
	M	SD
I was able to find a typical problem type in the Structural Dilemma Solutions component that was similar to my own problem.[c]	3.20	1.55
Moving from category to category in the Structural Dilemma Solutions component was easy.[c]	4.30	1.06

[a] These statements use scale:

Strongly Agree	Agree	Neutral	Disagree	Strongly Disagree
1	2	3	4	5

[b] These statements use scale:

Not at all helpful	Slightly helpful	Somewhat helpful	Considerably helpful	Extremely helpful
1	2	3	4	5

[c] These statements use scale:

Disagree				Agree
1	2	3	4	5

To test for differences between the PLATO counseling and standard counseling groups in their reactions to their respective programs, a multivariate analysis of variance (MANOVA) was conducted on the items. All items were compared simultaneously across the two groups, and then ANOVA F tests were conducted on each of the reaction items.

There is a significant multivariate F for the PLATO counseling and standard counseling group participants' reactions ($F_{(14, 42)}$ = 6.22, $p<.01$). Two of the reaction items have significant univariate F ratios: the item stating that PLATO/the counselor had encyclopedic knowledge ($F_{(1, 56)}$ = 3.89, $p<.05$), and the statement that PLATO/the counselor taught them a problem solving method they could use in the future ($F_{(1, 56)}$ = 9.81, $p<.01$). As can be seen in Table 12.2, the PLATO counseling group relative to the standard counseling group rated PLATO as having greater encyclopedic knowledge and rated PLATO as a better teacher of a problem solving method that could be used in the future.

CONCURRENT TREATMENT MEASURE

Responses to the questions dealing with use of additional forms of counseling during the experiment were analyzed. A series of six Chi-square tests was conducted in which the PLATO counseling, standard counseling, and outside counseling (private professional counselor, religious counselor, etc.) were compared. The percentage of each group indicating at the post session that they had used the specific types of counseling and Chi-square statistics are given in Table 12.4. Parallel sets of percentages and Chi-square statistics for the follow-up session are also given in Table 12.4. Only the Chi-square for friends as a specific form of additional outside counseling is significant, and it is significant at both the post and follow-up sessions. At both sessions, more standard counseling participants than control, and more control participants than PLATO, indicated they had used friends as an additional source of counseling.

FOLLOW-UP QUESTIONNAIRE MEASURE

The means and standard deviations of the items on the follow-up questionnaire for each of the three groups are given in Table 12.5 These items measure the status of subjects' problems after applying solutions.

An ANOVA was computed to examine differences between the PLATO counseling, standard counseling, and control group responses to the follow-up questionnaire items. This multivariate analysis was followed by a series of ANOVAs comparing the three groups on each of the items. Specific comparisons to determine if the PLATO counseling group scores on these items differed significantly from the standard counseling group scores were also made.

There is a significant difference between the three groups for the follow-up questionnaire items, $F (14, 134) = 1.92$, $p<.05$. Subsequent ANOVAs indicate that there are significant differences for three of the items: troublesomeness of the problem, $F (2, 75) = 3.92$, $p<.05$, manageableness of the problem, $F (2, 75) = 3.83$, $p<.05$, and overall improvement in the problem, $F (2, 75) = 4.76$, $p<.01$. The specific comparisons indicate that there is a significant difference, $F (7, 67) = 2.02$, $p<.05$, between the PLATO counseling and control groups on the items, but no significant difference, $F (7, 67) = 1.79$, between the PLATO counseling and standard counseling. Examination of the means displayed in Table 12.5 shows that the PLATO

TABLE 12.4. Use of additional sources of counseling by PLATO DCS Group, Standard Counseling Group, Control Group

	Post % answering "yes"				Follow-up % answering "yes"			
	PLATO DCS	Standard Counseling	Control	Chi-Square	PLATO DCS	Standard Counseling	Control	Chi-Square
Private Counselor	0	6.7	3.3	2.12n.s.	0	6.7	10.0	3.05n.s.
Religious Counselor	0	3.3	0	2.06n.s.	0	6.7	0	4.16n.s.
Family Physician	0	0	0		0	0	0	
Family	9.7	20.0	6.7	2.77n.s.	16.1	20.0	23.3	.50n.s.
Friends	16.1	56.7	43.3	11.03p<.01	25.8	56.7	53.3	7.10p<.05
Other	6.5	10.0	6.7	.33n.s	6.5	6.7	6.7	.01n.s.

TABLE 12.5. Follow-up questionnaire: means and standard deviations for PLATO DCS Group, Standard Counseling Group, Control Group

	PLATO DCS		Standard Counseling		Control	
	M	SD	M	SD	M	SD
After applying solution, troublesomeness of problem.	3.61	2.29	3.37	1.88	5.21	2.11
After applying solution, manageableness of the problem.	3.23	1.88	2.63	1.54	5.86	1.82
After applying solution, pleasantness of feelings about the problem.	3.68	1.87	3.43	1.63	4.79	1.83
After applying solution, good versus bad feelings about the problem.	3.55	1.86	3.50	1.61	4.43	1.93
How much free time spent on problem.	4.40	1.69	4.27	2.13	5.11	1.78
Effort expended applying solution to problem.	5.20	1.92	4.50	2.06	5.41	1.74
After applying solution, over-all improvement in problem.	2.57	.97	2.90	.86	5.36	.91

counseling group has lower scores than the control group on the troublesomeness of the problem, manageableness of the problem and over-all improvement in the problem, after applying solution, items.

Correlational Analyses

A series of correlational analyses was conducted to examine relationships among experimental variables. The first of these analyses concerned relationships between reaction variables and dependent variables.

REACTION ITEMS AND DEPENDENT MEASURES

Usefulness of program. For the PLATO counseling group, subjects who rated the program as more useful (a) had lower scores on the State Anxiety Inventory at the post session, $r(18) = .52$, $p<.01$, (b) had higher scores on the Coopersmith Self-Esteem Inventory at the post session, r(19) = .37, p<.05 and at the follow-up session, r(14) = .43, p<.05 and (c) had lower scores on the condition of problem measure at the follow-up session, r(10) = .51, p<.05. For the standard counseling group, subjects who rated the program as more useful, indicated at the post session that they had put more effort or time in applying their solutions to their problems, r(10) = .69, p<.01.

Liking of PLATO/Counselor More. Subjects who liked PLATO counseling more indicated, at the follow-up session, that they had less frequently discussed their problems with friends, r(12) = .46, p<.05. Subjects who liked the counselor more had higher scores on the Coopersmith Self-Esteem Inventory at the follow-up session, r(8) = .54, p<.05.

Program as more interesting. Subjects who rated the PLATO program as more interesting, (a) had lower scores on the frequency of problem measure at the post session, r(12) = .45, p<.05, (b) had lower scores on the troublesomeness of problem measure at the post session, r(12) = .45, p<.05 and (c) indicated, at the post session, r(14) = .57, p<.01 and at the follow-up session, r(14) = .57, p<.01, that they had less frequently sought professional consultation for their problems. For the standard counseling group, subjects who rated the counseling program as more interesting had lower scores on the feelings of anxiety and apprehension measure at the post session, r(7) = .59, p<.05.

FOLLOW-UP QUESTIONNAIRE AND DEPENDENT MEASURES

Management of Problems. For the PLATO counseling group, subjects who, on the follow-up questionnaire, indicated that they were more able to manage their problems by themselves, (a) had lower scores on the Brief Symptom Inventory at the post session, r(20) = .36, p<.05 and at the follow-up session, r(18) = .38, p.<.05, (b) had lower scores on the State Anxiety Inventory at the follow-up session, r(17) = .57, p<.01, (c) had lower scores on the Trait Anxiety Inventory at the follow-up session, r(21) = .48, p<.01, (d) had higher scores on the Coopersmith Self-Esteem Inventory at the follow-up session, r(30) = .41, p<.01, (e) had lower scores on the frequency of problem measure at the follow-up session, r(13) = .64, p.<.01, (f) had lower scores on the condition of problem measure at the follow-up session, r(9) = .74, p<.001, (g) had lower scores on the feelings of being trapped measure at the follow-up session, r(15)

= .56, p<.01, (h) had lower scores on the feelings of dejection and discouragement measure at the follow-up session, r(12) = .46, p<.05, (i) had lower scores on the feelings of pleasantness about the problem measure at the follow-up session, r(4) = .91, p<.001 and (j) had lower scores on the good versus bad feelings about the problem measure at the follow-up session, r(5) = .89, p<.001. For the standard counseling group, subjects, who, on the follow-up questionnaire, indicated that they were more able to manage their problems by themselves, (a) had higher scores on the Coopersmith Self-Esteem Inventory at the post session, r(16) = .40, p<.05, (b) had lower scores on the frequency of problem measure at the post session, r(18) = .52, p<.01, (c) had lower scores on the feelings of anxiety or apprehension measure at the follow-up session, r(10) = .69, p<.01, (d) had lower scores on the troublesomeness of problem measure at the follow-up session, r(7) = .60, p<.05, (e) had lower scores on the feelings of pleasantness about their problems measure at the follow-up session, r(5) = .68, p<.05 and (f) had lower scores on the good versus bad feelings about their problems measure at the follow-up session, r(5) = .66, p<.05. For the control group, subjects who, on the follow-up questionnaire, indicated that they were more able to manage their problems by themselves, (a) had lower scores on the State Anxiety Inventory at the post session, r(19) = .37, p<.05, (b) had lower scores on the feelings of physical upset measure at the post session, r(9) = .52, p<.05, (c) had lower scores on the troublesomeness of problem measure at the post session, r(9) = .73, p<.001 and at the follow-up session, r(11) = .63, p<.01, (d) had lower scores on the feelings of pleasantness measure at the post session, r(11) = .64, p<.01 and at the follow-up session, r(11) = .64, p<.01, (e) indicated, at the post session, that they had put more effort or time into solving their problems, r(11) = .48, p<.05, (f) had lower scores on the Brief Symptom Inventory at the follow-up session, r(18) = .38, p<.05, (g) had lower scores on the frequency of problem measure at the follow-up session, r(21) = .48, p<.01 and (h) indicated, at the follow-up session, that they had less often sought professional consultation for their problems, r(10) = .51, p<.05.

Comparisons between the PLATO counseling group and the standard counseling group with respect to coefficients of correlation between the manageableness of problem variable and (a) the feelings of pleasantness variable indicated a non-significant difference (z =

.77, p>.05) and (b) the good versus bad feelings variable indicated a non-significant difference (z = .71, p>.05). Comparisons between the PLATO counseling group and the control group with respect to coefficients of correlation between the manageableness of problem variable and (a) the frequency of problem variable indicated a non-significant difference (z = .62, p>.05) and (b) the feelings of pleasantness variable indicated a non-significant difference (z = .99, p>.05). Comparisons between the standard counseling group and the control group with respect to coefficients of correlation between the manageableness of problem variable and (a) the troublesomeness of problem variable indicated a non-significant difference (z = −.32, p>.05) and (b) the feelings of pleasantness variable indicated a non-significant difference (z = .99, p>.05).

PERSONALITY AND DEMOGRAPHIC MEASURES

The relationships between the personality and demographic items and other variables used in this study were examined. Both the personality and demographic items were correlated with the post and follow-up dependent measures.

PERSONALITY VARIABLES AND DEPENDENT MEASURES

Affiliation Scale. For the PLATO counseling group, subjects with higher scores on the affiliation scale had lower scores on the State Anxiety Inventory at the post session, r(18) = .38, p<.05. For the standard counseling group, subjects with higher scores on the affiliation scale, (a) had higher scores on the Coopersmith Self-Esteem Inventory at the post session, r(12) = .45, p<.05, and (b) indicated, at the post session, that they had more often sought professional consultation for their problems, r(7) = .58, p<.05 and at the follow-up session, r(7) = .60, p<.05. For the control group, subjects with higher scores on the affiliation scale had lower scores on the Coopersmith Self-Esteem Inventory at the follow-up session, r(18) = .38, p<.05.

Understanding Scale. For the PLATO counseling group, subjects with higher scores on the understanding scale, (a) had lower scores on the manageableness of problem measure at the post session, r(11) = .48, p<.05, (b) had lower scores on the feelings of anxiety or apprehension measure at the follow-up session, r(10) = .49, p<.05, and (c) had lower scores on the feelings of physical upset measure at the follow-up session, $r(16) = .55$, $p<.01$. For the standard counseling group, subjects with higher scores on the understanding scale, (a) had higher scores on the feelings of physical upset measure at the post session, $r(8) = .56$, $p<.05$ and (b) indicated, at the follow-up session, that they had put more effort or time into solving their problems, $r(8) = .71$, $p<.01$. For the control group, subjects with higher scores on the understanding scale had lower scores on the feelings of preoccupation with the problem measure at the follow-up session, $r(13) = .44$, $p<.05$.

Extroversion Scale. For the PLATO counseling group, subjects with higher scores on the extroversion scale, (a) had lower scores on the Brief Symptom Inventory at the post session, $r(20) = .36$, $p<.05$, (b) had lower scores on the State Anxiety Inventory at the post session, $r(23) = .46$, $p<.01$ and at the follow-up session, $r(24) = .45$, $p<.01$, (c) had lower scores on the Trait Anxiety Inventory at the post session, $r(14) = .42$, $p<.05$ and at the follow-up session, $r(20) = .49$, $p<.01$, (d) had higher scores on the Coopersmith Self-Esteem Inventory at the post session, $r(15) = .41$, $p<.05$, (e) had lower scores on the condition of problem measure at the follow-up session, $r(12) = .46$, $p<.05$, (f) had lower scores on the feelings of being trapped measure at the follow-up session, $r(13) = .59$, $p<.01$, (g) had lower scores on the feeling of preoccupation with the problem measure at the follow-up session, $r(12) = .46$, $p<.05$, (h) had lower scores on the feelings of pleasantness about the problem measure at the follow-up session, $r(11) = .48$, $p<.05$, and (i) had more good versus bad feelings about their problems at the follow-up session, $r(16) = .40$, $p<.05$. For the standard counseling group, subjects with higher scores on the extroversion scale, (a) had lower scores on the feelings of dejection or discouragement measure at the post session, $r(10) = .67$, $p<.01$ and (b) had lower scores on the manageableness of problem measure at the post session, $r(8) = .55$, $p<.05$.

Cognitive Structures Scale. For the PLATO counseling group, subjects with higher scores on the cognitive structures scale, (a) had higher scores on the Brief Symptom Inventory at the post session, $r(16) = .40$, $p<.05$, (b) had higher scores on the Trait Anxiety Inventory at the post session, $r(19) = .37$, $p<.05$ and (c) had higher scores on the State Anxiety Inventory at the follow-up session, $r(18) = .38$, $p<.05$. For the standard counseling group, subjects with higher scores on the cognitive structures scale, indicated at the follow-up session, that they had put less effort or time into solving their problems, $r(9) = .68$, $p < .01$.

DEMOGRAPHIC VARIABLES AND DEPENDENT MEASURES

Female versus Male. For the PLATO counseling group, female subjects as compared with male subjects, (a) had higher scores on the condition of problem measure at the follow-up session, $r(12) = .45$, $p < .05$, (b) had higher scores on the manageableness of problem measure at the follow-up session, $r(12) = .45$, $p < .05$ and (c) had higher scores on the good versus bad feelings measure at the follow-up session, $r(9) = .52$, $p < .05$. For the standard counseling group, female subjects as compared with male subjects, (a) had lower scores on the feelings of pleasantness measure at the post session, $r(6) = .61$, $p < .05$ and at the follow-up session, $r(7) = .79$, $p < .001$, (b) had lower scores on the condition of problem measure at the follow-up session, $r(7) = .58$, $p < .05$, (c) had lower scores on the manageableness of problem measure at the follow-up session, $r(7) = .58$, $p = .05$ and (d) had lower scores on the good versus bad feelings measure at the follow-up session, $r(7) = .78$, $p < .001$. For the control group, female subjects as compared with male subjects, (a) had lower scores on the Brief Symptom Inventory at the post session, $r(13) = .44$, $p < .05$, (b) had higher scores on the Coopersmith Self-Esteem Inventory at the post session, $r(13) = .44$, $p < .05$, (c) indicated, at the post session, that they had fewer discussions with friends about their problems, $r(12) = .46$, $p < .05$, (d) had lower scores on the feelings of being trapped measure at the follow-up session, $r(9) = .53$, $p < .05$, (e) had lower scores on the feelings of dejection or discouragement measure at the follow-up session, $r(12) = .45$, $p < .05$, (f) had lower scores on the feelings of being confused measure at the follow-up session, $r(13) = .44$, $p < .05$ and (g) had lower scores on the feelings of anxiety or apprehension measure at the follow-up session, $r(11) = .47$, $p < .05$.

Comparisons between the PLATO counseling group and the standard counseling group with respect to coefficient of correlation between the female-male variable and (a) the condition of problem variable indicated a significant difference ($z = 2.09$, $p < .05$), (b) the manageableness of problem variable indicated a significant difference (z = 2.09, p<.05) and (c) the good versus bad feelings variable indicated a significant difference (z = 2.77, p<.01).

MEASURE OF TECHNIQUES USED

The measure of techniques used items were correlated with other variables used in this study. The techniques used items were correlated with the post and follow-up dependent measures. The relationships between the measure of techniques used items and the reactions to the program items were also examined. The measure of techniques used items and the reactions to the program items were also examined. The measure of techniques used items were also correlated with the follow-up questionnaire items. The measure of techniques used items were then examined in relation to personality and demographic items. Finally, the inter-correlation matrix of the measure of techniques used items was computed.

Technique of Reassurance. The more frequently counselors used the technique of reassurance, (a) the higher clients' scores on the feelings of being confused measure at the post session, r(6) = .61, p<.05, (b) the higher the clients' scores on the feelings of anxiety or apprehension measure at the post session, r(7) = .60, p<.05, (c) the lower clients' scores on the State Anxiety Inventory at the follow-up session, r(9) = .69, p<.05, and (d) the higher subjects' scores on the order scale, r(12) = .45, p<.05.

Technique of Sympathy or Empathic Response. The more frequently counselors used the technique of sympathy or empathic response, the lower clients' scores on the State Anxiety Inventory at the follow-up session, r(6) = .63, p<.05.

Technique of Recognition and Clarification of Feelings. The more frequently counselors used the technique of recognition and clarification of feelings, (a) the lower clients' scores on the feelings of dejection or discouragement measure at the post session, r(5) = .68, p<.05, (b) the lower clients' scores on the frequency of problem measure at the post session, r(12) = .46, p<.05, (c) the lower clients' scores on the condition of problem measure at the post session, r(7) = .60, p<.05, (d) the lower clients' scores on the feelings of preoccupation with the problem measure at the post session, r(7) = .76, p<.01, and (e) the higher subjects' scores on the improvement in problem as a result of applying solution measure, r(14) = .42, p<.05.

Technique of Self-Disclosure Relationship. The more frequently counselors used the technique of self-disclosure relationship, (a) the higher clients' scores on the feelings of physical upset measure at the post session, $r(5) = .89$, $p<.001$, and at the follow-up session, $r(6) = .78$, $p<.01$, (b) the more clients indicated, at the post session, that they had discussed their problems with friends, $r(5) = .98$, $p<.001$, (c) the higher clients' scores on the State Anxiety Inventory at the follow-up session, $r(6) = .63$, $p<.05$ and (d) the higher clients' scores on the condition of problem measure at the follow-up session, $r(9) = .70$, $p<.01$.

Technique of Persuasion Relationship. The more frequently counselors used the technique of persuasion relationship, (a) the more clients indicated, at the post session, that they had discussed their problems with friends, $r(9) = .69$, $p<.01$, (b) the higher clients scores on the feelings of physical upset measure at the follow-up session, $r(7) = .60$, $p<.05$, (c) the higher subjects' scores on the extent to which solutions will be used measure, $r(11) = .47$, $p<.05$, and (d) the higher subjects' scores on the appropriateness of solutions measure, $r(12) = .46$, $p<.05$.

Technique of Directing Relationship. The more frequently counselors used the technique of directing relationship, (a) the higher clients' scores on the feelings of being confused measure at the post session, $r(9) = .70$, $p<.01$, (b) the higher clients' scores on the feelings of preoccupation with the problem measure at the post session, $r(9) = .70$, $p<.01$, (c) the higher clients' scores on the manageablenes of problem measure at the follow-up session, $r(8) = .54$, $p<.05$, and (d) the lower the frequency of use of the technique of client-centered relationship, $r(13) = .44$, $p<.05$.

Technique of Modeling Responses. The more frequently counselors used the technique of modeling responses, (a) the higher clients' scores on the feelings of physical upset measure at the post session, $r(9) = .68$, $p<.01$ and at the follow-up session, $r(7) = .60$, $p<.05$, (b) the more clients indicated, at the post session, that they had discussed their problems with friends, $r(10) = .66$, $p<.01$, (c) the lower subjects' scores on the grade point average measure, $r(6) = .63$, $p<.05$, (d) the higher the frequency of use of the technique of self-disclosure relationship, $r(10) = .67$, $p<.01$ and (e) the higher the frequency of use of the technique of persuasion relationship, $r(14) = .58$, $p<.01$.

Technique of Behavior Rehearsal. The more frequently counselors used the technique of behavior rehearsal, (a) the lower clients' scores on the frequency of problem measure at the post session, $r(8) = .71$, $p<.01$, (b) the lower clients' scores on the feelings of being confused measure at the post session, $r(10) = .66$, $p<.01$, (c) the lower clients' scores on the feelings of anxiety or apprehension measure at the follow-up session, $r(8) = .56$, $p<.05$, and (d) the lower subjects' scores on the succorance scale, $r(9) = .53$, $p<.05$.

Technique of Cognitive Restructuring. The more frequently counselors used the technique of cognitive restructuring, (a) the lower clients' scores on the troublesomeness of problem measure at the follow-up session, $r(7) = .59$, $p<.05$, (b) the lower subjects' scores on the authoritarianism scale, $r(10) = .49$, $p<.05$, (c) the lower subjects' scores on the locus of control scale, $r(8) = .55$, $p<.05$, (d) the lower subjects' scores on the order scale, $r(8) = .55$, $p<.05$ and (e) the higher the frequency of use of the technique of recognition and clarification of feelings relationship, $r(15) = .55$, $p<.01$.

Technique of Rational Emotive Therapy. The more frequently counselors used the technique of rational emotive therapy, (a) the lower clients' scores on the feelings of being trapped measure at the follow-up session, $r(10) = .67$, $p<.01$, (b) the more effort or time did clients indicate, at the follow-up session, that they had put into solving their problems, $r(7) = .60$, $p<.05$, (c) the higher subjects' scores on the troublesomeness of problem measure, $r(12) = .46$, $p<.05$, (d) the lower subjects' scores on the authoritarianism scale, $r(12) = .45$, $p<.05$, (e) the higher subjects' scores on the understanding scale, $r(12) = .45$, $p<.05$, and (f) the higher the frequency of use of the technique of cognitive restructuring, $r(13) = .59$, $p<.01$.

Technique of Providing Solutions. The more frequently counselors used the technique of providing solutions, (a) the higher clients' scores on the feelings of physical upset measure at the post session, $r(11) = .64$, $p<.01$, (b) the higher clients' scores on the manageableness of problem measure at the follow-up session, $r(8) = .55$, $p<.05$, (c) the higher subjects' scores on the usefulness of solutions measure, $r(17) = .53$, $p<.01$, (d) the higher subjects' scores on the extent to which solutions will be used measure, $r(15) = .61$, $p<.001$, (e) the higher subjects' scores on the applying learning in the future measure, $r(15) = .61$, $p<.001$, (f) the higher subjects' scores on the over-all liking of counseling received measure, $r(15) = .55$, $p<.01$, (g) the higher subjects' scores on the free time spent solving the problem measure, $r(23) = .46$, $p<.01$, (h) the higher subjects' scores on the effort expended applying solutions measure, r(18) = .52, p<.01, (i) the lower the frequency of use of the technique of client-centered relationship, r(13) = .60, p<.01 and (j) the higher the frequency of use of the technique of directing relationship, r(13) = .65, p<.001.

Technique of Discussing and Evaluating Solutions. The more counselors used the technique of discussing and evaluating solutions, (a) the higher clients' scores on the feelings of being trapped measure at the post session, r(6) = .63, p<.05, (b) the higher the frequency of use of the technique of persuasion relationship, r(13) = .44, p<.05, and (c) the higher the frequency of use of the technique of determining the problem r(15) = .41, p<.05.

Technique of Motivating Clients to Apply Solutions. The more frequently counselors used the technique of motivating clients to apply solutions, (a) the higher clients' scores on the frequency of problem measure at the follow-up session, r(11) = .47, p<.05, (b) the lower subjects' scores on the future job scale, r(6) = .62, p<.05, (c) the lower the frequency of use of the technique of client-centered relationship, r(16) = .54, p<.01, (d) the higher the frequency of use of the technique of persuasion relationship, r(12) = .66, p<.001, (e) the higher the frequency of use of the technique of providing solutions, r(16) = .54, p<.01, and (f) the higher the frequency of use of the technique of discussing and evaluating solutions, r(15) = .41, p<.05.

Technique of Interpretation of Current Dynamic. The more frequently counselors used the technique of interpretation of current dynamic, (a) the lower subjects' scores on the applying learning in the future measure, r(11) = .48, p<.05, (b) the higher subjects' scores on the pleasantness of problem measure, r(11) = .48, p<.05, (c) the higher the frequency of use of the technique of recognition and clarification of feelings relationship, r(12), = .46, p<.05, (d) the higher the frequency of use of the technique of rational emotive therapy, r(10) = .72, p<.001, and (e) the higher the frequency of use of the technique of paradoxical intention, r(8) = .50, p<.05.

Technique of Interpretation of Genetic Dynamic. The more frequently counselors used the technique of interpretation of genetic dynamic, (a) the lower the subjects' scores on the authoritarianism scale, r(8) = .54, p<.05, (b) the higher the frequency of use of the technique of rational emotive therapy, r(11) = .63, p<.01, and (c) the higher the frequency of use of the technique of interpretation of current dynamic, r(6) = .82, p<.001.

Adequacy of Solution. The higher counselors' ratings of adequacy of solution to subjects' problems, (a) the lower subjects' scores on the Trait Anxiety Inventory at the post session, $r(12) = .46$, $p<.05$ and at the follow-up session, $r(6) = .61$, $p<.05$, (b) the lower subjects' scores on the feelings of dejection or discouragement measure at the post session, $r(9) = .68$, $p<.01$, (c) the lower subjects' scores on the feelings of pleasantness measure at the follow-up session, $r(8) = .56$, $p<.05$, (d) the lower subjects' scores on the good versus bad feelings measure at the post session, $r(9) = .53$, $p<.05$, and at the follow-up session, $r(8) = .55$, $p<.05$, (e) the lower subjects' scores on the State Anxiety Inventory at the post session, $r(15) = .41$, $p<.05$, (f) the higher subjects' scores on the Coopersmith Self-Esteem Inventory at the post session, $r(16) = .40$, $p<.05$ and at the follow-up session, $r(7) = .57$, $p<.05$, (g) the lower subjects' scores on the manageableness of problem measure at the post session, $r(8) = .54$, $p<.05$, (h) the lower subjects' scores on the feelings of being confused measure at the follow-up session, $r(7) = .58$, $p<.05$, (i) the lower subjects' scores on the troublesomeness of problem measure, $r(23) = .46$, $p<.01$, (j) the lower subjects' scores on the pleasantness of problem measure, $r(24) = .46$, $p<.01$, (k) the lower subjects' scores on the good versus bad feelings measure, $r(10) = .40$, $p<.05$, (l) the higher subjects' scores on the extroversion scale, $r(22) = .47$, $p<.01$, (m) the higher subjects' scores on the year in college measure, $r(7) = .60$, $p<.05$ and (n) the lower the frequency with which the technique of paradoxical intention was used, $r(14) = .58$, $p<.01$.

Technique of Determining the Problem. The more frequently counselors used the technique of determining the problem, (a) the higher subjects' scores on the liking of the counselor as a teacher measure, $r(12) = .46$, $p<.05$, (b) the lower subjects' scores on the applying learning in the future measure, $r(18) = .38$, $p<.05$ and (c) the higher subjects' scores on the contact with computers in general measure, $r(6) = .64$, $p<.05$.

Technique of Providing Motivation for Applying Solutions. The more frequently counselors used the technique of providing motivation for applying solutions, (a) the higher subjects' scores on the usefulness of solutions measure, $r(16) = .54$, $p<.01$, (b) the higher subjects' scores on the over-all liking of counseling received measure, $r(21) = .48$, $p<.01$, (c) the higher subjects scores on how interesting was the counseling received measure, $r(28) = .42$, $p<.01$ and (d) the higher subjects' scores on the troublesomeness of problem measure, $r(17) = .39$, $p<.05$.

Technique of Client-Centered Relationship. The more frequently counselors used the technique of client-centered relationship, (a) the lower subjects' scores on the effort expended applying solution measure, $r(8) = .54$, $p<.05$, and (b) the higher subjects' scores on the grade point average measure, $r(5) = .65$, $p<.05$.

Technique of Paradoxical Intention. The more frequently counselors used the technique of paradoxical intention, (a) the lower subjects' scores on the authoritarianism scale, $r(9) = .68$, $p<.01$, (b) the lower subjects' scores on the order scale, $r(11) = .48$, $p<.05$ and (c) the higher the number of appointments, $r(8) = .55$, $p<.05$.

Extent to Which Problem was Solved. The greater the extent to which the problem was solved, as rated by counselors, (a) the lower the frequency of use of the technique of client-centered relationship, $r(11) = .48$, $p<.05$, (b) the higher the frequency of use of the technique of directing relationship, $r(17) = .53$, $p<.01$, (c) the higher the frequency of use of the technique of modeling, $r(9) = .52$, $p<.05$, (d) the higher the frequency of use of the technique of providing solutions, $r(18) = .76$, $p<.001$, (e) the higher the frequency of use of the technique of motivation for applying solutions, $r(17) = .53$, $p<.01$, (f) the lower subjects' scores on the how much did subjects change measure, $r(16) = .40$, $p<.05$, and (g) the higher subjects' scores on the improvement of subject, $r(4) = .92$, $p<.001$.

Discussion

Comparative Methods

PLATO DCS uses the single method of systematic dilemma counseling (see Chapters Ten and Eleven), but the human counselors (counseling psychologists), in this experiment, used multiple methods. PLATO DCS uses the same method across all clients and across all their problems. The counselors use multiple methods across clients and their problems.

In the present study, clients' problems are psychological dilemmas with a wide variety of content (from personal and inter-personal to vocational and educational), but all characterizable as dilemmas, i.e., psychological problems which involve difficult conflicts epitimized as avoidance-avoidance issues (see Chapters Nine, Ten, Eleven). The counselors were free to construe clients' problems from any theoretical stance they wished. PLATO DCS was confined to its particular theory (see Chapters Ten and Eleven).

As part of the research design, each counselor, following the final session with a client, responded to the measure of techniques used (see Figure 12.1). This instrument allowed counselors to indicate the frequency (including not at all) with which they used different techniques of counseling (e.g., recognition and clarification of feelings, interpretation of dynamics, cognitive restructuring, problem solving). It is intriguing to discover how the frequency of use of different techniques of counseling is related to changes in various experimental measures such as reaction, dependent, personality and demographic variables. More specifically, it is of interest to learn what different patterns of relationship between technique and experimental variables exists for problem solving and cognitive techniques, on the one hand, and client centered and inter-personal techniques on the other hand. In addition, since PLATO DCS uses problem solving and cognitive techniques, it would be of interest to discover whether it has patterns of relationships to experimental variables that are similar to the patterns found in counselors who frequently employ such techniques while different from counselors who employ client centered and inter-personal techniques. The correlational analyses presented in the Results section contain data relevent to these questions.

Counselors rated the adequacy of the solutions generated that resulted from counseling. As a significant rating of counseling outcome, it is of interest that adequacy of solutions is positively correlated with improvement on several general dependent measures (self-esteem, state anxiety, trait anxiety) and on a number of specific dependent measures (discouragement, confusion, troublesomeness, unmanageableness, unpleasant and bad feelings about the problem).

The technique of providing solutions is, at once, similar to the Specific and Structural Dilemma Solutions components of PLATO DCS and different from client-centered techniques. When therefore, the counselors' activity resembles that of the computer, it is of interest to learn which experimental variables are correlated and in what direction.

Frequency of counselors' use of the technique of providing solutions is positively correlated with the following client-rated variables: manageableness of problem, usefulness of solutions, over-all liking of counseling received, extent to which solutions will be used, apply learning in the future, free time spent solving the problem, effort expended in applying solutions. In addition, the frequency of use of the technique of directing relationship is negatively correlated with the frequency of use of the technique of client-centered relationship.

Measure of Techniques Used

To what extent did you use each of the following techniques or methods?

    I. Relationship techniques

        A. Client centered

1) Not at all   4) Considerably
2) Slightly   5) Predominantly
3) Moderately

        B. Reassurance

1) Not at all   4) Considerably
2) Slightly   5) Predominantly
3) Moderately

        C. Sympathy or empathic response

1) Not at all   4) Considerably
2) Slightly   5) Predominantly
3) Moderately

        D. Recognition and clarification of feelings

1) Not at all   4) Considerably
2) Slightly   5) Predominantly
3) Moderately

        E. Self-disclosure

1) Not at all   4) Considerably
2) Slightly   5) Predominantly
3) Moderately

        F. Persuasion

1) Not at all   4) Considerably
2) Slightly   5) Predominantly
3) Moderately

        G. Directing

1) Not at all   4) Considerably
2) Slightly   5) Predominantly
3) Moderately

  II. Behavioral

        A. Relaxation procedures

1) Not at all   4) Considerably
2) Slightly   5) Predominantly
3) Moderately

        B. Modeling

1) Not at all   4) Considerably
2) Slightly   5) Predominantly
3) Moderately

        C. Behavior rehearsal

1) Not at all   4) Considerably
2) Slightly   5) Predominantly
3) Moderately

        D. Desensitization

1) Not at all   4) Considerably
2) Slightly   5) Predominantly
3) Moderately

FIGURE 12.1. The measure of techniques used.
Counselors completed this instrument immediately after the final counseling session.

III. Cognitive

    A. Cognitive restructuring
       1) Not at all   4) Considerably
       2) Slightly   5) Predominantly
       3) Moderately

    B. Rational emotive
       1) Not at all   4) Considerably
       2) Slightly   5) Predominantly
       3) Moderately

    C. Paradoxical intention
       1) Not at all   4) Considerably
       2) Slightly   5) Predominantly
       3) Moderately

IV. Problem-solving

    A. Determining the problem
       1) Not at all   4) Considerably
       2) Slightly   5) Predominantly
       3) Moderately

    B. Providing solutions
       1) Not at all   4) Considerably
       2) Slightly   5) Predominantly
       3) Moderately

    C. Discussing and evaluating possible solutions
       1) Not at all   4) Considerably
       2) Slightly   5) Predominantly
       3) Moderately

    D. Motivation for applying solutions
       1) Not at all   4) Considerably
       2) Slightly   5) Predominantly
       3) Moderately

V. Psychodynamic

    A. Interpretation of current dynamic
       1) Not at all   4) Considerably
       2) Slightly   5) Predominantly
       3) Moderately

    B. Interpretation of genetic dynamic
       1) Not at all   4) Considerably
       2) Slightly   5) Predominantly
       3) Moderately

    C. Transference interpretation
       1) Not at all   4) Considerably
       2) Slightly   5) Predominantly
       3) Moderately

VI. Other

    A.
       1) Not at all   4) Considerably
       2) Slightly   5) Predominantly
       3) Moderately

FIG. 12.1. CON'T

B.   1) Not at all   4) Considerably
                                             2) Slightly   5) Predominantly
                                             3) Moderately

C.   1) Not at all   4) Considerably
                                             2) Slightly   5) Predominantly
                                             3) Moderately

VII. Similarity to clients seen for one, two or three interviews
  A. In general, how similar is the participant's problem to client's seen for
     one, two or three interviews?
     1) Essentially the same   4) Considerably different
     2) Slightly different   5) Extremely different
     3) Moderately different

  B. In general, how similar was your treatment of the research participant
     compared with treatment of clients seen briefly for one, two or three
     interviews:
     1) Essentially the same   4) Considerably different
     2) Slightly different   5) Extremely different
     3) Moderately different

VIII. Characterize the participant's problem as
      to its type

  A. Educational   1) Not at all   4) Considerably
                                    2) Slightly   5) Predominantly
                                    3) Moderately

  B. Vocational   1) Not at all   4) Considerably
                                    2) Slightly   5) Predominantly
                                    3) Moderately

  C. Personal-social   1) Not at all   4) Considerably
                                    2) Slightly   5) Predominantly
                                    3) Moderately

  IX. Change
  A. Problems can have several solutions varying in quality. With respect to the
     best solutions worked out for the problem of the research participant, rate
     its degree of adequacy on the following scale.

1   2   3   4   5   6   7   8

Completely inadequate for solving
this problem
                                 Perfectly   adequate   for   solving   this
                                 problem

Fig. 12.1. CON'T

B. To what extent is the problem of the research participant a circumscribed adjustment problem in an otherwise healthy personality, and to what extent is the problem embedded in a generally neurotic personality?
   1) Not at all embedded in a neurotic personality
   2) Slightly embedded in a neurotic personality
   3) Moderately embedded in a neurotic personality
   4) Considerably embedded in a neurotic personality
   5) Essentially embedded in a neurotic personality

C. In general, compared with most clients seen for one, two or three interviews, how much did the research participant change as a result of counseling?
   1) Research participant improved more than most clients
   2) Research participant improved about as much as most clients
   3) Research participant improved less than most clients

D. How much did the research participant improve as a result of counseling?
   1) Not at all   4) Considerably
   2) Slightly   5) Extremely
   3) Moderately

E. To what extent do you believe the problem of the research participant was solved as a result of counseling?
   1) Not solved at all   4) Considerably solved
   2) Slightly solved   5) Essentially solved
   3) Moderately solved

F. As a result of counseling, to what extent has general distress associated with the problem been reduced in the life of the research participant?
   1) Not reduced at all   4) Considerably reduced
   2) Slightly reduced   5) Extremely reduced
   3) Moderately reduced

X. Prediction
   A. In general, compared with most clients seen for one, two or three interviews, how much will the research participant change as a result of counseling?
      1) Research participant will improve more than most clients
      2) Research participant will improve about as much as most clients
      3) Research participant will improve less than most clients
   B. How much will the research participant improve as a result of counseling?
      1) Not at all   4) Considerably
      2) Slightly   5) Extremely
      3) Moderately

FIG. 12.1. CON'T

C. To what extent do you believe the problem of the research participant will be solved as a result of counseling?

    1) Not solved at all   4) Considerably solved
    2) Slightly solved   5) Essentially solved
    3) Moderately solved

D. As a result of counseling, to what extent will general distress associated with the problem be reduced in the life of the research participant?

    1) Not reduced at all   4) Considerably reduced
    2) Slightly reduced   5) Extremely reduced
    3) Moderately reduced

XI. Comments II

FIG. 12.1. CON'T

As indicated in the Results section, subjects in the standard counseling condition did not differ from subjects in the PLATO DCS counseling in the extent to which they evaluated their respective programs as useful in solving their problems. It would appear, therefore, that a procedure of providing solutions whether produced by a computer or a counselor is a satisfactory method of resolving dilemmas as judged by subjects who had been troubled by their psychological dilemmas. The positive correlation of the counselor technique of providing solutions with the counselor technique of directing relationship and the negative correlation of the former technique with the counselor technique of client-centered relationship suggests the affinity of the former counseling technique to the Specific and Structural Dilemma Solutions components of PLATO DCS.

In addition to the solutions components, PLATO DCS contains the Dilemma Counseling component which teaches a set of procedures for formulating or determining the dilemma (see Chapter Ten). It is of interest, therefore, that the more frequently counselors use the technique of determining the problem, the higher subjects' scores on the liking of counselor as a teacher.

It also should be noted that the greater the extent to which the problem was solved, as rated by counselors, the lower the frequency of use of the technique of client-centered relationship, the higher the frequency of use of the technique of directing relationship, the higher the frequency of use of the technique of providing solutions and the higher the scores on the improvement of participant scale (see Figure 12.1).

Comparative Reactions

It is both important and interesting to learn how reactions to a computer counseling system such as PLATO DCS compared with reactions to standard counseling as traditionally performed by human professional counselors. To achieve this purpose, a series of fourteen reaction items was administered to PLATO DCS counseling and standard counseling subjects as described in the Methods section. As indicated in the Results section, although these two treatment methods are ostensively quite different, strikingly different in the personna of the counselor (computer versus human) and less impressively different in their techniques of counseling (systematic dilemma counseling versus a wide variety of counseling techniques), the two treatment groups shared equivalent reactions by their subjects for twelve of the fourteen items (see Table 12.2). Items can be grouped into two categories. The first category is concerned with the technical effectiveness of PLATO DCS or the counselor. The second category is concerned with affective aspects of PLATO DCS or of the counselor. The category of technical effectiveness contains items that refer to over-all usefulness of the program, usefulness of the solutions generated by PLATO DCS or the counselor, usefulness of the problem-solving method for future problems, encyclopedic knowledge of PLATO DCS or the counselor. The category of affective aspects contains items that refer to how interesting was counseling by PLATO DCS or by the counselor, feelings of dependency on PLATO DCS or on the counselor, feelings that PLATO DCS or the counselor intruded too much into privacy, feelings that PLATO DCS or the counselor is objective or has a problem-solving orientation, feelings of being hurried by PLATO DCS or the counselor. It would be difficult to state, a priori, which of these two categories is more significant and which one would be more capable of differentiating between the computer and a human, when each is consulted by a human. It might have been supposed that consultation of a human by a human would involve uniquely affective aspects that would be absent in the consultation of a computer by a human (see Appendix). Yet, it is the category of affective aspects that is common to both counseling modalities. Thus, the computer is no more intrusive into personal privacy than is the counselor, just as capable of producing feelings of dependency and involvement and just as patient. With respect to the category of technical effectiveness, the modalities do not differ with respect to generating useful solutions to subjects' problems. However, with respect to technical acumen, subjects evaluated the computer as possessing greater encyclopedic knowledge than the counselor and as surpassing the counselor in teaching a method that subjects could apply to future problems.

Subjects in the PLATO DCS counseling group were asked to react to a series of items that concern comparisons of counseling by PLATO DCS with counseling by professional human counselors. As may be seen from Table 12.2, PLATO DCS subjects agreed that, as compared with professional human counselors, PLATO DCS allows more freedom to choose their own solutions to their problems and PLATO DCS allows them more control over the direction their counseling will take. In addition, PLATO DCS subjects agreed that they liked the objectivity of PLATO DCS in working on their problems and that it is advantageous that they can use their own values in solving problems on PLATO DCS. Taken together, these results would seem to suggest that a computer counselor enables subjects to experience an augmentation of their autonomy beyond that typically experienced in standard counseling. However, subjects in the PLATO DCS group also agreed that it would be helpful to see a counselor and use PLATO DCS to work on a problem. Overall, the data in Table 12.3 supports the conclusion of a very favorable reaction by subjects who received counseling from PLATO DCS for their personal problems.

Personality Variables

The personality variables were included in the experiment for exploratory purposes. It seemed possible that the understanding or cognitive structure scales of the Personality Research Form (see Methods section) with their emphasis on logic, precision and system might be positively correlated with computer methodology, in general, and with PLATO DCS, in particular, and might be negatively correlated with methods of counseling that presumably contain a large share of inter-personal attitudes and empathic responses, which, in turn, would have a closer affinity to personality measures such as the affiliation and succorance scales of the Personality Research Form. In a similar vein, perhaps high authoritarianism, with its need for structure and external locus of control (see Methods section), with its need for control might be accomodative of a computer-based counseling methodology. Therefore, as indicated in the Results section, correlations between the personality variables, on the one hand, and dependent variables, on the other hand, were calculated. Several of the more interesting sets of correlations will now be briefly discussed.

For subjects in the standard counseling condition, affiliation scale scores are positively correlated with Coopersmith's Self-Esteem measure scores at the post session, suggesting the possibility that the counseling relationship was meeting their affiliative needs, except that, for these subjects, affiliation scores are also positively correlated with frequency, at both post and follow-up sessions, of seeking additional professional consultation (in addition to their research participation) for their problem. Perhaps, the importance of the affiliation need is indicated by the finding, for the control group subjects, that high affiliation scale scores are negatively correlated with Coopersmith's Self-Esteem scores at the follow-up session. However, the implied association between affiliative scale score and need for human counseling is not supported by the finding that, for the PLATO DCS counseling group, subjects with higher scores on the affiliation scale have lower scores on the State Anxiety Test at the post session. One interpretation is that the computer, at least the PLATO DCS computer program, can reduce the strong anxiety associated with high affiliative needs.

Perhaps an example of the putative relationship between personality and type of treatment is the finding that, for the PLATO DCS counseling group, subjects with higher scores on the Understanding scale (analytic, logical, rational) improved more on the manageableness, feelings of anxiety or apprehension and feelings of physical upset dependent measure. However, it is not just treatment type that may be related to personality, since it was also found that, for the control group, subjects with higher scores on the understanding scale improved more on the feelings of preoccupation with the problem dependent measure.

Demographic Variables

Among demographic variables, the gender variable was the only one to show significant relationships with dependent measures. For the PLATO DCS counseling group, female subjects as compared with male subjects improved less on the condition of problem, manageableness, and good versus bad feelings dependent measures. In contrast, for the standard counseling group, female subjects as compared with male subjects improved more on the feelings of pleasantness-unpleasantness, condition of problem, manageableness, and good versus bad feelings dependent measures. However, gender is associated not only with type of treatment, but with no treatment, i.e., for the control group, female subjects as compared with male subjects, improved more on the Brief Symptom Inventory, Coopersmith's Self-Esteem measure, feelings of being trapped, feelings of dejection or discouragement, feelings of being confused, and feelings of anxiety or apprehension dependent measures.

Comparing the PLATO DCS counseling and standard counseling groups with respect to those scales on which gender differences were present in both groups, it is interesting that the results of the comparisons between correlation coefficients (see Results section) indicated significant differences for the condition of problem variable and for the manageableness of problem variable and for the good versus bad feelings variable. With respect to these variables, it appears that female subjects as compared with male subjects improved less in the PLATO DCS counseling condition and improved more in the standard counseling condition.

Several studies (Kerber, 1983; Wagman, 1983) have found a general gender difference in favorability of attitudes toward the use of computers in health, education and counseling settings. It appears that males as compared to females have more favorable attitudes toward these types of computer applications (see Appendix).

Comparative Effectiveness

In this experiment, the effectiveness of PLATO DCS as an experimental method was studied with respect to the standard method and to a control condition, employing a research design that included both a post-session and a follow-up session and a set of dependent measures that included both general scales and specific research scales.

It is of interest that, at the post session, PLATO DCS counseling and standard counseling groups do not differ in effectiveness, as measured by the Brief Symptom Inventory, Coopersmith's Self-Esteem measure, the State and Trait Anxiety Scales; but at the follow-up session, PLATO DCS counseling is less effective than standard counseling with respect to these dependent measures. Three sets of issues are involved: immediate and later effects of treatment, general versus specific dependent measures, the treatments themselves. Regarding the issue of the treatments themselves, it is appropriate to compare treatment by PLATO DCS with the control condition.

Although at the post-session, there is a significant difference between PLATO DCS counseling and the control condition, the two groups do not differ significantly at the follow-up session. At the post-session, the PLATO DCS counseling condition, relative to the control condition, is more effective in ameliorating low self-esteem, general symptoms and trait anxiety, but less effective in ameliorating state anxiety. At the follow-up session, these significant differences in effectiveness are no longer apparent. However, the PLATO DCS counseling group tends to have lower scores than the control group on the State and Trait Anxiety Inventories and a higher score on the Coopersmith Self-Esteem Inventory.

In summary, with respect to the general dependent measures, it would appear that at the post-session, PLATO DCS counseling is as effective as standard counseling and more effective than the control condition. At the follow-up session, PLATO DCS is not as effective as standard counseling with respect to the four general dependent measures, but PLATO DCS tends to be more effective than the control condition with respect to the State Anxiety, Trait Anxiety, and Coopersmith Self-Esteem Inventories. It is now of interest to inquire as to whether these findings hold when the specific research measures are employed as dependent variables.

The PLATO DCS counseling, standard counseling and control groups do no differ significantly with respect to the frequency, condition, pleasantness-unpleasantness of feelings dependent measures. However, at the follow-up session, PLATO DCS counseling tended to be more effective than standard counseling and PLATO DCS counseling tended to be more effective than the control condition in ameliorating scores on the frequency of problem dependent measure.

At the post-session, the PLATO DCS counseling, standard counseling and control groups did not differ significantly with respect to the troublesomeness, manageableness and good versus bad feelings dependent measures. These findings also hold for the follow-up session.

In summary, with respect to the frequency, condition, pleasantness-unpleasantness feelings, troublesomeness, manageableness, and good versus bad feelings dependent measures, there is no significant difference among the PLATO counseling, standard counseling and control groups at either the post session or follow-up session. However, there is a tendency, at the follow-up session, for the PLATO DCS counseling condition, as compared with each of the other two conditions, to be more effective in ameliorating scores on the frequency of problem dependent measure.

At both the post-session and the follow-up session, the PLATO DCS counseling group does not differ from the standard counseling group and the PLATO DCS counseling group does not differ from the control condition with respect to feelings of being trapped, feelings of discouragement or dejection, feelings of consusion, feelings of anxiety or apprehension, preoccupation with the problem, and feelings of physical upset dependent measures.

Concurrent Treatment

The concurrent treatment measure was included in the experiment as an indirect means of assessing the comparative effectiveness of PLATO DCS counseling and standard counseling, under the assumption that differential concurrent treatment frequencies reflect differential satisfaction of clients with their respective programs. As indicated in the Results section, differential concurrent treatment frequencies were found for only one of the six possible categories (see Table 12.4). With respect to the category of discussing their problems with friends, research participants differed. The frequency for this category is significantly higher for standard counseling participants than for control participants and for control participants than for PLATO DCS participants. The differential frequencies may reflect differential effectiveness or differential satisfaction. For example, as indicated in the Results section, participants who liked the PLATO DCS program more, less frequently consulted friends about their problems. Also, participants who evaluated PLATO DCS counseling as more interesting, less frequently had concurrent professional counseling. It is of interest that for the standard counseling condition, higher affiliation scales are associated with higher frequency of concurrent professional counseling. The finding that for the control condition, the more that participants were able to manage their problems by themselves, the less frequently they had concurrent professional counseling, may imply some support for the assumption that research participants who obtained concurrent treatment were responding to the failure of their counseling programs to enable them to manage their problems. Additional research that would focus more sharply on the issues of the meaning of differential and non-differential concurrent treatment frequencies would seem to be appropriate.

Status at Follow-up

At the follow-up session, subjects in the PLATO DCS counseling, standard counseling and control groups responded to a series of items regarding the status of their problems after applying solutions (see Table 12.5). Subjects in the PLATO DCS counseling group, as compared with subjects in the control group, evaluated their problems as less troubling, more manageable and generally more improved after applying the solutions that they had generated during interaction with the computer program. This finding is in line with results of previous research that compared PLATO DCS with a control group (Wagman, 1980a; Wagman & Kerber, 1980). In the present study, there is no difference between subjects in the PLATO DCS counseling group and subjects in the standard counseling group with respect to the status of their problems at the follow-up session as measured by the troublesomeness, manageableness and improvement scales.

Conclusion

The research described in this chapter is generally supportive of PLATO DCS counseling whether compared with standard counseling or with a control condition. Comparisons of the two types of counseling concerned methods, reactions, effects, personality and demographic variables. Further research can usefully be concerned with the cross-validation of the findings. The conduct of this research by other investigators is greatly facilitated by the recent (1985) extension of PLATO DCS availability to several types of personal computers (e.g., IBM PC, APPLE II).

CHAPTER THIRTEEN

Conclusion: Problems and Prospects of Computer Counseling

Introduction

In this chapter, we shall discuss various approaches and problems in the design of computer counseling systems. General concepts will be considered with respect to the major components of knowledge input and knowledge processing.

In a computer counseling system, the knowledge input component refers to the computer's comprehension of client communications and includes concepts such as fidelity in computer comprehension and semantic input limitations. Knowledge processing, at a general level, consists of data structures and operational procedures in a given problem domain and may include concepts such as modes of reasoning and algorithmic formalisms.

Computer counseling represents an integration of concepts in the field of artificial intelligence and in the field of psychotherapy. As an amalgam of concepts from these two fields, the development of computer counseling will, inevitably, have to consider the assets and liabilities of each field and the constraints they impose on approaches to system designs.

Knowledge Input

Constraints Imposed by Artificial Intelligence Concepts

A basic approach to the development of computer counseling systems is the recognition that they are varieties of expert systems (see Chapter Seven). In this section, comparisons of computer counseling

193

and expert systems will be made with respect to problems of knowledge input.

In considering approaches to the design of computer counseling systems, comparisons can be made with several types of artificial intelligence systems (expert systems, consultative systems, tutorial systems). In each of these systems, a human professional person is modeled. The individual modeled may be a research chemist (the DENDRAL programs), a research mathematician (the MACSYMA system), a psychologist or psychiatrist (computer psychometry programs), a medical consultant (the MYCIN programs) or educator (the WHY system). In the case of computer counseling systems, the professional person modeled is a psychological counselor (psychotherapist).

The knowledge input to be comprehended by the computer counselor are psychological beliefs (carrying cognitive and affective import) concerning variegated and idiosyncratic personal and interpersonal problem situations. By several orders of magnitude the range of this knowledge input is more extensive than the knowledge input delivered to any of the artificial intelligence systems mentioned above, in each of which knowledge to be comprehended by the system is specified (molecular structures, infectious diseases) and in a standard format (e.g., mathematical equations, psychodiagnostic checklists).

It is clear that artificial intelligence systems (expert, consultative, tutorial) are dedicated with respect to specific knowledge input, corresponding to specific problems or topics in chemistry or mathematics or medicine or education. Topics and problems that exceed their scope of dedication can not be comprehended by the artificial intelligence systems. Further research and development can, of course, broaden their scope, by creating programs for additional topics and problems. However, in such an expanding library of programs, it is still the case that the conceptual approach is one of specialization in topic or problem. It is also the case that the knowledge necessary for the selection from an existing library of a program suitable for a specific topic or problem is possessed not by the computer, but by the professional researcher or practitioner (chemist, mathematician, physician, psychologist, psychiatrist, educator). A professional person needs to exercise judgement in program selection for a given client or client problem. In this respect, a computer counseling system would be an expert in, for example, marital or divorce decisions, just as MYCIN, a medical consultation system, is dedicated only to certain types of infectious diseases (e.g., bacteremia, meningitis). In effect, then, it is not the general human counselor that the computer counselor would be modeling, but, rather, an expert or specialist counselor. It would then be the case that the persons referred to the expert computer counselor would be referred for a previously indentified and specific psychological problem.

In summary, the constraint exercised by artificial intelligence research on the development of computer counseling systems is that the systems be composed of a library of programs dedicated to specific psychological problems, that the system is a specialist or expert in counseling only certain psychological problems and that the recommendation of clients for computer counseling programs depends upon the knowledge of human professional counselors.

Constraints Imposed by Psychotherapy Concepts

Perhaps, the most general constraint exercised by the nature of psychotherapy concepts on the development of computer counseling systems is that theories of psychotherapy lack the rigor of mathematical and chemical sciences and even lack the biological base of the inexact medical sciences. Theories of psychotherapy are not always clear as to the relative contribution of efforts of the psychotherapist, efforts of the client and environmental ameliorations that result in therapeutic change or improvement. The problems of attribution of therapeutic change (incremental or decremental) to specific conditions (a particular therapeutic method or even a particular therapist) or to general conditions (knowledge, guidance, persuasion, support, benevolence, interest, reinstatement of hope and courage) and the problem of the quantity, quality and duration of change over and above that due to spontaneous remission effects have been extensively researched for many years without definitive resolution, often without agreement as to what constitutes acceptable measures of the effects of psychotherapy (Erdman, et al, 1981; Strupp, 1977; Hersen, Michelson & Bellack, 1984). These problems are not confined to long term psychotherapy, but significantly, because computer-based counseling is likely to be brief in duration (given the limitations of current artificial intelligence research to represent complex knowledge input such as that produced in the free association and dreams of psychoanalysis), are characteristic of planned short term therapy (PSTT) as indicated by Bloom (1980, p. 119):

> While it is beyond the scope of this review to provide a comprehensive comparative analysis of the various approaches to PSTT that have appeared in the literature, that literature has an enormous intellectual richness. The issues discussed in these works include; (a) optimal length of PSTT; (b) therapeutic attitudes and skills needed to do successful PSTT; (c) patient characteristics associated with favorable PSTT outcome; (d) therapeutic techniques and strategies particularly appropriate for PSTT; (e) limitations of PSTT; (f) training for PSTT; and (g) a variety of special topics, such as short-term therapy of inpatients. The authors are seldom in agreement with each other regarding any of these issues, and perhaps because of that, a wealth of important testable hypotheses can easily be generated from this literature.

Other Constraints on Knowledge Input

There are constraints on the development of computer counseling systems which derive from an interaction of characteristics of psychotherapy and artificial intelligence. These constraints on knowledge input refer, on the one hand, to the varying attitudes which different systems of psychotherapy take toward the matter of clients asking questions and, on the other hand, the limitations on the range of questions that can be comprehended by a given artificial intelligence system.

Clients' questions may be handled differently in different psychotherapy systems. In psychoanalysis, questions may be considered part of free association productions or otherwise responded to (or not responded to) in terms of latent meaning rather than factual content. In client-centered psychotherapy, questions may be parried with attention directed to the possible feelings associated with the question. Problem-solving , cognitive and behavior therapies may construe queries only with respect to their factual content. The client in each of these systems may be directly or indirectly instructed regarding queries and may be subtly discouraged in raising them. However, in any psychotherapy, some factual questions will be raised by the client and answered by the therapist (if only matters of fees and other logistics). Clients can feel frustrated by therapists' disregard or re-interpretation of their queries, but they would experience a different type of frustration in being required to eliminate many types of queries from their general input to the computer counselor because the computer can not comprehend queries beyond those for which it has been specifically programmed. The consequences of this limitation for computer psychotherapy effectiveness constitute an interesting research problem.

Knowledge Processing

It was indicated above that theories of computer counseling represent an integration or amalgam of concepts from the fields of artificial intelligence and psychotherapy. It was also indicated that the content of the theories of computer counseling with respect to knowledge input consists of psychological beliefs concerning personal and interpersonal problem situations. The psychological beliefs are variegated and idiosyncratic and are compounds of cognitive, affective and motivational aspects of individual personality.

At a general level, it might appear that a theoretical amalgam of information processing concepts (artificial intelligence) and affective and motivational concepts (psychotherapy) would possess inherent inconsistencies that would weaken the integration of the theoretical structure. It might also appear that a theoretical structure based on uniform information processing concepts common to artificial intelligence and psychotherapy would be highly consistent and generally robust.

An information processing model of psychotherapy implies a theory of human personality that places less emphasis on long-standing emotional and motivational predispositions (e.g., a chronic need for dependence and approval, a chronic need to rebel) and more emphasis on contemporaneous adaptable and flexible problem-solving competencies and coping schema. Beginning around 1950, psychological theory, in general, (Hebb, 1949) and personality and psychotherapy theory, in particular, (Blake & Ramsey, 1951; Kelly, 1955) have experienced an accelerated emphasis on cognitive and information processing concepts. Pervin (1985, p. 96) draws the following contrasts between information processing and traditional theories of personality:

Whereas traditional personality theory tends to emphasize stability and consistency, current cognitive, information-processing theory emphasizes discriminativeness and flexibility; whereas the former emphasizes generalized predictions about a person, the latter emphasizes predictions specific to situations; whereas the former emphasizes concepts such as dispositions and needs, the latter emphasizes concepts such as category structures and inferential strategies; whereas the former emphasizes motivation and dynamics, the latter emphasizes cognitive economics and the limitations of everyday cognitive processes; whereas the former emphasizes the self as causal agent and a unitary concept, the latter emphasizes the self as a compound of multiple schema. Taking liberally from the concepts and methods of cognitive psychology, this new approach to personality has begun to dominate the literature in the field.

The concepts of cognitive psychology include the attentional, encoding, data storage and retrieval aspects of information processing (Simon, 1979). In cognitive psychology research (Bower, 1978; Neisser, 1967; Norman & Rumelhart, 1975), these concepts have been applied, primarily, to natural rather than social categories. It is not entirely clear that an information processing approach to natural phenomena is equally appropriate for personal and interpersonal phenomena (Cohen, 1981). The uncritical transfer of information processing concepts to the areas of personality and psychotherapy theory carries with it a serious neglect of affective (Fiske, 1982; Holyoak & Gordon, 1984), motivational (Neisser, 1980; Norman, 1980) and unconscious (Mahoney, 1980) processes. While some theory and research assign to cognition an antecedent and determinative status with respect to affect (Mandler, 1982; Weiner, 1982) and while other theory and research point to the significance of emotion as prior to and determinative of cognitive processes (Bower & Cohen, 1982; Clark & Teasdale, 1982; Wright & Mischel, 1982), it would appear that the question of whether affect or cognition has permanent causation influence is best approached by the fluid position that, depending on many conditions, sometimes cognition determines affective and motivational processes and sometimes the converse holds (Coyne & Gotlib, 1983; Hilgard, 1980; Izard et al., 1984; Kiesler, 1982; Teasdale, 1983). Moreover, in significant human problems, it is likely to be the case that a cognitive theory and psychotherapy carry some admixture of affective and motivational processes and that a motivational and affective theory of psychotherapy contain some admixture of cognitive processes.

Knowledge processing in a computer counseling system that attempts to model primarily traditional motivational and affective systems of psychotherapy or primarily recent cognitive and problem solving systems would appear to have differentiable characteristics. The pertinent characteristics will next be examined.

Knowledge Processing and Traditional Psychotherapy

There are two levels of demand that could be made upon a computer counseling system with respect to processing knowledge about its own behavior and that of the client. At level one, the computer would possess a general model of its own reasoning that included a specific model of the client's neurotic personality that would adjust to the changes taking place during the course of psychotherapy. At level two, the computer would not be guided by models of itself reasoning as a therapist about its conceptual model of the client's neurotic personality dynamics. Instead, knowledge processing in the computer counselor would focus on techniques of counseling (e.g., pointing out feelings, presenting clarifications, offering interpretations of comparison or contrast). The distinction between the two levels is the difference between theory and technique. A level one computer counselor possesses a theory of its own reasoning that includes a representation of the client's personality structure and dynamics and applies techniques as tactics within the overall structure of its model of its therapeutic domain. For a level two computer counselor, techniques are applied in the absence of the computer counselor's possession of models of its therapeutic domain and the effects of the techniques are processed largely by the client's models of therapy and personality problem domains.

A level one computer counseling system with a conceptual model of its therapeutic domain bears a closer relationship to the knowledge processing of the traditional human psychotherapist than does a level two computer counseling system. However, a level one system requires more complex knowledge representation and processing capability. The requirements are for individualized models of initial and changing status of clients' problems during the course of psychotherapy and the relationship of these models to the timing, quality and quantity of therapeutic techniques and methods. Moreover, these general models are not sufficient, but must be supplemented by control mechanisms that continuously monitor the nature of the therapeutic situation at any given time.

Researchers in artificial intelligence interested in the development of a level one computer counseling system may find useful the concepts and methods of computer psychometry (see Chapter Seven) for developing models of therapy, client personality dynamics and structure, and the concepts of the SHRDLU (see Chapter Five) and PLANNER language (see Chapter Six), MYCIN and WHY systems (see Chapter Seven) for models of reasoning, and the monitoring concepts of the Neurotic Program (see Chapter Eight) for control mechanisms in the therapeutic domain.

Knowledge Processing and Cognitive Psychotherapy

In general, cognitive psychotherapies construe clients' problems (e.g., avoidance-avoidance dilemmas, depression) as largely a consequence of inappropriate patterns of thought, inadequate problem-solving competencies and deficient coping styles. This information processing problem-solving oriented conception is quite different from traditional psychotherapy and personality conceptions as discussed above. Theories in cognitive psychotherapy (Eysenck, 1982; Mahoney, 1980) represent not so much historically conditioned models of personality dynamics and structure, but models of current thinking and reasoning about personal situations (Wagman, 1979, 1984a). The theoretical stance of cognitive psychotherapies frequently results in a technique dominated and didactic approach.

Level two computer counseling systems are likely to be especially suitable for cognitive psychotherapy approaches. Techniques that diagnose faulty assumptions, thinking and problem solving methods and that prescribe effective information processing methods can be represented as computer routines and algorithmic procedures (e.g., PLATO DCS, MORTON).

Researchers in artificial intelligence interested in developing cognitive computer counseling systems may find useful the concepts and methods of the WHY system (see Chapter Seven) for problems of individualizing the teaching of reasoning and problem solving strategies.

Researchers are likely to find the PLATO DCS System (see Chapters Ten-Twelve) and the MORTON System (see Chapter Nine) valuable as models of level two computer counseling systems.

Summary

In this chapter, fundamental approaches and problems in the design of computer counseling systems were discussed. General concepts of computer counseling were examined with respect to the major functions of knowledge input and knowledge processing.

It was indicated that computer counseling systems constitute an integration of concepts from the fields of artificial intelligence and psychotherapy. Constraints on the development of computer counseling systems that result from characteristics and limitations of the fields of artificial intelligence and psychotherapy were considered.

In examining approaches to the design of computer counseling systems, consideration was given to several types (expert, consultative, tutorial) and examples (DENDRAL, MACSYMA, MYCIN, computer psychometry and WHY) of artificial intelligence systems. It was indicated that the domain of the knowledge input (psychological beliefs) to be comprehended by the computer counselor is more extensive and less exact than the knowledge input accommodated by artificial intelligence systems. The constraints exercised by artificial intelligence research include the need for an extensive library of computer counselor programs dedicated to circumscribed psychological problems, the recognition that the system is a specialist or expert (rather than a generalist) in the counseling of only certain specified psychological problems and the application of the knowledge of human professional counselors in the referal of clients to computer counseling systems.

It was suggested that the most general constraint exercised by the nature of psychotherapy concepts on approaches to the design of computer counseling systems is that theories of psychotherapy lack the rigor of theories in science that have been embodied in artificial intelligence systems. Unresolved problems concerned with the determinants of psychotherapeutic change were discussed and examples of theoretical confusion in planned short term therapy were cited.

It was indicated that, with respect to knowledge input and knowledge processing, the content of theories of computer counseling consists of psychological beliefs that are concerned with personal and interpersonal situations and that are idiosyncratic compounds of cognitive, affective and motivational aspects of individual personality. Recently developed cognitive information processing models of personality were contrasted with traditional motivational and affective theories and implications for approaches to the design of computer counseling systems were discussed. The issue of predominant direction of causation between cognition and affect was considered.

It was indicated that there are two conceptual levels that distinguish computer counselors with respect to processing knowledge about their own behavior and that of clients. A level one computer counselor possesses a model of its own reasoning that includes a representation of the client's personality dynamics and structure and employs techniques as tactics within the overall theoretical structure of its therapeutic domain. A level two computer counselor is not guided by models of itself reasoning as a psychotherapist, but, instead, focuses on techniques of counseling. It was indicated that the distinction between the two levels is the difference between theory and technique. The relationship between level one computer counseling systems and traditional psychotherapy and the relationship between level two (PLATO DCS, MORTON) computer counseling systems and recent cognitive information processing psychotherapy was discussed and brief suggestions concerning the direction of artificial intelligence research for the two levels were presented.

Time lines

At a theoretical level, advances in computer counseling have paralleled advances in artificial intelligence and psychotherapy in that the development of each field has been marked by increased specificity and precision in problem-solving methods. The time lines presented in the following table comprise a concise longitudinal description of the major advances in each field.

TABLE 13.1. Time lines for advances in the specificity of problem-solving in aritficial intelligence, psychotherapy and computer counseling

Artificial Intelligence		Psychotherapy		Computer Counseling	
1936–1964	classical artificial intelligence, directed toward the totality of human cognition	1885–1951	classical period of psychotherapy, characterized by treatment directed toward the total personality	1965–1978	classical period of computer counseling characterized by the attempt to model the counselor or psychotherapist
1936	development of the abstact mathematical theory of the digital computer	1885	development of the theory of repression and abreaction of unconscious emotions	1965	the DOCTOR program, employed the ELIZA natural language understanding system to model a client-centered psychotherapist
1946	first functioning general electronic computer	1905	development of the theory of psycho-sexual fixations and their relationship to psychoneuroses	1966	computer interview program, attempted to use natural language communication in modeling the initial session of pscyhoanalytic psychotherapy
1956	development of the Logic Theorist, a computer program that proved various theorems of Principia Mathematica	1921	development of the theory of personality structure and dynamics (ego, super-ego, id)		
1958	development of the General Problem Solver, a program that attempted the emulation of general human mental ability	1939	development of the theory of mechanisms of defense		
		1945	theoretical integration of topographic, dynamic and economic components of psychoanalysis		

TABLE 13.1. (Cont.)

Artificial Intelligence	Psychotherapy	Computer Counseling
1964–present modern artificial intelligence, characterized by expert systems directed toward specific knowledge domains and designed to perform at a professional level	1951–present modern period of psychotherapy characterized by treatment directed toward specific sectors of the personality and the development of specific problem-solving methods	1978–present modern period of computer counseling, characterized by the attempt to model the techniques of counseling or psychotherapy, emphasis on problem-solving methods
1964 molecular analysis in chemistry (the DENDRAL program)	1951 psychoanalytically-oriented pscychotherapy	1978 PLATO Dilemma Counseling System (PLATO DCS), an expert system that provides counseling and solutions for difficult avoidance-avoidance personal problems and teaches a method of problem-solving for psychological dilemmas
1974 psychiatric diagnosis (the DIAGNO program)	1951 client-centered psychotherapy	
1976 prescription of pharmaceutical therapy for infectious diseases (the MYCIN program)	1969 behavior therapy	
	1970 cognitive therapy	
	1979 systematic dilemma counseling	1982 MORTON, a computer program for the treatment of mild depression, employing psycho-educational methods

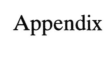
Appendix

A Factor Analytic Study of the Psychological Implications of the Computer for the Individual and Society

The consequences of the expansion of computer presence had led Simon (1977) to refer to the changes in society due to the introduction of computers as "the information revolution" (p. 1,186). Others (Abelson & Hammond, 1977; Davis, 1977) refer to the "information revolution" as comparable to the earlier Industrial Revolution. The impact of computers upon society has been extensive. The increasing presence of the computer and of electronics has also led to debates and disputes, sometimes extremely vociferous.

The impact of the computer upon man and upon various sectors of society has caused some to rejoice (see Sagan, 1977) and some to advise caution (see Weizenbaum, 1976). In general, there is agreement that the introduction of electronics and computers into society has had and will have many consequences. Simon (1977) sees four major areas in which the consequences will be felt: "First, there are the economic consequences that follow an innovation that increases human productivity.... Second, there are consequences for the nature of work and leisure —for the quality of life. Third, the computer may have special consequences for privacy and individual liberty. Fourth, there are consequences for man's view of himself, for his picture of the universe and of his place and goals in it" (Simon, 1977, p. 1,189).

This research was supported by a grant from the University of Illinois Graduate College Research Board. The author wishes to acknowledge the assistance of Patricia Cavanee and William Ross in collecting and analyzing the experimental data.

Reactions to computers have spawned a vast literature that argues both for and against their presence and usage. The general points made in each specific context are often repeated in numerous other contexts. In each context, the debate is between those in favor of computers and those against their introduction into that specific sector. In any sector, there is the question of the nature of the computer, and the consequences of its presence.

In general terms, those who are against the introduction of the computer decry its dehumanizing effects. Often they point to the limits and boundaries of its applicability. Weizenbaum (1976) points to the necessity of recognizing its limitations.

In an earlier study (Wagman, 1976), the general literature concerned with the impact of the computer on man and society was analyzed concisely in each of 10 sectors of society. In each sector, the contrasting viewpoints of behavioral and social scientists advocating or criticizing the use of computers in that sector were analyzed with respect to their major differences. Analyses of these major issues were presented for the following sectors: computer and (1) society, (2) values, (3) cognition, (4) education, (5) medicine, (6) counseling, (7) mathematics, (8) banking, (9) politics, and (10) the criminal justice system. Thus, in the earlier study (Wagman, 1976), an attempt was made to clarify and reduce the general literature by a summary analysis of contending viewpoints within specific sectors.

In the present article, a further clarification and reduction is achieved by representing, insofar as feasible, the specific contending viewpoints as sets of attitude scale items, each set representing advocacy or criticism of the use of computers in a specific sector of society.

Method

Subjects

63 male and 58 female undergraduate students at the University of Illinois served as subjects in connection with course requirements.

Materials

The Cybernetics Attitude Scale (Wagman, 1977) comprises 100 items, ten items on each of ten subscales. Each subscale is designed to measure attitudes toward computers in a specific sector of society. A subscale is composed of five statements representing positive attitudes toward computers. For each of these five statements, there is a converse statement that expresses a negative attitude toward computers. The complete Cybernetics Attitude Scale is arranged to depict groupings of items under each of the subscales (see Table A1). (As administered to subjects, items are not grouped with respect to subscales.)

Responses are scored on a 7-point Likert scale (1 = strongly agree with the favorable items; 1 = strongly disagree with the converse items). A high score represents negative attitudes toward computers; a low score represents positive attitudes.

Procedure

The Cybernetics Attitude Scale was administered to subjects in groups of 20 or 30. The subjects were allowed up to one hour to complete the scale. Responses were coded and anonymous. Following completion of the study, the subjects were fully debriefed.

Results

Descriptive Statistics

Means and standard deviations were computed for the total scale score and for each of the ten subscale total scores. These statistics were computed for the total sample and for men and women separately. Analyses were performed on the CYBER 170 at the University of Illinois at Urbana-Champaign. The FREQUENCIES program of the Statistical Package for the Social Sciences (Nie, Hull, Jenkins, Steinbreener, & Bent, 1975) was employed.

The mean (M) and the standard deviation (SD) for all subjects (N = 121) on the total Cybernetics Attitude Scale (100 items) were 404.36 and 56.80, respectively. The mean and standard deviation for each subscale (10 items) of the Cybernetics Attitude Scale, ranked in order from most favorable attitudes toward computer applications for that sector of society to least favorable attitudes, were: criminal justice system (M = 32.66, SD = 7.32), mathematics and statistics (M = 34.31, SD = 7.83), politics (M = 34.36, SD = 7.35), society (M = 35.60, SD = 9.18), finance and banking (M = 35.86, SD = 7.56), cognition (M = 42.72, SD = 8.78), values (M = 44.05, SD =

TABLE A1. The Cybernetics Attitude Scale (100 items)

Statements	Converse

Society

1. The complexity of the problems of modern society require computers for their solutions. (69)
2. There is really no reason to fear computers. (39)
3. Computers increase human freedom and allow us to become more human. (72)
4. Compared with the industrial revolution, the computer is less threatening to society. (47)
5. What is threatening to society is not the computer, but people's use of the computer. (77)

6. Computers increase the complexity of modern life. (60)
7. Computers are justifiably feared. (94)
8. Computers are beginning to make us less human. (37)
9. The widespread use of computers in society theatens civilization more than any other innovation. (81)
10. The most threatening thing about computers is their very existence. (98)

Values

1. It is good that computers do only what they are programmed to do. (61)
2. It is not important that computers do not exercise discretionary judgment over the purpose that may have been intended. (78)
3. The dependability that a computer provides is more important than the human flexibility that is lost. (86)
4. It does not matter that computers cannot reflect upon the meaning of their personal experience. (53)
5. Computers can never change the value of being human. (95)

6. It would be nice if computers didn't always do only what they are programmed to do. (21)
7. Even computers should use discretionary judgment in solving social problems. (38)
8. A computer cannot replace man's flexibility in solving problems. (13)
9. The ability to reflect upon personal experience separates man from computers. (26)
10. The more we use computers the more we will devalue people's worth. (87)

Cognition

1. Computers are valuable because they save people from mental drudgery. (23)
2. Just because people use a computer for arithmetic problems does not mean that people will forget how to do arithmetic problems. (65)
3. It is a good idea to use computers to teach concepts to grade school children. (1)
4. People's mental abilities are actually increased by interacting with the computer. (99)
5. No matter how much society uses computers, the mental capacity of society will remain as good as ever. (17)

6. People have begun to rely too heavily upon computers. (31)
7. If people do all of their math problems on a computer, people will forget how to do these problems by hand. (5)
8. Learning concepts on the computer sacrifices children's grasp of the meaning of these concepts. (63)
9. A computer simply cannot increase a person's mental abilities. (71)
10. If society uses computers too often and too much, the mental capacity of society will begin to decrease. (89)

TABLE A1. *(Cont.)*

Statements	Converse

Counseling

1. I would feel more at ease solving a personal problem with a computer than with a counselor. (45)
2. I would feel more independent solving a personal problem on a computer than with a counselor. (55)
3. I think a computer could have more information to help me solve my problems than a counselor could have. (6)
4. Compared with a counselor, a computer would be more patient and reliable in helping to solve a personal problem. (41)
5. As compared with a counselor, a computer could generate a greater number of solutions to my personal problems. (80)

6. I would rather talk to a counselor than try to solve my personal problems with a computer. (40)
7. I would feel more in control discussing my problems with a counselor than with a computer. (18)
8. A counselor could know me better than a computer ever could. (44)
9. Too many things could go wrong with a computer that couldn't go wrong with a counselor as I try to solve my personal problems. (22)
10. A counselor could help me more than a computer could with my personal problems because a counselor would have more experience with my type of problem. (9)

Education

1. I would feel more at ease learning from a computer than from a teacher. (59)
2. I would feel more independent learning from a computer than learning from a teacher. (100)
3. I would like learning with a computer because I can work at my own pace. (97)
4. I would like learning from a computer because I wouldn't feel embarrassed when I didn't know the answer. (35)
5. I would like working with a computer because it doesn't play favorites as a teacher might. (8)

6. I would rather learn from a teacher than from a computer. (82)
7. A computer can never match the human contact a teacher provides. (20)
8. A computer structures the learning situation too much. (88)
9. I would not like to feel that a computer is smarter than I am. (91)
10. Learning from a computer would be a cold and impersonal experience. (56)

TABLE A1. *(Cont.)*

Statements	Converse

Medicine

1. I would be more at ease answering health questions from a computer than from a doctor. (68)
2. I could be more frank and open when answering a computer's health questions than questions from a doctor. (10)
3. I feel that a computer health survey would be more systematic than a health survey taken by a doctor. (49)
4. I think that personal answers to a computer health survey would be kept in stricter confidence than answers to a doctor's survey. (14)
5. In medical diagnosis, I believe that computers are faster and more accurate than a doctor. (4)

6. I would be more comfortable talking to a doctor than to a computer about my health problems. (3)
7. I would be more honest when answering questions about my health from a doctor than from a computer. (42)
8. A doctor would be less likely to miss important facts about my health than would a computer. (96)
9. I could not be sure who would see my answers to a computer health survey. (46)
10. A computer can never replace the experience and intuition of a good doctor. (62)

Politics

1. I think it is valuable to have computers to forecast the outcomes of elections. (25)
2. When computers report the outcomes of elections, the democratic process is made more effective. (74)
3. I have more confidence when votes are counted by a computer than when they are counted by an election official. (34)
4. When a computer keeps records of contributions to politicians, elections are made fairer. (52)
5. When a computer, instantaneously reports public opinion, both citizens and government benefit. (50)

6. Forecasting the outcomes of elections by computers interferes with the election process. (27)
7. When computers report the outcomes of elections instantaneously, the possibility of naming the wrong person as a winner increases. (2)
8. An election official would be less likely to make a mistake in counting ballots than a computer would. (11)
9. Keeping a computer accounting of political contributions does not deter illegal contributions. (75)
10. Reporting public opinion by computer may interfere with the functioning of the government. (54)

TABLE A1. *(Cont.)*

Statements	Converse

Criminal Justice System

1. I think it is desirable to have information about criminals stored in computers. (12)
2. The use of computers in keeping crime statistics benefits the public. (15)
3. I feel safer knowing the police can use the computer's high speed and extensive memory to help in the apprehension of criminals. (51)
4. I do not think my freedom is reduced by the widespread use of computers in the justice system. (64)
5. There is really no way in which innocent citizens can be harmed by the wide use of computers in the justice system. (76)

6. I don't think computers have a place in the justice system. (85)
7. The crime statistics kept on computers are too misleading to be much good. (36)
8. The use of the speed and memory of computers to help apprehend criminals does not really help to deter crime. (90)
9. The widespread use of computers in the justice system violates my rights. (70)
10. It is too easy to make a mistake and harm an innocent person when computers are used in the justice system. (67)

Finance and Banking

1. As compared with people, computers are more accurate in keeping records of personal financial transactions. (57)
2. Credit and other financial transactions are faster when done through a computer than when done through people. (32)
3. Personal credit information can be kept just as private and confidential on computers as through any other medium. (24)
4. I do not think that personal credit information stored in computers will interfere with my rights to privacy. (83)
5. The danger of theft of personal funds is not increased by the use of computers in banking and credit operations. (92)

6. Computers can never match the accuracy of trained people in keeping records of financial transactions. (66)
7. There are more important things to consider about financial transactions than the speed a computer can give. (16)
8. The use of computers to record personal credit information increases the possibility of other people getting hold of personal information about me. (29)
9. My rights are more easily violated when computers store personal credit information about me. (33)
10. Theft of personal funds has greatly increased since computers were introduced into credit and banking operations. (7)

Table A1. *(Cont.)*

Statements	Converse

Mathematics and Statistics

1. The computer's lightening swift calculating ability and nearly infinite memory are entirely desirable. (19)
2. It would be desirable to learn statistics from a computer because most statistics are calculated on computers. (30)
3. It is better to solve math or statistics problems by computer than by hand. (73)
4. I would have more trust in statistics processed by a computer than by hand. (93)
5. I would feel more comfortable doing math or statistics by computer than by hand. (79)

6. Inaccuracy is often the price paid for the speed and memory of a computer. (48)
7. Statistics should be learned and understood before a computer is used for their calculation. (58)
8. Solving statistics or math problems by hand is often better than using the computer to solve these problems. (84)
9. I would use more caution in using computer-calculated statistics than hand-calculated statistics. (43)
10. All in all, I would prefer to do math or statistics myself than use a computer. (28)

6.80), medicine (M = 45.73, SD = 7.20), education (M = 47.05, SD = 9.23), counseling (M = 51.84, SD = 8.74).

Five subscales — society, values, cognition, education, and criminal justice-yielded significant differences between men and women. For each of these subscales, men had more favorable attitudes toward computer applications in that sector of society. Specific attitude scale scores were: (1) for the society subscale, men (M = 33.11, SD = 8.61), women (M = 38.31, SD = 9.04) (p<.01); (2) for the values subscale, men (M = 42.40, SD = 6.50), women (M = 45.85, SD = 6.71) (p<.01); (3) for the cognition subscale, men (M = 40.98, SD = 8.34), women (M = 44.60, SD = 8.93) (p<.05); (4) for the education subscale, men (M = 45.03, SD = 9.38), women (M = 49.24, SD = 8.61) (p<.05); and (5) for the criminal justice system subscale, men (M = 31.25, SD = 7.02), women (M = 34.19, SD = 7.40) (p<.05). The total scale scores were also different across sex: The mean equaled 392.52 (SD = 53.62) for men versus 417.22 (SD = 57.79) for women (p<.05).

Before one concludes that each of the subscales is truly different across sex, one must consider the correlations between the subscales. If the subscales are highly related, then the t tests might be measuring the same variance several times.

The correlations between subscales ranged between .23 for criminal justice and counseling to .67 for society and values. The average correlation was .45. Most correlations were above .40.

Principal-Components Analysis

To further test for the independence of the subscales, two principal-components analyses were conducted on the subscale total scores. SPSS was again used. The first analysis revealed three factors.

Factor 1 had high loadings on two subscales: values (loading = .79) and cognition (loading = .82). Society and education also had highest loadings on Factor 1 compared with loadings on other factors. Society had a loading of .76 on Factor 1 and a loading of .35 on Factor 2. Education loaded .70 on Factor 1 and .44 on Factor 3.

Factor 2 included the politics subscale (with a loading of .76). Criminal justice and finance also had their highest loadings on Factor 2. Criminal justice loaded .34 on Factor 1 and .74 on Factor 2; finance loaded .79 on Factor 2 and .35 on Factor 3.

Medicine loaded .81 on Factor 3. The counseling and mathematics subscales had split loadings: Counseling loaded .84 on Factor 3 and .34 on Factor 1. Mathematics loaded .57 on Factor 1, .37 on Factor 2, and .33 on Factor 3. The criterion used for identifying a subscale with a particular factor was a loading above .4 on that factor and loadings below .3 on all other factors. The subscales that showed sex differences also tended to have high loadings on Factor 1. The only exception was criminal justice.

The second principal-components analysis included sex as a variable. Sex had a loading of .85 on Factor 3. So the third factor in this analysis was virtually identical to the sex variable. This analysis had the effect of separating the variance shared by the society, values, cognition, and education subscales into two parts; (1) variance shared by those variables, and also shared with the sex variable; and (2) variance shared by those variables due to reasons other than the sex variable (such as content similarity). All of the subscales of interest (except for criminal justice) still had moderate factor loadings on Factor 1. But they also showed high loadings on the sex factor (Factor 3). These results suggest that some of the sex differences found by the t tests were reflecting common variance.

Differences Between Subscales

Dependent t tests were computed (using SPSS) within the three samples. Each of these revealed that most of the subscale means were significantly different from one another. These subscales did not appear to group together on the basis of the principal-components analysis.

For the total sample, the t values ranged in absolute magnitude from .33 for society versus finance (not statistically significant) to 20.05 for counseling versus mathematics (p<.001). For men, the absolute values range from .18 for the t test comparing subscales medicine and education (not significant) to 17.25 for counseling versus criminal justice (p<.001). For women, the lowest t value in absolute magnitude occurred between the pair finance and mathematics (t = .08, n.s.). The largest absolute t value was 13.42, between education and criminal justice (p<.001).

Factor Analysis

A factor analysis was conducted on the 100 items constituting the Cybernetics Attitude Scale. Oblique rotation using DAPPFER (hyperplane fitting — Tucker, 1980) and parallel analysis (Humphreys & Montinelli, 1975) suggested the presence of five major factors. The same criterion for identifying an item with a factor was used with this analysis that had been used with the principal-components analysis. Recall that this criterion was a factor loading above .4 on one factor and loadings below .3 on all other factors. The factor analysis revealed 32 items with loadings on only one factor. These items, their factor loadings, and the subscales for which they were written are presented below.

Factor 1. The first factor was a general dimension. Computers were seen as servants of man. Four of the five items are from the values and society subscales. The fifth item (with the lowest loading) was a general mathematics item.

For Factor 1, items, subscales, and factor loadings were: "The more we use computers the more we will devalue people's worth" (values, .70); "Computers increase human freedom and allow us to become more human" (society, .64); "Compared with the industrial revolution, the computer is less threatening to society" (society, .56); "Computers can never change the value of being human" (values, .49); "I would feel more comfortable doing math or statistics by computer than by hand" (mathematics and statistics, .45).

Factor 2. The second factor had three items. This factor contains items from values and counseling subscales. It appears to emphasize the difference between computers and humans.

For Factor 2, items, subscales, and factor loadings were: "The ability to reflect upon personal experience separates man from computer" (values, .60); "Too many things could go wrong with a computer that couldn't go wrong with a counselor as I try to solve my personal problems" (counseling, .44); "I would feel more at ease solving a personal problem with a computer than with a counselor" (counseling, .43).

Factor 3. Two areas contributed items to the third factor: (1) items based on affective reactions, and (2) items dealing with health (mental and physical) and education. The affective items often use phrases such as "I would feel more *at ease* learning from a computer than from a teacher," and "I would like learning from a computer because I wouldn't feel embarrassed when I didn't know the answer." Items also appear to be similar in content. This factor consisted totally of items from the counseling, education and medicine subscales.

For Factor 3, items, subscales, and factor loadings were: "I would like learning with a computer because I can work at my own pace" (education, .62); "I would be more at ease answering health questions from a computer than from a doctor" (medicine, .60); "Compared with a counselor, a computer would be more patient and reliable in helping to solve a personal problem" (counseling, .57); "I would feel more in control discussing my problems with a counselor than with a computer" (counseling, .55); "I would like learning from a computer because I wouldn't feel embarrassed when I didn't know the answer" (education, .53); "I would feel more independent solving a personal problem on a computer than with a counselor" (counseling, .51); "As compared with a counselor, a computer could generate a greater number of solutions to my personal problems" (counseling, .48); "I think a computer could have more information to help me solve my problems than a counselor could have" (counseling, .46); "I would be more comfortable talking to a doctor than to a computer about my health problems" (medicine, .41); "I would like working with a computer because it doesn't play favorites as a teacher might" (education, .41).

Factor 4. The accuracy of computers is reflected in the fourth factor. Although items come from subscales as diverse as finance, politics, and mathematics, all deal with the speed and accuracy computers offer.

For Factor 4, items, subscales, and factor loadings were: "Computers can never match the accuracy of trained people in keeping records of financial transactions" (finance and banking, .61); "I would have more trust in statistics processed by a computer than by hand" (mathematics and statistics, .61); "I have more confidence when votes are counted by a computer than when they are counted by an election official" (politics, .52); "Inaccuracy is often the price paid for the speed and memory of a computer" (mathematics and statistics, .52); "When computers report the outcomes of elections instantaneously, the possibility of naming the wrong person as a winner increases" (politics, .42); "I would use more caution in using computer-calculated statistics than hand-calculated statistics" (mathematics and statistics, .41).

Factor 5. The fifth factor might be considered a "memory" factor. Four of the eight items pertain to the ability of a computer to store large quantities of information. However, computer memory is not all that is reflected in Factor 5. The use of computers to benefit society could also be found in almost all of the items. This is also shown in the fact that six of the items came from the criminal justice and politics subscales.

For Factor 5, items, subscales, and factor loadings were: "I feel safer knowing the police can use the computer's high speed and extensive memory to help in the apprehension of criminals" (criminal justice, .63); "The use of computers in keeping crime statistics benefits the public" (criminal justice, .56); "When a computer instantaneously reports public opinions, both citizens and government benefit" (politics, .55); "I do not think that personal credit information stored in computers will interfere with my rights to privacy" (banking and finance, .51); "I think it is valuable to have computers forecast the outcomes of elections" (politics, .47); "Forecasting the outcomes of elections by computers interferes with the election process" (politics, .47); "I think it is desirable to have information about criminals stored in computers" (criminal justice, .46); "A computer simply can not increase a person's mental abilities" (cognition, .42).

Discussion

The data can be used to examine the question of whether, among the ten sectors of society, there exist generally differentiable rankings of advocacy or criticism of the use of computers. It appears from the data that there is advocacy for the use of computers in such sectors as the criminal justice system and mathematics and statistics, and criticism of the use of computers in such sectors as counseling and medicine. There are a number of possible explanations of these differences: There is a historical hypothesis, there is a sociological hypothesis, and, finally, there is a psychological hypothesis.

With respect to the historical hypothesis (Goldstine, 1972; Randall, 1979), the development of the analog computer and the subsequent development of the modern digital computer had as their goal the execution of complex mathematical and statistical analyses that, without the aid of computers, would be exceedingly difficult or impossible. Begun during World War II and, because of their expense, initially restricted to only a few scientific, university, and government settings, digital computer applications in mathematics, science, and statistics have become highly prevalent and, indeed, indispensable. Thus, in the mathematics and statistics sector of society, computers have the longest history and represent a functional use that is equivalent to their definition, that is, a computing function. This computing function was early extended beyond scientific systems to social and government systems such as the criminal justice system and to business organizations such as financial and banking systems, in each of which there is a continuity of the historical use for statistical and data-processing purposes. On the other hand, the uses of computers in psychiatry and psychology, and especially in the areas of counseling and medical diagnosis, depart from the historic purpose of computers (numerical analysis) and represent much more recent applications and, by comparison, are probably still pioneering efforts.

A sociological hypothesis for the slow acceptance of or, indeed, resistance to the use of computers in medical history taking and diagnosis, psychiatry, and counseling might include the concept of cultural lag (Ogburn, 1922), which states that the symbolic acceptance of technological innovation requires a time delay for the overcoming of the strain induced in customary behavior patterns in a particular cultural enterprise. Related sociological hypotheses are those of vested interest and social evolution (Parsons & Smelser, 1956). As pointed out by Parsons and Smelser (1956, pp. 246-249), a vested interest within a social system may require the rejection of innovative threats to its customary behavior patterns by institutionalized rationalizations (Parsons, 1951, pp. 505–520).

A psychological hypothesis is the threat computers offer in the fields of medical diagnosis (Bleich, 1979; Card, Nicholson, & Crean, 1974; Grossman, Barnett, McGuire, & Swedlow, 1979), psychiatry (Erdman, Greist, Klein, Jefferson, & Getto, 1981; Lucas, Mullin, Luna, & McInroy, 1977), psychotherapy (Colby, 1980; Greist, 1980; Slack & Slack, 1977), and counseling (Harris, 1974; Wagman, 1980a, 1982a, 1984a,b; Wagman & Kerber, 1980, 1984). The threat is to professionals' pride in possessing unique intellectual and judgmental abilities (Blois, 1980; McDonald, 1976). This psychological hypothesis of injury to professional pride has been offered as a more general explanation of the initial resistance to the Copernican heliocentric theory, the Darwinian evolutionary theory of the descent of man, and the Freudian psychodynamic theory of unconscious determination of behavior, which initially were considered to be insults to mankind's unique dignity and significance.

The results of the factor analysis indicate clusters of attitudes that cut across several subscales or sectors of society. One such cluster is Factor 3, which represents similarity of attitudes toward computers in the medicine, education, and counseling sectors. This cluster appears to represent affective reactions toward the use of the computer in traditional professional roles, such as those of physician, teacher, psychologist, and psychiatrist. This clustering of items represents highly personal and ego-involved reactions.

Whereas Factor 3 cut across the education, medicine, and counseling sectors, Factor 5 represents a cluster of attitudes that cut across the criminal justice system and the politics sectors. It would appear that attitudes toward the use of computers in these sectors of society reflect storage and retrieval functions in which the computer's memory is used for the benefit of society. However, as may be seen from the converse items of the Cybernetics Attitude Scale (Table A1) for these sectors, these positive uses may imply possible deleterious uses that result in intrusion into privacy and threats to personal freedom in these sectors of society.

In Factor 4, there is a cluster of attitudes that cut across the mathematics and statistics and the finance and banking sectors. Common to this attitude cluster is the recognition of the fundamental hallmarks of the computer, namely, its speed and accuracy in data processing. This efficiency cluster represents the power of the computer's contributions to mathematical, scientific, and engineering applications.

In contrast to Factors 4 and 5, which seem to refer to the specific technical uses of the computer, such as its speed, accuracy, and memory, Factors 1 and 2 search out the meanings of these technical functions of the computer with respect to values and society in general. These factors seem to reflect the concern that, somehow, the intelligent functions of the computer threaten an eventual possible control, in an undesirable direction, of the human social system, or, at least, a diminution in the uniqueness of those higher cognitive processes by which the humanistic and scientific disciplines have been advanced. It is of interest that scholars in the humanities are beginning to relate themselves to the computer in such a way that its mere technical functions become an adjunct to the scholar's inquiry and judgment. Contemporary examples might include proving the authorship of poems, plays, or religious tracts by identifying common elementary features present in a set of written productions, tracing etymological changes in classical languages over several centuries (Dilligan, 1982) and computer-aided investigations by art historians and conservators into the restoration of paintings by old masters (Cherlin, 1982).

Glossary

affective psychotherapeutic relationship: a psychotherapeutic relationship characterized by emotional interpersonal relationship between therapist and client (see transferance and also countertransference).

agoraphobia: a fear of open places frequently extending to relative or absolute inability to leave one's residence.

algorithms: logical and mathematical formulas that regulate automatic information processing in computer programs.

analysand: the technical term for the patient in the psychoanalytic interview.

analytically-oriented psychotherapy: an abbreviated form of classical psychoanalysis that while guided by psychoanalytic theory may employ eclectic techniques in the interest of reducing the duration of treatment.

anxiety neurosis: a psychological problem characterized by chronic pervasive anxiety, usually without clear knowledge of the impulses that provoke the anxiety.

aphasia: a relative or absolute inability to speak or to perform some other act of communication.

artificial intelligence: a division of computer science concerned with developing the capacity in machines to perform tasks which if performed by human beings would require intelligence.

automata: self-governing systems, typically of a mechanical or electronic nature that perform tasks (e.g., clocks) or execute control and command functions (e.g., computers).

avoidance-avoidance situation: this is the dilemma situation characterized by the necessity to choose between two unpleasant alternatives.

behavior therapy: a set of variagated techniques designed to modify a broad range of maladaptive behavior in children and adults.

Boolean alegebra: a type of symbolic logic in which propositions have only two values (true or false) and mathematical operations are conducted in the binary system of numbers. In computers, the logic of binary numbers controls the physical logic and operations of differences in voltage.

case endings: a syntactical term that refers to the modification of the ends of words as a function of their belonging to a particular grammatical case (e.g., computer in the nominative case is modified to computer's in the genitive case).

cathexis: in psychoanalytic theory, the strength of an emotional attitude directed toward a person or object. Cathexes may be of a positive, negative or ambivalent nature.

client-centered psychotherapy: a system of psychotherapy in which the therapist's activity is non-directive and focused on the affective components of the client's communication.

client-centered system: see DOCTOR program.

CLIENT—1: a program that models a client's psychological problems and that responds to the inputs of a counselor attempting to treat it.

cognitive behavior system: see MORTON program.

cognitive psychotherapeutic relationship: a psychotherapeutic relationship characterized by didactic orientation and content (e.g., therapist teaching client more effective ways of thinking about problem situations).

cognitive therapy: a system of psychotherapy that applies a range of techniques to change problem-producing patterns of thinking.

computer adaptive system: an expert system which, depending on the quality of the previous response, branches to one of a particular set of interview or test questions.

computer counseling: an expert system that provides counseling or psychotherapy services.

computer counselor: see computer counseling.

computer interview system: an expert system that interviews psychiatric patients regarding their symptoms and problems.

computer modeling: the representation of real world problems and possible solutions in the form of computer programs that can symbolically operate on the data of problems and solutions.

computer program: the symbolic data and procedures in a computer that control its physical operations.

computer psychodiagnostic system: an expert system that deterimines the psychological or psychiatric status of a person with respect to a diagnostic system of classification.

computer psychometry system: an expert system that performs some of the diagnostic and assessment functions of a professional psychologist or psychiatrist.

computer psychotherapist: see computer counseling.

computer report writing system: an expert system that produces a narrative report of its psychodiagnostic findings.

computer simulation: see computer modeling.

computer testing system: an expert system that administers intelligence, personality and other tests.

conceptual dependency theory: a theory that language and thought can be reduced to a few basic or primitive concepts. The theory is used in research with translation systems and with story understanding systems.

conflict resolution: a set of procedures that determines temporal priorities for the sequence of operations in a production system.

consultative systems: expert systems that provide advice and recommendations to professionals regarding solutions to problems (e.g., recommend type of anti-biotic treatment that minimizes undesired side effects).

countertransference: innappropriate (positive or negative) attitudes or behaviors on the part of the psychoanalyst (or psychotherapist) toward the patient (or client).

cybernetics: the science of command and control by machines and, more narrowly, control processes based on information feedback such as thermostat control of a furnace based on feedback of temperature information.

declarative representation: knowledge that is represented in a computer by data structures as opposed to knowledge that is represented by procedures (see procedural representation).

default reasoning: a type of reasoning in which it is assumed that, in the absence of other information, the usual or typical conditions hold.

DENDRAL system: an expert system used in complex chemical analyses.

derivation tree: a hierarchical arrangement of nodes and links in a semantic net in which lower branches on the tree derive their knowledge from higher branches (e.g., from the root psychopathology to the branches, neroses, psychoses, and from neuroses to the branches obsession, compulsion, hysteria, phobia).

diffuse psychological problem: a psychological problem with far-reaching effects (e.g., generalized anxiety and dependency manifested in multiple situations).

digital computer: a computer based on symbolic logic in contrast to an analog computer based on physical operations.

dilemma: a conflict characterized by the necessity to choose between two unpleasant alternatives.

dilemma component: in the theory of systematic dilemma counseling, any psychological dilemma can be subdivided into five components, each of which constitutes a part of the confronting problem.

dilemma counseling: see systematic dilemma counseling.

dilemma counseling component: see PLATO DCS system.

dilemma formulation: in the PLATO DCS system, a set of standard procedures for recasting a personal problem into correct dilemma form.

DOCTOR program: a computer program that takes the role of a client-centered psychotherapist.

ELIZA system: a natural language understanding system based on pattern recognition that included the DOCTOR script that simulates a client-centered psychotherapist.

empathic response: a response of the psychotherapist characterized by emotional sharing and grasp of the client's difficulties.

ENIAC: the first successful computer and used for military and scientific research during and immediately after World War II.

existential psychotherapy: a system of psychotherapy that emphasizes present rather than past and self rather than other determinants of personal problems.

expert system: a computer program developed through the collaboration of human experts and computer programmers and intended to perform at a high level of professional proficiency in such domains as counseling, psychological diagnosis, medical diagnosis, molecular analysis, etc.

focal psychological problem: a psychological problem confined to a circumscribed situation (e.g., test anxiety).

frames: the representation of stereotypical information about a specific object or situation.

free association: a method used in psychoanalysis in which the patient says whatever comes to mind without censoring the content or temporal ordering of the report.

generalized dilemma matrix: a symbolic system of extrication routes from psychological dilemmas (see PLATO DCS and systematic dilemma counseling).

General Problem Solver: an early computer program that employed heuristic procedures to solve a range of problems.

Godel's theorem: a mathematical theorem which demonstrated the inevitable incompleteness of mathematics. This limitation on mathematics has sometimes been used to propose limits for artificial intelligence.

heuristics: procedures applied to a problem that while not guaranteed to produce a solution assist in the process of problem solving.

idiographic understanding: an understanding based on the unique or specific characteristics of a person or situation.

imitation game: a procedure in which the goal is to determine whether or not computers can imitate human thinking behavior well enough so that thinking can be ascribed to them (see Turing's test).

information processing system: an abstract set of data structures and procedural operations that, according to some psychological theory and research, describes the symbol processing activities of both computers and people as they solve problems.

isolation: in psychoanalytic theory, the separation of emotions from thought in order to reduce anxiety (see mechanisms of defense).

knowledge engineer: a computer programmer who develops expert systems (see expert system).

knowledge representation: a basic research and practical problem in artificial intelligence that is concerned with methods of representing, in computers, knowledge (information) about real world data, objects and processes.

latent level: in psychoanalytic theory, the unconscious meaning of a dream, symptom or behavior (e.g., poor academic performance might at the latent level, signify hostile retaliation towards the student's parents).

links: see semantic networks.

LISP: a very powerful programming language characterized by flexibility and logical clarity.

logic-based representation: the representation of knowledge (data and procedures) in computer programs by logical symbols and operations such as the predicate calculus.

Logic Theorist: an early computer program used in psychological research to model and study human problem solving with logic type problems.

logotherapy: a system of psychotherapy that emphasizes the discovery of new meanings in a person's life that may contribute to a more satisfactory existence.

LUNAER system: a natural language understanding system that provided geological information concerning the surface of the moon.

manifest level: a term used in psychoanalytic theory to refer to the conscious meaning of a psychological experience. The manifest level of meaning is often contrasted with the unconscious meaning (see latent level).

MACSYMA system: an expert system that provides assistance in the solution of mathematical problems.

means-ends analysis: a heuristic procedure serially applied to reduce the difference between any state of a problem and its final solution state.

mechanisms of defense: in psychoanalytic theory, the cognitive procedures by which anxiety-laden beliefs are modified.

modularity: a condition in which elements can be added or subtracted from a set of elements without effecting the functioning of the original elements.

MORTON program: a computer program that takes the role of a cognitive behavior psychotherapist.

MYCIN system: an expert system providing consultation to physicians regarding diagnosis and treatment of diseases (see consultative systems).

natural language: ordinary language (e.g., English) in contrast to programming language (e.g., LISP).

natural language understanding system: a computer program that receives and produces natural language and whose understanding of this communication is a matter of theoretical debate and research in the field of artificial intelligence.

neo-Freudian psychotherapy: systems of psychotherapy that modified classical psychoanalysis by changing theory or technique (e.g., Adlerian individual psychology that emphasized problems of inferiority and narcissism rather than problems of sexuality and aggression).

Neurotic Program: a program that simulates the belief system of a neurotic person.

nodes: see semantic networks.

nomothetical understanding: an understanding based on general or universal characteristics of a person or situation.

non-directive psychotherapy: see client-centered psychotherapy.

PARRY system: a natural language understanding system incorporating a number of semantic analyzers that understand an interviewing psychiatrist and a number of semantic synthesizers that produce paranoid responses.

personal counseling: a term used interchangeably with the term psychotherapy and thus to be distinguished from educational counseling or vocational counseling.

PLATO DCS system: an expert system that conducts systematic dilemma counseling. The program has three integrated components: dilemma counseling, specific dilemma solutions, structural dilemma solutions.

predicate calculus: a system of logic used in computer programs to represent knowledge about specific facts or relationships.

problem-solving psychotherapy: a type of psychotherapy emphasizing an objective evaluation of a problem or situation and the specification of specific solution steps.

problem-solving system: see PLATO DCS system.

procedural representation: knowledge that is represented in a computer program by instructions as to conditions and sequences of operations.

production rule: a rule composed of a condition to be met and an action to be taken when the condition is fullfilled (see production system).

production system: a computer program using the methodology of production rules (see production rule).

propositional calculus: a system of logic with rules of inference that lead to valid conclusions concerning truth or falsity of propositions (sentences that are properly formed).

PROSPECTOR system: an expert system used in the analysis of oil or mineral bearing geological formations.

psychoanalysis: a system of psychotherapy characterized by an extensive intensive and lengthy course of treatment directed towards a drastic restructuring of the patient's personality and behavior.

psychoanalytic system: see psychotherapy interview program.

psychodynamics: in psychoanalytic theory, the changing patterns of anxiety and defense within the structure of the personality (see mechanisms of defense).

psychological dilemma: see dilemma.

psychotherapy: a professional field of psychology, psychiatry and social work directed towards the treatment and amelioration of psychological difficulties of a personal or interpersonal character.

psychotherapy interview program: a computer program that simulates the role of an analytically-oriented psychotherapist.

representation of knowledge: see knowledge representation.

SAM system: a computer program that answers questions about stories.

SCHOLAR system: a tutorial system that guides the learning of South American geography (see tutorial system).

scripts: the representation of knowledge about stereotypical action expected in a specific situation.

semantic networks (nets): a method of representing knowledge in computer programs by a configuration (see derivation tree) of nodes (containing knowledge about objects and events) and links (containing knowledge about relationships between the nodes).

semantics: the meaning of language.

SHRDLU system: a natural language understanding system that converses with a human partner about its miniature world of blocks. SHRDLU demonstrates its understanding by providing reasons for its behavior as it manipulates the blocks.

simple phobia: a fear confined to a specific object (e.g., spiders) or situation (e.g., public speaking).

Specific Dilemma Solutions Component: see PLATO DCS system.

Structural Dilemma Solutions Component: see PLATO DCS system.

sub-routine: a subsidiary computer program that accomplishes a subordinate portion of an over-all problem-solving task.

symbolic logic: a discipline of mathematics and philosophy in which sentences and their validity are reduced to symbolic expressions and rules of inference. Symbolic logic in the form of the predicate calculus and theorem proving procedures is employed in the problem solving function of computers.

syntax: the grammer or structure of language.

systematic desensitization: a procedure used in behavior therapy to reduce fears of an object or situation by pairing the mental imagery of the situation with deep muscle relaxation. The pairing of feared aspects of the situation and muscle relaxation are arranged in a hierarchy from least to most feared (e.g., from reading about the plans for the construction of hospitals to clearly imagining the details of an impending surgical procedure on oneself).

systematic dilemma counseling: a system of psychotherapy in which problems are resolved through the systematic procedures of dilemma formulation and dilemma matrix (see dilemma formulation and generalized dilemma matrix).

technique of cognitive restructuring: a technique in which a psychotherapist reconstructs the faulty thought patterns of a client.

tecnnique of interpretation of current dynamic: in analytically-oriented psychotherapy, an interpretation designed to reveal the nature of the patient's patterns of defense and anxiety regarding a current problem (see mechanisms of defense).

technique of interpretation of genetic dynamic: in psychoanalysis and analytically-oriented psychotherapy, an interpretation that reveals the childhood origins of a patient's symptoms.

technique of paradoxical intention: in logotherapy, a method of dealing with anticipatory anxiety whereby the feared situation is intentionally exaggerated with the paradoxical result that the person achieves a calm and even humorus perspective on the situation.

technique of self-disclosure: a technique in which the psychotherapist reveals information about his/her behavior or thoughts to the client.

technique of transference interpretation: in psychoanalysis, an interpretation of the patient's behavior as a transfer to the psychoanalysist of attitudes originally held or expressed toward the analysand's parents.

theorem-proving: a strategy used in computer programs to obtain solutions to problems. The strategy often employs a reductio ad absurdum (contrary to fact) tactic to prove the theorem.

theorem resolution method: theorem proving in which theorems are proven by demonstrating that, if certain conditions were not true, a logical inconsistency would be demonstrated.

transference: a term used in psychoanalysis and in psychotherapy to describe excessive emotional behavior (positive or negative) directed by the patient (or client) toward the psychoanalysist (or psychotherapist). The behavior was originally directed towards parents and is transferred in the psychotherapeutic relationship.

transform: the computer program equivalent of mechanism of defense (see Neurotic Program and mechanisms of defense).

truth table: a table from which the truth or falsity of a composite statement can be determined from the values of the components of the statement.

Turing's test: a behavior test of whether a computer can think based on the discriminability of computer and person responses to a carefully guided interrogation.

tutorial system: an expert system that patterns its teaching according to limitations and progress of the student.

WHY system: a tutorial system that guides reasoning about the nature of rainfall through the use of the Socratic method (see tutorial system).

Bibliography

Abelson, P., & Hammond, A. (1977). The electronics revolution. *Science*, *195*, 1087−1092.

Adorno, T.W., Frenkel-Brunswik, E., Levinson, D.J., & Sanford, R.N. (1950). *The authoritarian personality*. New York: Harper.

Alpert, D. & Bitzer, D.L. (1970). Advances in computer-based education. *Science*, *167*, 1582−1590.

American Personnel and Guidance Association. (1981). *Ethical standards*. Washington, D.C.: American Personnel and Guidance Association.

American Psychological Association. (1981). Ethical principles of psychologists. *American Psychologist*, *36*, 633−638.

Bar-Hillel, Y. (1960). The present status of automatic translation of languages. In F.L. Alt (ed.), *Advances in computers*. New York: Academic Press, 91−163.

Barr, A. & Feigenbaum, E.A. (1981). *The handbook of artificial intelligence (Vol. 1)*. Los Altos, CA: William Kaufman, Inc.

Barstow, D.R. (1979). *Knowledge-based program construction*. New York: American Elsevier.

Beck, A.T. (1976). *Cognitive therapy and the emotional disorders*. New York: International Universities Press.

Bernstein, M.I. (1977). *Knowledge-based systems: A tutorial* (Report No. TM-(L)-5903/000/00A). Santa Monica, CA: Systems Development Corporation.

Biglan, A., Villowock, C., & Wick, S. (1979). The feasibility of a computer controlled program for the treatment of test anxiety. *Journal of Behavior Therapy and Experimental Psychiatry*, *10*, 47−49.

Blake, R.R. & Ramsey, G.V. (eds.). (1951). *Perception: An approach to personality*. New York: Ronald Press Co.

Bleich, H.L. (1979). The computer as a consultant. *New England Journal of Medicine*, *284*, 141−147.

231

Blois, M.S. (1980). Clinical judgement and computers. *New England Journal of Medicine, 303*, 192–197.

Bloom, B.L. (1980). Social and community interventions. *Annual Review of Psychology, 31*, 111–142.

Bobrow, D.G. (1968). Natural language input for a computer problem-solving system. In M. Minsky (ed.), *Semantic information processing*, Cambridge, MA: MIT Press.

Bobrow, D.G., & Winograd, T. (1977). Experience with KRL-one cycle of a knowledge representation language. *International Joint Conferences on Artificial Intelligence 5*, 213–222.

Boden, M. (1977). *Artificial intelligence and natural man.* New York: Basic.

Bolter, J.D. (1984). Artificial intelligence. *Daedalus, 113*, 1–18.

Bower, G.H. (1978). Contacts of cognitive psychology with social learning theory. *Cognitive Therapy and Research, 2*, 123–146.

Bower, G.H., & Cohen, P.R. (1982). Emotional influences in memory and thinking: Data and theory. In M.S. Clark & S.T. Fiske (eds.), *Affect and cognition*. Hillsdale, NJ: Erlbaum.

Brachman, R.J. (1978). *A structural paradigm for representing knowledge* (Report No. 3605). Cambridge, MA: Bolt, Beranek and Newman, Inc.

Brachman, R.J., & Smith, B.C. (1980). *Association for Computing Machinery Special Interest Group on Artificial Intelligence Newsletter 70* (special issue on knowledge representation).

Bromberg, W. (1959). *The mind of man.* New York: Harper & Row.

Buchanan. (1976, November). In *Three reviews of J. Weizenbaum's "Computer power and human reason"* (Memo AIM–219). Stanford Artificial Intelligence Laboratory.

Byers, A.P. (1981). Psychological evaluation by means of an on-line computer. *Behavior Research Methods & Instrumentation, 13*, 585–587.

Byrne, D. (1974). *An introduction to personality: Research, theory, and applications.* Englewood Cliffs, NJ: Prentice Hall, Inc.

Byrnes, E. & Johnson, J.H. (1981). Change technology and the implementation of automation in mental health care settings. *Behavior Research Methods & Instrumentation, 13*, 572–580.

Carbonell, J.R. (1970a). AI in CAI: An artificial intelligence approach to computer-assisted instruction. *Institute for Electrical and Electronic Engineers Transactions on Man-Machine Systems, MMS-II*, 190-202.

Carbonell, J.R. (1970b). *Mixed-initiative man-computer instructional dialogues* (BBN Report No. 1971). Cambridge, MA: Bolt, Beranek and Newman, Inc.

Carbonell, J.R., & Collins, A.M. (1974). Natural semantics in artificial intelligence. *International Joint Conferences on Artificial Intelligence, 3*, 344–351.

Card, W.I., Nicholson, M., & Crean, G.P. (1974). A comparison of doctor and computer interrogation of patients. *International Journal of Biomedicine and Computers*, *3*, 175–187.

Carr, A.C. & Ghosh, A. (1983). Response of phobic patients to direct computer assessment. *British Journal of Psychiatry*, *142*, 60.

Chapuis, A., & Droz, E. (1958) (trans. Alec Reid). *Automata*. Neuchatel: Editions du Griffon.

Charniak, E. (1969). Computer solution of calculus word problems. *Proceedings of the International Joint Conferences on AI*, Mitre Corp.

Cherlin, M. (1982, June). Computer-aided investigations into old master paintings. *Datamation*, pp. 92-94.

Clancey, W.J. (1978). *An antibiotic therapy selector which provides for explanations*. Heuristic Programming Project Memo HPP-78–26, Computer Science Dept., Stanford University.

Clark, D.M. & Teasdale, J.D. (1982). Diurnal variation in clinical depression and accessibility of memories of positive and negative experiences. *Journal of Abnormal Psychology*, *91*, 87–95.

Cochran, D.J., Hoffman, S.C., Strand, K.H., & Warren, P.M. (1977). Effects of client/computer interaction on career decision-making process. *Journal of Counseling Psychology*, *24*, 308–312.

Cohen, (1981). C. Goals and schemata in person perception: Making sense from the stream of behavior. In N. Cantor & J.J. Kihlstrom (eds.), *Personality, cognition, and social interaction* (pp. 45–68). Hillsdale, NJ: Erlbaum.

Colby, K.M. (1951). *A primer for psychotherapists*. New York: Ronald Press Co.

Colby, K.M. (1963). Computer Simulation of a Neurotic Process. In S.S. Tomkins and S. Messick (eds.), *Computer simulation of personality: Frontier of psychological research* (pp. 165–180). New York: John Wiley and Sons, Inc.

Colby, K.M. (1964). Experimental treatment of neurotic computer programs. *Archives of General Psychiatry*, *10*, 220–227.

Colby, K.M. (1965). Computer simulation of neurotic processes. In R.W. Stacy and B.D. Waxman (eds.), *Computers and biomedical research, Vol. 1* (pp. 491–503). New York: Academic Press, Inc.

Colby, K.M. (1968). Computer-aided language development in nonspeaking children. *Archives of General Psychiatry*, *19*, 641.

Colby, K.M. (1973). The rationale for computer-based treatment of language difficulties in nonspeaking autistic children. *Journal of Autism and Childhood Schizophrenia*, *3*, 254–260.

Colby, K.M. (1975). *Artificial paranoia: A computer simulation of paranoid processes*. New York: Pergamon Press, Inc.

Colby, K.M. (1980). Computer psychotherapists. In J.B. Sidowski, J.H. Johnson, & T.A. Williams (eds.), *Technology in mental health care delivery systems*. Norwood, NJ: Ablex.

Colby, K.M., & Gilbert, J.P. (1964). Programming a computer model of neurosis. *Journal of Mathematical Psychology, 1*, 220–227.

Colby, K.M., Watt, J.B., & Gilbert, J.P. (1966). A computer method of psychotherapy: Preliminary communication. *Journal of Nervous and Mental Disease, 142*, 148–152.

Colby, K.M., Weber, S., & Hilif, F. (1971). Artificial paranoia. *Artificial Intelligence, 2*, 1–25.

Cole, E.B., Johnson, J.H., & Williams, T.A. (1976). When psychiatric patients interact with computer terminals: Problems and solutions. *Behavior Research Methods & Instrumentation, 8*, 92.

Collins, A. (1978). Fragments of a theory of human plausible reasoning. *Workshops on Theoretical Issues in Natural Language Processing, 2*, 194–210.

Coopersmith, S. (1967). *The antecedents of self-esteem*. San Francisco: W.H. Freeman & Co.

Coyne, J.C., & Gotlib, I.H. (1983). The role of cognition in depression: A critical appraisal. *Psychological Bulletin, 94*, 472–505.

Davis, R.M. (1977). Evolution of computers and computing. *Science, 195*, 1096–1101.

Davis, R., Buchanan, B.G., & Shortliffe, E.H. (1977). Production rules as a representation for a knowledge-based consultation system. *Artificial Intelligence, 8*, 15–45.

Davis, R., & King, J.J. (1977). An overview of production systems. In E. Elcock and E. Michie (eds.), *Machine intelligence 8* (pp. 300–322). Chichester, England: Ellis Horwood.

Derogatis, L.R. (1975). Brief Symptom Inventory. Towson, MD: Clinical Psychometric Research.

DeWeaver, K.L. (1983). Evolution of the microcomputer: Technological implications for the private practitioner. *Psychotherapy in Private Practice, 1*, 59–69.

Dilley, J.S. (1967). Decision-making: A dilemma and a purpose for counseling. *Personnel and Guidance Journal, 45*, 547–551.

Dilligan, R. (1982, August). Literary studies enter the computer age. *Personal Computing*, pp. 60–61.

Dreyfus, H.L. (1972). *What computers can't do*. New York: Harper and Row.

Dunn, T.G., Lushene, R.E., & O'Neil, H.F. (1972). Complete automation of the MMPI and a study of its response in latencies. *Journal of Consulting and Clinical Psychology, 39*, 381–387.

Erdman, H.P., Greist, J.H., Klein, M.H., Jefferson, J.W., & Getto, C. (1981). The computer psychiatrist: How far have we come: Where are we heading: How far dare we go? *Behavior Research Methods & Instru-mentation*, *13*, 393–398.

Erdman, H.P., Klein, M.H., & Greist, J.H. (1985). Direct patient com-puter interviewing. *Journal of Consulting and Clinical Psychology*, *53*, 760–773.

Eysneck, H.J. (1959). *Maudsley personality inventory*. London University: London Press, Ltd.

Eysneck, H.J. (1982). *Personality genetics and behavior*. New York: Praeger.

Feigenbaum, E.A. (1977). The art of artificial intelligence: Themes and case studies of knowledge engineering. *International Joint Conferences on Artificial Intelligence*, *5*, 1014–1029.

Feigenbaum, E.A. & McCorduck, P. (1983). *The fifth generation*. Reading, MA: Addison-Wesley.

Fikes, R.E., Hart, P., & Nilsson, N.J. (1972). Learning and executing generalized robot plans. *Artificial Intelligence*, *3*, 251–288.

Findler, N.V. (ed.). (1979). *Associative networks: The representation and use of knowledge by computers*. New York: Academic Press.

Finley, W.W., Etherton, M.D., Dickman, D., et al. (1981). A simple EMG-reward system for biofeedback training of children. *Biofeedback and Self-Regulation*, *6*, 169.

Finn, F.D. (1972). *Multivariance: Univariate and multivariate analysis of variance, covariance, and regression (Version 5)*. Ann Arbor, MI:National Education Resources, Inc.

Finney, J.C. (1966). Programmed interpretation of MMPI and CPI. *Archives of General Psychiatry*, *15*, 75–81.

Fiske, S.T. (1982). Schema-triggered affect: Applications to social perception. In M.S. Clark & S.T. Fiske (eds.), *Affect and cognition*. Hillsdale, NJ: Erlbaum.

Flavell, J.H. (1979). Metacognition and cognitive monitoring: A new area for cognitive-developmental inquiry. *American Psychologist*, *34*, 905–911.

Ford, W.E. (1976). A client-coding system to maintain confidentiality in a computerized data system. *Hospital and Community Psychiatry*, *27*, 624–625.

Fowler, R.D. (1980). The automated MMPI. In J.B. Sidowski, J.H. Johnson, & T.A. Williams (eds.), *Technology in mental health care delivery systems*. Norwood, NJ: Ablex.

Fowler, R.D. (1985). Landmarks in computer-assisted psychological assess-ment. *Journal of Consulting and Clinical Psychology*, *53*, 748–759.

Freud, S. (1926). *Inhibitions, symptoms, and anxiety*. London: Hogarth Press.

Freud, S. (1935). *A general introduction to psycho-analysis*. New York: Liveright.

Friedman, R.M. (1980). The use of computers in the treatment of children. *Child Welfare*, *59*, 152.

Gaschnig, J. (1977). Computer "therapy". *Science, 198,* 880.

Gedye, J.L., & Miller, E. (1969). The automation of psychological assessment. *International Journal of Man-Machine Studies, 1,* 237−262.

Gentner, D. & Grudin, J. (1985). The evolution of mental metaphors in psychology: A 90−year old retrospective. *American Psychologist, 40,* 181−192.

Ghosh, A. (1981). *Therapeutic interaction and outcome in phobia.* Unpublished doctoral dissertation, Institute of Psychiatry, London.

Ghosh, A., Marks, I.M., & Carr, A.C. (1984). Controlled study of self-exposure treatment for phobics: preliminary communication. *Journal of the Royal Society of Medicine, 77,* 483−487

Gilberstadt, H., Lushene, R., & Beugel, B. (1976). Automated assessment of intelligence: The TAPAC test pattern and computerized report writing. *Perceptual and Motor Skills, 43,* 627−635.

Godel, K. (1931). Uber formal unentscheidbare Satz der Principia Mathematica und verwandter System, I, *Monatshefte fur Mathematica und Physics,* 173−189.

Goldfried, M.R., & Davidson, G.C. (1976). *Clinical behavior therapy.* New York: Holt, Rinehart & Winston.

Goldstine, H. (1972). The computer from Pascal to von Neumann. Princeton University Press.

Gough, H.G. (1976). Personality and personality assessment. In M.D. Dunnette (ed.), *Handbook of industrial and organizational psychology.* Chicago: Rand McNally.

Green, B.F. (1983). Computer testing. *Science, 222,* 1181.

Green, C.C. (1969). The application of theorem-proving to question-answering systems. *International Joint Conferences on Artificial Intelligence I,* 219−237.

Greist, J.H. (1980). Computer therapy. In R. Herenk (Ed.), *The psychotherapy handbook.* New York: New American Library.

Greist, J.H., Gustafson, D.H., Strauss, F.F., Rowse, G.L., Langren, T.P., & Chiles, J.A. (1973). A computer interview for suicide-risk prediction. *American Journal of Psychiatry, 130,* 1327−1332.

Greist, J.H., & Klein, M.H. (1980). Computer programs for patients, clinicians, and researchers in psychiatry. In J.B. Sidowski, J.H. Johnson, & T.A. Williams (Eds.), *Technology in mental health care delivery systems.* Norwood, NJ: Ablex.

Greist, J.H., Klein, M.H., & Erdman, H.P. (1976). Routine on-line psychiatric diagnosis by computer. *American Journal of Psychiatry, 133,* 1405−1408.

Greist, J.H., Klein, M.H., Gurman, A.S., & Van Cura, L.J. (1977). Computer measures of patient progress in psychotherapy. *Psychiatry Digest, 38,* 23.

Grossman, J., Barnett, G.O., McGuire, M.T., & Swedlow, D. (1979).

Computer acquired patient histories. *Journal of American Medical Association, 215,* 1286−1291.

Harper, F.A. (1959). *Psychoanalysis and psychotherapy: 36 systems.* Englewood Cliffs, NJ: Prentice-Hall.

Harris, H. (1974). The computer: Guidance tool of the future. *Journal of Counseling Psychology, 21,* 331−339.

Harvey, O.J., Hunt, D.E., & Schroeder, H.N. (1969). *Conceptual systems and personality organization.* New York: John Wiley and Sons, Inc.

Haugeland, J., (Ed.). (1981). *Mind design: Philosophy, psychology, artificial intelligence.* Cambridge, MA: MIT Press.

Hayes, P.J. (1977). In defence of logic. *International Joint Conferences on Artificial Intelligence, 5,* 559−565.

Hayes, P.J. & Reddy, D.R. (1983). Steps toward graceful interaction in spoken and written man-machine communication. *International Journal of Man-Machine Studies, 19,* 231−234.

Hayes-Roth, F. (1984, June). The machine as partner of the new professional. *Institute for Electrical and Electronic Engineers Spectrum,* 28−31.

Hebb, D.O. (1949). *The organization of behavior: A neuropsychological theory.* New York: John Wiley and Sons, Inc.

Hedl, J.J., O'Neil, H.F., & Hansen, D.H. (1973). Affective reactions toward computer-based intelligence testing. *Journal of Consulting and Clinical Psychology, 40,* 217−222.

Heppner, P.P. (1978). A review of the problem-solving literature and its relationship to the counseling process. *Journal of Counseling Psychology, 25,* 366−375.

Hersen, M., Michelson, L., & Bellack, A. (Eds.). (1984). *Issues in Psychotherapy Research.* New York: Plenum Press.

Hewitt, C. (1972). *Description and theoretical analysis (using schemata) of PLANNER, a language for proving theorems and manipulating models in a robot* (Report No. TR−258). Massachusetts Institute of Technology, AI Laboratory.

Hewitt, C. (1975). How to use what you know. *International Joint Conferences on Artificial Intelligence, 4,* 189−198.

Hilgard, E.R. (1980). The trilogy of mind: Cognition, affection, and conation. *Journal of the History of the Behavioral Sciences, 16,* 107−117.

Hofer, P.J., & Green, B.F. (1985). The challenge of competence and creativity in computerized psychological testing. *Journal of Consulting and Clinical Psychology, 53,* 826−838.

Holden, C. (1977). The empathic computer. *Science, 198,* 32.

Hollander, M. (1975). Behavior therapy approach. In C. Loew, N. Grayson, and G. Loew (Eds.), *Three Psychotherapies.* New York: Brunner/Mazel.

Holt, R.W. (1983). The PLATO IV System in psychological research: An introduction to the PLATO CAI system. *Behavior Research Methods & Instrumentation, 15,* 142−144.

Holyoak, J.J., & Gordon, P.C. (1984). Information processing and social cognition. In R.S. Wyer, T.K. Srull, and J. Hartwick (Eds.), *Handbook of social cognition*. Hillsdale, NJ: Erlbaum.

Houck, J.H. (1982). Psychiatry for the 80's: Old problems, new prospects. *Association of Life Insurance Medical Directors of America Transactions*, *65*, 119.

Hummel, T.J., & Shaffer, W.F. (1979). Three experiments using an algorithm for empathic responses. *Journal of Counseling Psychology*, *26*, 279−284.

Hummel, T.J., Lichtenberg, J.W., & Shaffer, W.F. (1975). CLIENT 1: A computer program which simulates client behavior in an initial interview. *Journal of Counseling Psychology*, *22*, 164−169.

Humphreys, L.G., & Montinelli, R.G. (1975). An investigation of parallel analysis criterion for determining the number of common factors. *Multivariate Behavioral Research*, *10*, 193−205.

Inhelder, B., & Piaget, J. (1958). *The growth of logical thinking*. New York: Basic Books.

Izard, C., Kagan, J., & Zajonc, R. (Eds.). (1984). *Emotions, cognition, and behavior*. New York: Cambridge University Press.

Jackson, D.N. (1967). *Manual for the personality research form*. Goshen, N.Y.: Research Psychologists Press.

Johnson, J.H. (1979). Technology. In T.A. Williams & J.H. Johnson (Eds.), *Mental health in the 21st century*. Lexington, MA: Heath.

Johnson, J.H. & Williams, T.A. (1980). Using on-line computer technology to improve service response and decision-making effectiveness in a mental health admitting system. In J.B. Sidowski, J.H. Johnson, & T.A. Williams (Eds.), *Technology in mental health care delivery systems*. Norwood, NJ: Ablex.

Johnson-Laird, P.N., & Wason, P.C. (1970). A theoretical analysis of insight into a logical relation. *Cognitive Psychology*, *1*, 134−148.

Jones, E. (1975, April). Psychotherapists shortchange the poor. *Psychology Today*, 24−28.

Karasu, T.B. (1977). Psychotherapies: An overview. *American Journal of Psychiatry*, *132*, 851−863.

Karson, S., & O'Dell, J.W. (1975). A new automated interpretation system for the 16PF. *Journal of Personality Assessment*, *39*, 256−260.

Kelly, G.A. (1955). *The psychology of personal constructs*. New York: W.W. Norton.

Kelley, R.S. & Tuggle, F.D. (1981). In the blink of an electronic eye: A prospectus. Behavior Reseach Methods & Instrumentation, 13, 434−435.

Kerber, K.W. (1983). Attitudes towards specific uses of the computer: Quantitative, decision-making, and record-keeping applications. Behavior and Information Technology, 2, 197−209.

Kiesler, C. (1982). Comments. In M.S. Clark & S.T. Fiske (eds.), *Affect and Cognition*. Hillsdale, NJ: Erlbaum.

Kleinmuntz, B. (1975, March). The computer as clinician. *American Psychologist*, 379–387.

Klinge, V., & Rodziewicz, T. (1976). Automated and manual intelligence testing of the Peabody Picture Vocabulary Test on a psychiatric adolescent population. *International Journal of Man-Machine Studies, 8*, 253–256.

Kolata, G. (1982). How can computers get common sense? *Science, 217*, 1237–1238.

Krumboltz, J.D. (1965). Behavioral counseling: Rationale and research. *Personnel and Guidance Journal, 44*, 383–387.

Lang, P.J. (1969). The on-line computer in behavior therapy research. *American Psychologist, 24*, 236–239.

Lang, P.J. (1980). Behavioral treatment and bio-behavioral assessment: Computer applications. In J.B. Sidowski, J.H. Johnson, & T.A. Williams (eds.), *Technolgy in mental health care delivery systems*. Norwood, NJ: Ablex.

Lang, P.J., Melamed, B.G., & Hart, J. (1970). A psychophysiological analysis of fear modification using an automated desensitization procedure. *Journal of Abnormal Psychology, 76*, 220.

Lanyon, R.I. (1971). Mental health technology. *American Psychologist, 26*, 1070–1076.

Lanyon, R.I., & Johnson, J.H. (1980). Technology in mental health: A conceptual overview. In J.B. Sidowski, J.H. Johnson, & T.A. Williams (eds.), *Technology in mental health care delivery systems*. Norwood, NJ: Ablex.

Lawrence, G.H. (1981). *The use of home computers to enhance homework adjuncts to psychotherapy*. Unpublished doctoral dissertation, Rutgers University, The State University of New Jersey, Rutgers.

Leahey, T.H., & Wagman, M. (1974). The modification of fallacious reasoning with implication. *Journal of General Psychology, 91*, 277–285.

Lederberg, J. (1976, November). Review of J. Weizenbaum's computer power and human reason. In *Three reviews of J. Weizenbaum's "Computer power and human reason"*: (Memo AIM–219). Stanford Artificial Intelligence Laboratory.

Lefkowitz, M.B. (1973). *Statistical and clinical approaches to the identification of couples at risk in marriage*. Unpublished doctoral dissertation, University of Florida.

Lester, D. (1977). *The use of alternative modes for communication in psychotherapy*. Springfield, IL: Charles C. Thomas.

Lichtenberg, J.W., Hummel, T.J., & Shaffer, W.F. (1984). CLIENT 1: A computer simulation for use in counselor education and research. *Counselor Education and Supervision, 24*, 155–167.

Lindsay, R.K., Buchanan, B.G., Feigenbaum, E.A., & Lederberg, J. (1980). *Applications of artificial intelligence for organic chemistry: The DENDRAL project.* New York: McGraw-Hill.

London, P. (1974, June). The psychotherapy boom. *Psychology Today,* 63–68.

Lucas, R.W., Mullin, P.J., Luna, C.D., & McInroy, D.C. (1977). Psychiatrists and a computer as interrogators of patients with alcohol related illnesses: A comparison. *British Journal of Psychiatry, 131,* 160-167.

MacKay, D. (1952). Mentality in machines. *Proceedings of the Aristotelian Society, 26,* 61–86.

Mahoney, M.J. (1974). *Cognition and behavior modification.* Cambridge, MA: Ballinger.

Mahoney, M.J. (1977). Reflections on the cognitive learning trend in psychotherapy. *American Psychologist, 32,* 5–13.

Mahoney, M.J. (1980). Psychotherapy and the structure of personal revolutions. In M.J. Mahoney (ed.), *Psychotherapy process; Current issues and future directions.* New York: Plenum.

Mandler, G. (1982). Cognitive underpinnings of affect. In M.S. Clark & S.T. Fiske (eds.), *Affect and cognition.* Hillsdale, NJ: Erlbaum.

Matarazzo, J.D. (1983). Computerized psychological testing. *Science, 221,* 323.

Maultsby, M.O., & Slack, W.V. (1971). A computer based psychiatry history system. *Archives of General Psychiatry, 25,* 570-571.

McCatrhy, J. (1976, November). An unreasonable book. In *Three reviews of J. Weizenbaum's "Computer power and human reason"* (Memo AIM-219). Stanford Artificial Intelligence Laboratory.

McCarthy, J. (1977). Epistomological problems of artifical intelligence. *International Joint Conferences on Artificial Intelligence 3,* 1038–1044.

McCarthy, J., & Hayes, P.J. (1969). Some philosophical problems from the standpoint of artificial intelligence. In D. Michie and B. Meltzer (eds.), *Machine intelligence, 4.* Edinburgh University Press.

McCorduck, P. (1979). Machines who think. San Francisco: Freeman.

McCracken, D. (1976, April). Review, "Computer power and human reason" by Joseph Weizenbaum. *Datamation,* 51–57.

McDonald, C.L.J. (1976). Protocol-based reminders, the quality of care and the non-perfectability of man. *New England Journal of Medicine, 295,* 1351–1355.

McEnmore, C.W., & Fantuzzo, J.W. (1982). CARE: Bridging the gap between clinicians and computers. *Professional Psychology, 13,* 501–510.

Menninger, K. (1955). *The human mind.* New York: Alfred Knopf.

Miller, G.A. (1981). Trends and debates in cognitive psychology. *Cognition, 10,* 215–225.

Miller, R.A., Pople, H., & Myers, J.D. (1982). Internist–1, an experimental computer-based diagnostic consultant for general internal medicine. *New England Journal of Medicine, 307,* 468–476.

Minsky, M. (1975). A framework for representing knowledge. In P. Winston (ed.), *The psychology of computer vision*. New York: McGraw-Hill.

Moses, J. (1971). Symbolic integration: The stormy decade. *Association for Computing Machinery*, *14*, 548−560.

National Research Council, Automatic Language Processing Advisory Committee (1966). *Language and machines: Computers in translation and linguistics* (Publication No. 1416). Washington, D.C.: National Academy of Sciences, National Research Council.

Neisser, U. (1967). *Cognitive psychology*. New York: Appleton-Century-Crofts.

Neisser, U. (1980). On "social knowing." *Personality and Social Psychology Bulletin*, *6*, 601−605.

Newell, A., & Simon, H.A. (1956, September). The logic theory machine. *Western Conference of the Institute for Radio Engineers*, *2*, 61−79.

Newell, A., Shaw, J.C., & Simon, H.A. (1960). Report on a general problem-solving program for a computer. *Information Processing*: *Proceedings of the International Conference of Information Processing*, 256−264.

Newell, A., & Simon, H.A. (1972). *Human problem solving*. Englewood Cliffs, NJ: Prentice-Hall.

Nie, N.H., Hull, C.H., Jenkins, J.G., Steinbrenner, K., & Bent, D.H. (2nd ed, 1975). *Statistical Package for the Social Sciences*. New York: McGraw-Hill.

Norman, A.C. (1975). On computing with formal power series. *Association for Computing Machinery Transactions on Mathematical Software*, *1*, 346−356.

Norman, D.A. (1980). Twelve issues for cognitive science. *Cognitive Science*, *4*, 1−32.

Norman, D.A., & Rummelhart, D.E. (1975). *Explorations in cognition*. San Francisco: Freeman.

Oettinger, A.G. (1955). The design of an automatic Russian-English technical dictionary. In W.N. Locke and A.D. Booth (eds.), *Machine translation of languages*. New York: Technology Press of MIT and Wiley.

Ogburn, W.F. (1922). *Social change*. Gloucester, MA: Smith.

Paitich, D. (1973). Computers in behavioral science: A comprehensive automated psychological examination and report (CAPER). *Behavioral Science*, *108*, 131−136.

Palmen, J. (1978). Sympathetic computers or programmers. *Science*, *199*, 934.

Parkison, R.C., Colby, K.M., and Faught, W.W. (1977). Conversational language comprehension using integrated pattern-matching and parsing. *Artificial Intelligence*, *9*, 111−134.

Parloff, M.B. (1975, October). *Twenty-five years of research in psychotherapy*. New York: Albert Einstein College of Medicine, Department of Psychiatry.

Parloff, M.B. (1976, February). Shopping for the right therapy. *Saturday Review*, pp. 14−20.

Parsons, T. (1951). *The social system*. New York: Free Press of Glencoe.

Parsons, T., & Smelser, N.J. (1956). *Economy and society*. New York: Free Press of Glencoe.

Pervin, L.A. (1985). Personality: Current controversies, issues, and directions. *Annual Review of Psychology, 36*, 83–114.

Pople, H. (1977). The formation of composite hypotheses in diagnostic problem solving-an exercise in synthetic reasoning. *International Joint Conferences on Artificial Intelligence*, 1030–1037.

Quillian, M.R. (1968). Semantic Memory. In M. Minsky (ed.), *Semantic information processing*. Cambridge, MA: MIT press.

Randall, B. (1979). Annotated bibliography of the origins of computers. *Annals of the History of the Computer, 1*, 107–207.

Raphael, B. (1968). SIR: A computer program for semantic information retrieval. In M. Minsky (ed.), *Semantic information processing*. Cambridge, MA: MIT Press.

Reiter, R. (1978). On reasoning by default. *Workshops on Theoretical Issues in Natural Language Processing, 2*, 210–218.

Richards, S.C., & Perri, M.G. (1978). Do self-control treatments last? An evaluation of behavioral problem solving and faded counselor contact as treatment maintenance strategies. *Journal of Counseling Psychology, 25*, 376–383.

Roberge, J.J. (1971). An analysis of response patterns for conditional reasoning schemes. *Psychonomic Science, 22*, 338–339.

Rogers, C. (1951). *Client centered therapy: Current practice, implication and theory*. Boston: Houghton-Mifflin.

Rotter, J.B. (1966). Generalized expectancies for internal vs. external control of reinforcement. *Psychological Monographs, 8*, 1–28.

Ruesch, J. (1968). Psychotherapy in the compter age. *Proceedings of the 7th International Congress of Psychotherapy, Wiesbaden, 1967, Part II: Community Psychiatry-Therapeutic Community, Psychother., Psychosom., 16*, 32.

Rychlak, J. (1965). The motives to psychotherapy. *Psychotherapy: Theory, Research, & Practice, 2*, 151–157.

Rychlak, J. (1969). Lockean vs. Kantian theoretical models and the "cause" of therapeutic change. *Psychotherapy: Theory, Research, & Practice, 6*, 214–222.

Sagan, C. (1977). *The dragons of Eden: Speculations on the evolution of human intelligence*. New York: Ballentine Books.

Sampson, J.P. (1983). Computer-assisted testing and assessment: Current status and implications for the future. *Measurement and Evaluation in Guidance, 15*, 293–299.

Sampson, J.P. Jr., & Pyle, K.R. (1983). Ethical issues involved with the use of computer-assisted counseling, testing, and guidance systems. *The Personnel and Guidance Journal, 61*, 283–287.

Schank, R.C. (1975). *Conceptual information processing*. New York: North-Holland.

Schank, R.C., and Abelson, R.P. (1977). *Scripts, plans, goals, and understanding*. Hillsdale, NJ: Lawrence Erlbaum.

Scissons, E.H. (1976). Computer administration of the California Psychological Inventory. *Measurement and Evaluation in Guidance*, 9, 22−25.

Scriven, M. (1953). The mechanical concept of mind. In A.R. Anderson (ed.), *Minds and machines*. Englewood Cliffs, NJ: Prentice-Hall.

Selmi, P.M. (1983). *Computer-assisted cognitive-behavior therapy in the treatment of depression*. Unpublished doctoral dissertation, Illinois Institute of Technology.

Selmi, P.M., Klein, M.H., Greist, J.H., Johnson, J.H., & Harris, W.G. (1982). An investigation of computer-assisted cognitive-behavior therapy in the treatment of depression. *Behavior Research Methods & Instrumentation*, 14, 181−185.

Seron, X., Deloche, G., Mouland, G., & Rousselle, M. (1980). A computer-based therapy for the treatment of aphasic subjects with writing disorders. *Journal of Speech and Hearing Disorders*, 45, 45.

Shortliffe, E.H. (1976). *Computer-based medical consultations: MYCIN*. New York: Elseview/North-Holland.

Simon, H.A. (1977). What computers mean for man and society. *Science*, 195, 1186−1190.

Simon, H.A. (1979). Information processing models of cognition. *Annual Review of Psychology*, 30, 363−396.

Sines, J.O. (1980). The use of computers in the delivery of mental health care: The necessary background conditions. In J.B. Sidowski, J.H. Johnson, & T.A. Williams (eds.), *Technology in mental health care delivery systems*. Norwood, NJ: Ablex.

Slack, W.V., Hicks, G.P., Reed, C.Z., & VanCura, L.J. (1966). A computer based medical history system. *New England Journal of Medicine*, 274, 194−198.

Slack, W.V., & Slack, C.L.W. (1977). Talking to a computer about emotional problems: A comparative study. *Psychotherapy: Theory, Research, Practice*, 14, 156−164.

Smith, S.G., & Sherwood, B.A. (1976). Educational uses of the PLATO computer system. *Science*, 192, 344−352.

Smith, D.H., Buchanan, B.G., Engelmore, R.S., Adlercreutz, H., & Djerassi, C. (1973). Applications of artificial intelligence for chemical inference IX. Analysis of mixtures without prior separation as illustrated for estrogens. *Journal of the American Chemical Society*, 95, 6076.

Sondheimer, N.K., & Relles, N. (1982). Human factors and user assistance in interactive computing systems: An introduction. *Institute for Electrical and Electronic Engineers Transactions on Systems*, 12, 102−107.

Space, L.G., & Huntzinger, R.S. (1979). A microprocessor-based psychopathology laboratory: III. Hardware. *Behavior Research Methods & Instrumentation, 11*, 247–252.

Spero, M.H. (1978). Thoughts on computerized psychotherapy. *Psychiatry, 41*, 279–288.

Spielberger, S.D., Gorsuch, R.L., & Lushene, R. (1968). *State-trait anxiety scale.* Palo Alto, CA: Consulting Psychologist Press.

Spitzer, R.L., Endicott, J., Cohen, J., & Fleiss, J.L. (1974). Constraints on the validity of computer diagnosis. *Archives of General Psychiatry, 31,* 197–203.

Stead, W.W., Heyman, A., Thompson, H.K., & Hammond, W.E. (1972). Computer-assisted interview of patients with functional headache. *Archives of Internal Medicine, 129,* 950–955.

Stevens, A.L., & Collins, A. (1977). *The goal structure of a socratic tutor* (BBN Report No. 3518). Cambridge, MA: Bolt, Beranek and Newman, Inc.

Stevens, A.L., Collins, A., & Goldin, S. (1978). *Diagnosing student's misconceptions in causal models* (BBN Report No. 3786). Cambridge, MA: Bolt, Beranek and Newman, Inc.

Stevens, G.C. (1983). User-friendly computer systems? A critical examination of the concept. *Behavior & Information Technology, 2,* 3–16.

Stone, L.A., & Kristjanson, R.W. (1975). Computer-assisted group encounter. *Small Group Behavior, 6,* 457.

Stout, R.L. (1981). New approaches to the design of computerized interviewing and testing systems. *Behavior Research Methods & Instrumentation, 13,* 436–442.

Strupp, H.H. (1975). Psychoanalysis, "focal psychotherapy," and the nature of the therapeutic influence. *Archives of General Psychiatry, 32,* 127–135.

Strupp, H.H. (1977). Psychotherapy for better or worse. New York: J. Aronson.

Sullivan, H.S. (1954). *The psychiatric interview.* New York: W.W. Norton.

Sutherland, N. (1976, July 30). The electronic oracle. Times Literary Supplement.

Teasdale, J.D. (1983). Negative thinking in depression: Cause, effect, or reciprocal relationship? *Advances in Behavior Research and Therapy, 5,* 3–25.

Trapple, J.D. (1983). Computer psychotherapy: Is it acceptable, feasible, advisable? *Cybernetics and Systems: An International Journal, 12,* 385.

Tucker, L.R. (1980). *DAPPFER: Direct artificial personal probability factor rotations.* Unpublished manuscript and computer program, University of Illinois at Urbana-Champaign, Department of Psychology.

Turing, A. (1936). On computable numbers, with an application to the Entscheudungs problem. *Proceedings of the London Mathematics Society, 52,* 230–265.

Turing, A. (1963). Computing machinery and intelligence. In E.A. Feigenbaum & J. Feldman (eds.), *Computers and Thought*. New York:
McGraw-Hill.

Vale, C.D. (1981). Design and implementation of a micro-computer based
adaptive testing system. *Behavior Research Methods and Instrumentation,
13*, 399–406.

Vanderplas, J. (1977). Computer "therapy". *Science, 198*, 880.

Wagman, M. (1976). *Conceptual analysis of the psychological meaning of
the computer in ten sectors of society*. Unpublished manuscript, University
of Illinois at Urbana-Champaign, Department of Psychology.

Wagman, M. (1977). *The cybernetics attitude scale*. Unpublished manuscript,
University of Illinois at Urbana-Champaign, Department of Psychology.

Wagman, M. (1978). The comparative effects of didactic correction and self-
contradiction on fallacious scientific and personal reasoning. *Journal of
General Psychology, 99*, 67–80.

Wagman, M. (1979). Systematic dilemma counseling: Theory, method,
research. *Psychological Reports, 44*, 55–72.

Wagman, M. (1980a). PLATO DCS, an interactive computer system for
personal counseling. *Journal of Counseling Psychology, 27*, 16–30.

Wagman, M. (1980b). Systematic dilemma counseling: Transition from
counselor mode to autonomous mode. *Journal of Counseling Psychology,
27*, 171–178.

Wagman, M (1981). Autonomous mode of systematic dilemma counseling.
Psychological Reports, 48, 231–246.

Wagman, M. (1982). A computer method for solving dilemmas. *Psychological Reports, 50*, 291–298.

Wagman, M. (1983). A factor analytic study of the psychological implications of the computer for the individual and society. *Behavior Research
Methods & Instrumentation, 15*, 413–419.

Wagman, M. (1984a). *The dilemma and the computer: Theory, research,
and applications to counseling psychology*. New York: Praeger.

Wagman, M. (1984b). Using computers in personal counseling. *Journal of
Counseling and Development, 63*, 172–176.

Wagman, M., & Kerber, K.W. (1978). *Dilemma counseling system*.
Minneapolis, MN: Control Data Corporation.

Wagman, M., & Kerber, K.W. (1979). DCS, an interactive computer
system for personal counseling: Technical description and performance
data. *JSAS Catalog, of Selected Documents in Psychology, 9*, 20, MS
1827.

Wagman, M., & Kerber, K. W. (1980). PLATO DCS, an interactive
computer system for personal counseling: Further development and
evaluation. *Journal of Counseling Psychology, 27*, 31–39.

Wagman, M., & Kerber, K.W. (1984). Computer-assisted counseling: Problems and prospects. *Counselor Education and Supervision, 24*, 147–154.

Wang, P., & Rothschild, L. (1975). Factoring multivariate polynomials over the integers. *Mathematics of Computation*, *29*, 935−950.

Wason, P.C. (1964). The effect of self-contradiction on fallacious reasoning. *Quarterly Journal of Experimental Psychology*, *15*, 30−34.

Wason, P.C., & Johnson-Laird, P.N. (1972). *Psychology of reasoning*: *Structure and content*. London: Batsford.

Weaver, W. (1955). Translation. In W.N. Locke and A.D. Booth (eds.), *Machine translation of languages*. New York: Technology Press of MIT and Wiley.

Weiner, B. (1982). The emotional consequences of causal attributions. In M.S. Clark & S.T. Fiske (eds.), *Affect and cognition*. Hillsdale, NJ: Erlbaum.

Weiss, D.J. (1985). Adaptive testing by computer. *Journal of Consulting and Clinical Psychology*, *53*, 774−789.

Weizenbaum, J. (1965). ELIZA — A computer program for the study of natural language communication between man and machine. *Communication of the Association for Computing Machinery*, *9*, 36−45.

Weizenbaum, J. (1967). Contextual Understanding by Computers. *Communications of the Association for Computer Machinery*, *10*, 474−480.

Weizenbaum, J. (1976). *Computer power and human reason*: *From Judgement to calculation*. San Francisco: Freeman.

Weizenbaum, J. (1977). Computer as therapist. *Science, 198,* 354.

Whitehead, A.N., & Russell, B. (1910−1913).*Principia Mathematica* (2nd ed.). Cambridge, England: Cambridge University Press.

Wilkes, M. (1953). Can machines think? *Proceedings of the Institute for Radio Engineers*, *41*, 1230−1234.

Wilks, Y.A. (1973). An artificial intelligence approach to machine translation. In R.C. Schank and K.M. Colby (eds.), *Computer models of thought and language*. San Francisco: Freeman.

Wilks, Y.A. (1977a). Time flies like an arrow. *New Scientist*, *76*, 696−698.

Wilks, Y.A. (1977b). Methodological questions about artificial intelligence: Approaches to understanding natural language. *Journal of Pragmatics*, *1*, 69−84.

Wilson, G.T., & Franks, C.M. (eds.), (1982). *Contemporary behavior therapy: Conceptual and empirical foundations*. New York: Guilford.

Winograd, T. (1972). *Understanding natural language*. New York: Academic Press.

Winograd, T. (1980a). Extended inference modes in reasoning by computer systems. *Artificial Intelligence*, *13*, 5−26.

Winograd, T. (1980b). What does it mean to understand language: *Cognitive Science*, *4*, 209−241.

Wolberg, L.R. (1965). *Short-term psychotherapy*. New York: Grune & Stratton.

Wolpe, J. (1969). *The practice of behavior therapy*. New York: Pergamon Press.

Woods, W.A. (1973). An experimental parsing system for transition network grammars. In R. Rustin (ed.), *Natural language processing*. New York: Algorithmics Press.

Wright, J., & Mischel, W. (1982). Influence of affect on cognitive social learning person variables. *Journal of Personality and Social Psychology*, *43*, 401–414.

Zarr, M.L. (1984). Computer-mediated psychotherapy: Toward patient-selection guidelines. *American Journal of Psychotherapy*, *38*, 47–62.

Zippel, R. (1976). Univariate power series expansions in algebraic manipulation. *Proceedings of the Association for Computing Machinery Symposium on Symbolic and Algebraic Computation*.

Author Index

Subject Index

Adequacy of solution, *see also* Measure of techniques used
  correlations with experimental variables, 177–178
Affiliation scale, 152–154; *see also* PLATO Dilemma Counseling System
  and dependent measures, 171–172
Artificial intelligence
  and applications of logic, 60–63
  compared with human intelligence, 8–11; and computer translation, 34–37
  and constraints on computer counseling, 195–197
  and consultative systems, 77–78
  and expert systems, 72–77
  and general characteristics of representation methods, 58–59; and grammars, 38–39
  limits of, 11; and natural language understanding systems, 39–55
  orienting concepts of 3–5
  and parsers, 38–39
  and problem solving, 3–5
  and the representation of knowledge, 57–69
  and representation methods, 59–69
  research in, 31–81
  and timelines for increases in the

  specificity of problem solving, 203–204
  and Turing's test, 8–11
  and tutorial systems, 78–81
  and understanding of natural language, 33–56

CLIENT I, *see* Computer models
Client centered computer system, 99–102
Client selection and preferences in
  computer counseling, *see* Computer counseling
Cognitive behavior computer system, 103–105
Cognitive structures scale, 154–155; *see also* PLATO Dilemma Counseling System
  and dependent measures, 173
Computer assisted solutions
  compared with self-generated solutions, 145–146
Computer counseling
  affective relationships in, 14–17
  attitudes toward, 207–221
  client centered system of, 99–102
  cognitive behavior system of, 103–105
  counter transference in, 16–18
  diffuse problems in, 14–17

255

About the Author

Morton Wagman is Professor Emeritus of Psychology at the University of Illinois, Urbana-Champaign. Professor Wagman is a diplomate in Counseling Psychology, American Board of Professional Psychology.

Dr. Wagman is co-originator of the PLATO computer-based Dilemma Counseling System. PLATO DCS, published by Control Data Corporation, has been internationally used at colleges and universities for research, service and instructional purposes.

Dr. Wagman's research on computer counseling has been published widely in scientific and professional journals. Professor Wagman's most recent book is THE DILEMMA AND THE COMPUTER: Theory, Research, and Applications to Counseling Psychology (Praeger, 1984).

Dr. Wagman was graduated Phi Beta Kappa from Columbia University with honors and special distinction in mathematics. Dr. Wagman holds a M.A. and Ph.D. in psychology from the University of Michigan.

Professor Wagman has held faculty positions in the departments of psychology at University of Michigan and University of Illinois, where he has also held the professional position of clinical counselor. Dr. Wagman is a member of the American Psychological Association and of the American Association for the Advancement of Science.

Milton Keynes UK
Ingram Content Group UK Ltd.
UKHW031146141024
449569UK00024B/1042